FAILURE OF A MISSION

SIR NEVILE HENDERSON

Failure of a Mission

Berlin 1937-1939

BY THE RIGHT HONORABLE

Sir Nevile Henderson

P. C., G. C. M. G.

FOUNDED 1838

GPPS

G. P. PUTNAM'S SONS, NEW YORK

Designed by Robert Josephy
MANUFACTURED IN THE UNITED STATES OF AMERICA

CONTENTS

PROLOGUE   vii

PART I: THE BACKGROUND OF THE STORY

I. Buenos Aires to Berlin   3

II. The Background of My Mission   9

III. Arrival in Berlin   29

IV. The Background of Germany in May, 1937   51

V. Attempts to Improve Anglo-German Relations   62

VI. Goering   76

VII. Further Attempt to Improve Anglo-German Relations   93

PART II: THE DRAMA

I. Prelude   105

II. *Act I:* Austria   119

III. First Entr'acte   129

IV. *Act II:* Czechoslovakia
Scene I: Prague   136

V. *Act II:* Czechoslovakia
Scene II: Munich   148

v

Contents

VI. *Second Entr'acte:* Hitler's Reactions after
Munich   176

VII. *Interlude:* Return to Berlin After Four Months   189

VIII. The Parting of the Ways   199

IX. *Act III:* The Occupation of Prague   208

X. *Act IV:* Poland
Scene I: The Anglo-Polish Agreement   224

XI. Third Entr'acte   235

XII. *Act IV:* Poland
Scene II: War   258

XIII. Departure from Berlin   302

APPENDIXES   311

PROLOGUE

I labour for peace, but when I speak unto them thereof they make them ready to battle.

6TH VERSE OF PSALM CXX OF
THE BOOK OF COMMON PRAYER.

IT was the stationmaster at Grantham who finally overcame my scruples about the writing of this book. Mr. Gardner was kind enough to invite me into his office, where there was a fire, one cold morning when I was waiting for a train for London, which was late. We spoke of this and that, about the war and its origins; and his final remark to me was that he and people like him knew nothing of the facts of the case.

I have attempted in this volume, the main purpose of which is historical, to give the facts of the case; and to those who read it I should wish, first of all, to make it quite clear that, whereas all the observations, comments, and opinions expressed in this volume are purely personal and therefore fallible and controversial, the sequence of events and the facts themselves are taken entirely from telegrams, dispatches, and letters written at the time, and are consequently, humanly speaking, strictly exact.

In a book of this nature, written so soon after the events recorded therein, there must necessarily be certain reticences. In the first place, I occupied an official position at Berlin, and was then, and still am, in the service of His Majesty's Government.

vii

Prologue

In the second place, if circumstances had been normal, nothing would have induced me to write—at least at this early stage—about people who had so recently been uniformly courteous and hospitable to me personally.

Unfortunately, circumstances are not normal; and, whatever my personal inclinations may be, I have felt that, having regard to the fact that it is British public opinion which ultimately determines the character of our foreign policy, it is my duty to give to the people of this country an account of my stewardship of the mission which was entrusted to me by the King in April, 1937, as his Ambassador at Berlin.

The first commandment of a diplomatist is faithfully to interpret the views of his own government to the government to which he is accredited; and the second is like unto it: namely, to explain no less accurately the views and standpoint of the government of the country in which he is stationed to the government of his own country.

The first commandment is much easier to keep than the second; and its fulfillment can, or should, be taken for granted. The second is sometimes far more difficult of performance. I went to Berlin resolved, in spite of my own doubts and apprehensions and in spite of many of its detestable aspects, to do my utmost to see the good side of the Nazi regime as well as the bad, and to explain as objectively as I could its aspirations and viewpoint to His Majesty's Government. Hitler and the Nazi party governed Germany, and with them it was my duty to work. But above all, I was determined to labor for an honorable peace and to follow the example of the Prime Minister in never wearying of that labor.

For two years I hoped against hope that the Nazi revolution, having run its course, would revert to a normal and civilized conduct of internal and international life, that there was a limit to Hitler's ambitions and a word of truth in some at least of his assurances and statements. Many may regard my persistence as convicting me of the lack of any intellectual understanding of Nazi or even German mentality. That may be true; but even today I do not regret having tried to believe in Germany's honor and good sense. Whatever happens, I shall always persist in thinking that it was right to make the attempt, that nothing was lost by making it, but that, on the contrary, we should never have entered upon this war as a united Empire and nation, with the moral support of neutral opinion behind us, if the attempt had not been made. Anyway, the fact remains that up to the fifteenth of March, 1939, and in spite of the shocks of Godesberg and Munich in 1938, I refused to abandon that hope. After the occupation of Prague on the Ides of last March I still struggled on, though all hope, except in a miracle, was dead.

No miracle occurred, and on September 1st the German armies and Air Force invaded Poland. There was no declaration of war, and a clearer case of unprovoked aggression there can never be. Indeed, in spite of all my hopes and efforts, it is possible now to say that for a year and a half before that date I had been obsessed with the idea that we were moving remorselessly through the pages of a Greek tragedy to its inevitably disastrous and sinister end. Those who take the trouble to read this book will realize what I mean. Hitler never intended the ultimate end to be other than war. It seems inconceivable that the will and lust for power of one man should plunge an unwilling Europe into war. But so it is; and hundreds of thousands of men, women, and children have to suffer and to die for it. So long as Germany, the home of the most numerous, disciplined, and hard-working race in Europe, is governed by Hitler and his secret police (Gestapo) and by all that Hitlerism stands for, there can be no confidence in international agreements and no civilized conduct in national and international life.

That is my profound conviction after living in the Germany of Hitler for over two years. I like and admire the German people; I feel myself very much at home among them and find them less strangers than almost any other foreign people. A prosperous, contented, and happy Germany is a vital British interest. But today the Germans are serving a false god, and their many good and great qualities are being debauched for ends which are evil. Germany can neither be prosperous nor happy till she recovers her individual and personal freedom of life and thought and has learned that the true responsibility of strength is to protect and not to oppress the weak.

I have lived abroad for a third of a century. The last year in which I spent as much as six months in England was 1905. In December of that year I was sent to my first post at St. Petersburg. Since then I have never spent more than four months in England in any one year, generally much less; and in the course of some years I have never returned to England at all. Yet, whenever I do so, I am always struck by the fundamental common sense, sound judgment, and critical faculty of the great mass of the British people, of John Citizen and Jane Citizeness in their simplest form. Never was I more impressed by this than in September of this year and in the

Prologue

months which preceded the declaration of war. I may tell of my personal experiences at Berlin during the past two years; but nothing in such a record can add to, or detract from, the instinctive appreciation by the British public of the realities of the struggle upon which we have now entered.

There is no material gain in it for ourselves. True to our own spirit of freedom, we are fighting for the moral standards of civilized life, in the full realization of our responsibilities and of the cost which we must pay for shouldering them. All that is best in this generation of the British nation, and particularly of its youth, has dedicated itself to the higher cause of humanity in the future; and it is in humble recognition of that marvelous fact that I myself dare to dedicate this book to the people of the British Isles, to the men and women of its streets and factories, shores and countrysides.

Rauceby Hall,
Sleaford.
October, 1939.

PART I

THE BACKGROUND
OF THE STORY

CHAPTER I. BUENOS AIRES TO BERLIN

IN January, 1937, when I had been just over a year at Buenos Aires as His Majesty's Ambassador to the Argentine Republic, I received a telegram from Mr. Eden, then Foreign Secretary in Mr. Baldwin's Cabinet, offering me the post of Ambassador at Berlin in succession to Sir Eric Phipps, who was being transferred to Paris in April. As the telegram was marked "personal," I asked my secretary, Mr. Pennefather, to help me decode it; and I can still vividly recall my first reactions on ascertaining its contents. They were threefold. In the first place a sense of my own inadequacy for what was obviously the most difficult and most important post in the whole of the diplomatic service. Secondly, and deriving from the first, that it could only mean that I had been specially selected by Providence with the definite mission of, as I trusted, helping to preserve the peace of the world. And thirdly there flashed across my mind the Latin tag about failure and success which ominously observes that the Tarpeian Rock, from which failures were thrown to their doom, is next to the Capitol, where the triumph of success was celebrated. I might have hesitated more than I did about accepting Mr. Eden's offer if I had not been persuaded of the reality of my second

3

Failure of a Mission

reaction, which seemed to me to outweigh every other consideration.

I left Buenos Aires in the middle of March. Though I had had a German governess as a small boy and had spent the best part of two years in Germany while preparing for the diplomatic examination, I had never during my thirty-two years' service abroad been in a post where German was the spoken language, so that my knowledge of it was extremely rusty. It was partly for that reason that I took my passage back to England on the German liner *Cap Arcona* and provided myself with two copies of Hitler's *Mein Kampf* to study on the way. The one had been given me by the German Ambassador at Buenos Aires, the other was an unexpurgated edition which I obtained privately. Though it was in parts turgid and prolix and would have been more readable if it had been condensed to a third of its length, it struck me at the time as a remarkable production on the part of a man whose education and political experience appeared to have been as slight, on his own showing, as Herr Hitler's.

The Captain of the *Cap Arcona* was a certain Niejahr, who was afterward promoted to be Commodore of the North German Lloyd. He was a great favorite with all the British passengers on board, of whom there were a number, including the late Lord Mount Temple, who was at that time President of the Anglo-German Fellowship, but who resigned from that position after the Jewish persecutions in November, 1938. I had several talks with Captain Niejahr; and, on one occasion, pointing to his own high cheek bones, he drew my attention to the considerable admixture of Slav blood in many of the Germans and particularly of the Prussians. It is no co-

4

incidence that in the last war it was the Prussians rather than the Germans whom we regarded as our real enemies and that in the present one it is the Nazis, or followers of Hitler, and again not the Germans as a race. Though but few of the actual leaders of the National Socialist party are Prussians by origin, it is the Prussian ideology and particularly their methods which are no less dominant today in Germany than they were in 1914 or in 1870.

In a democracy the state is subordinated to the service of its citizens. In National Socialism, as interpreted by Hitler, the state is all in all; while the citizen has no individual personality and is but the obedient servant and slave of the state as personified in its leader, whose will is absolute (the *Führerprinzip*). The "leader" principle is derived directly from Fascism; but otherwise this conception of national philosophy is based entirely on the old Prussian theory of service to the state and obedience to command, as preached in the writings of its apostle, Immanuel Kant. In what proportion militant Prussianism is due to its Slavic blood mixture, to the harsh northeastern German climate, or to the militarism imposed on it by its old indefensible eastern frontiers is an open question. But the fact remains that the Prussians, of whom even Goethe spoke as barbarians, are a distinctive European type, which has imposed itself and its characteristics upon the rest of Germany. Also, from the point of view of the western world, it has prostituted or is prostituting the great qualities of order and efficiency, probity and kindliness of the purer German of Northwest, West, and South Germany, with whom an Englishman on his travels abroad finds himself in such natural sympathy.

Failure of a Mission

Among the German passengers on board the *Cap Arcona* were Count and Countess Dohna, with whom, as I shall relate, I afterward stayed at their castle of Finckenstein in East Prussia; and Princess Frederick Leopold of Prussia, a sister of the late Empress, who was traveling with her only surviving son, destined later to be imprisoned by the Nazi Government. Apart, however, from having occasion to make my first attempt at a speech in German at a small dinner given to the Captain, by far the most interesting incident of the journey was our meeting with the new German airship *Hindenburg*, which, in the following May, was to become a total casualty with considerable loss of life at Lakehurst in the United States. She caught us up on her return journey from South America to Germany, and setting her engines as she reached us to the same speed as those of the *Cap Arcona*, she hung over our heads at about one hundred and fifty feet, a most impressive spectacle, for fully five or ten minutes while wireless messages were exchanged between the two craft. When she started her engines at full speed again, it was almost incredible how quickly she disappeared once more from view.

I reached Southampton on one of the last days of March and spent a hectic month in London seeing as many people as possible and occupied in all the numerous preparations which are necessary before one takes over a new post. My most important interview was, of course, with Mr. Neville Chamberlain, who was at that time Chancellor of the Exchequer but who was already Prime Minister designate, as Mr. Baldwin had some time previously announced his intention of retiring immediately after the Coronation, which was to take place on May 12th. Both he and Mr. Baldwin, whom

6

Buenos Aires to Berlin

I had seen earlier, agreed that I should do my utmost to work with Hitler and the Nazi party as the existing government in Germany. In democratic England the Nazis, with their disregard of personal freedom and their persecution of religion, Jews, and trade unions alike, were naturally far from popular. But they were the government of the country, and an ambassador is not sent abroad to criticize in a country the government which it chooses or to which it submits. It was just as much my duty honorably to try to co-operate with the Nazi Government to the best of my ability as it would be for a foreign ambassador in London to work with a Conservative Government, if it happened to be in power, rather than with the Liberal or Labor opposition, even though his own sympathies might possibly lie rather with the policy or ideologies of the latter. I was fully alive to the probability that the attempts which I intended to make to work with the Nazis and to understand their point of view would be criticized by many people in my own country. "Do what thy conscience bids thee do, from none but self expect applause." Burton's rule of conduct in life is not a bad one, provided one is a fairly strict critic of oneself, has a few real and candid friends, and does not easily applaud. Certainly, if one observes it, one is to a great extent armed against criticism.

Be that as it may, Mr. Chamberlain outlined to me his views on general policy toward Germany; and I think I may honestly say that to the last and bitter end I followed the general line which he set me, all the more easily and faithfully since it corresponded so closely with my private conception of the service which I could best render in Germany to my own country. I remember making but one reservation to Mr.

Chamberlain, namely, that, while doing my utmost to work as sympathetically as possible with the Nazis, it was essential that British rearmament should be relentlessly pursued, since no argument could count with the government of Hitler except that of force. Mr. Chamberlain assured me that he equally appreciated this and that such was his own firm intention.

Inasmuch as any public attempt to co-operate with the Nazi Government would constitute somewhat of an innovation, I remember also asking Mr. Chamberlain whether, as Prime Minister, he would object to my being, if I thought it necessary, slightly indiscreet on first arrival in Berlin. His reply was to the effect that a calculated indiscretion was sometimes a very useful form of diplomacy and that he had himself recently had experience of its value.

CHAPTER II. THE BACKGROUND
OF MY MISSION

FORTIFIED by this understanding attitude on the part of the future Prime Minister, I left for Germany on April 29th. Before, however, describing the dramatic events of the next two years, I wish to make quite clear to my readers the principles which guided me in undertaking my mission to Berlin.

I was, above all, convinced that the peace of Europe depended upon the realization of an understanding between Britain and Germany. I was consequently determined: firstly, to do all in my power to associate with the Nazi leaders, and if possible to win their confidence and even sympathy; and, secondly, to study the German case as objectively as possible and, where I regarded it as justified, to present it as fairly as I could to my own government. To those two rules I adhered throughout my two and a quarter years in Berlin. I honestly endeavored, where I could do so without sacrificing the principles or the interests of my country, both to understand the German external viewpoint and to see what was good in its social experiment, without being blind to what was bad. My mission to Germany was a tragic failure, but at least my own conscience in this respect is clear. The modern ambassador is but a small cog in the machinery of a

9

twentieth-century government, but nobody strove harder for an honorable and just peace than I did. That all my efforts were condemned to failure was due to the fanatical megalomania and blind self-confidence of a single individual and of a small clique of his self-interested followers. I say this in no spirit of bitterness, but with the conviction drawn from the experience of two years' close observation and contact. For the fact of the matter is that one of the things for which we have gone to war today is to decide whether, in the future, the fatal arbitrament of peace or war, not only for a great nation but for the world, is again to rest in the hands of a single individual, and, as in this case, an abnormal one. In other words, this is a war for the principles of democracy.

What I wish here to stress, however, is the honesty of the intentions which inspired me when I went to Berlin in 1937, and which afforded the Nazi Government every opportunity for frank co-operation with me. I may have erred in optimism, but not in cynicism, in hoping as long as possible for the best and in refusing to be convinced, until the worst proved me wrong, that the intentions of others were as evil as they seemed.

Nor did I lose any time in making clear to the Germans the standpoint which I proposed to adopt. Just a month after my arrival the German-English Society of Berlin, which corresponded to the Anglo-German Fellowship in London, were so good as to give a dinner in my honor. The President of this Society was, very suitably, H.R.H. the Duke of Saxe-Coburg-Gotha, whom, as Duke of Albany, I had known as an Eton boy and afterward as a German student at Bonn, where I had spent three months in 1903 when studying for my diplomatic examination. A large number of the leading Nazis attended the banquet; and, taking advantage of the license granted me by Mr. Chamberlain, I committed the indiscretion of making there a speech which aroused considerable criticism in certain circles in England, and which earned for me in some British journals the application of "our Nazi British Ambassador at Berlin." I have never felt the least remorse about that speech. It may have been prejudicial to the usefulness of my reports on Germany, to be regarded by some of my own countrymen as "pro" anything except British. But that was inevitable at a moment when everyone was being labeled "pro" something or other.

Before ever I went to Germany, I had twice had experience of the same superficiality of judgment. When I was at Constantinople, in the days of Chanak and the Lausanne Conference, General Harington and myself were both labeled as pro-Turk. Both he and I would gladly accept that reputation today. Again, when I was Minister at Belgrade in the early nineteen thirties, and largely because I happened to be a friend of the late King Alexander, I was condemned as being pro-Yugoslav and pro-dictator. People in England sometimes forget that there are "less happier lands" than theirs, and fail to realize that even dictators can be, up to a point, necessary for a period and even extremely beneficial for a nation. I say "up to a point" because the ancient Romans, who were the first to invent dictators to deal with crises, were wiser than their successors today, in that they carefully restricted dictatorial powers to a limited period of months. Few impartial historians would deny the uses of Cromwell, even in England, after the troubles of the civil war; and the crop of dictators which sprang up in Europe after the chaos of the 1914-1918 world war is explicable for the same reasons. It is a curious fact, parenthetically, that Hitler himself, who is a great reader of history, and especially so since his accession to power (Baron von Neurath once told me that his Führer knew far more history than he did himself), at one time made a particular study of Cromwell, who, among other things, died in his bed. Goering, too, mentioned to me on one occasion the names of two books which he also had read on the life of the Protector. The fact, indeed, is that dictators only become an unqualified evil for their own subjects and a danger for their neighbors when power goes to their heads and ambition and the desire for permanence drives them to oppression or adventure. Nor are all dictatorships, even if prolonged, reprehensible. Ataturk (Mustapha Kemal) built up a new Turkey on the ruins of the old; and his expulsion of the Greeks, which perhaps suggested to Hitler that he should do the same in Germany with the Jews, has already been forgotten and forgiven. One cannot, just because he is a dictator, refuse to admit the great services which Signor Mussolini has rendered to Italy; nor would the world have failed to acclaim Hitler as a great German if he had known when and where to stop; even, for instance, after Munich and the Nuremberg decrees for the Jews. Dr. Salazar, the present dictator of Portugal, who has set himself his own limitations and abided by them, is assuredly one of the wisest statesmen which the postwar period has produced in Europe. Dictatorships are not always evil; and, however anathematic the principle may be to us, it is unfair to condemn a whole country or even a whole system because

The Background of My Mission

parts of it are bad. Many dogs have been hanged simply for their bad name; and who was I to condemn the Nazis offhand or before they had finally proved themselves incurably vicious? Anyway, I do not concede to anyone the right to label me as anything but pro-British. I had told Mr. Eden before I left London that I should probably incur the appellation of pro-German; and if there were people who continued to regard me, till the end of my time at Berlin, as too pro-Nazi or pro-German or pro-anything at all except British, theirs was the mistake.

Moreover, whatever the detriment may have been of having such a reputation in certain quarters in England, it was outweighed, from the point of view of my work on behalf of British interests, by the sympathy which the sincerity of my attitude immediately won for me with the general public in Germany. With one rather interesting exception the text of my speech at the dinner of the German-English Society was published in full in all the German papers. Toward the end of it, with a view to enlisting the support of German women for the peace for which I pleaded, I quoted a verse of a song which, if I remember rightly, had been popular in America during the antiwar Wilson election there in 1916. It ran as follows:

> I did not raise my son to be a soldier,
> I brought him up to be my pride and joy.
> Who dares to put a musket on his shoulder
> To kill some other Mother's darling boy?

I was told afterward that it had been purposely omitted, lest German mothers should really think that their sons were not solely born to die for Hitler and for Germany.

Failure of a Mission

Admittedly, foreign relations are an ambassador's sole concern; and it is no business of his to refer in speeches to the internal affairs of the country in which he is living. But Germany was no normal state, and one could not ignore Nazism when referring to Germany. In point of fact, my reference to the Nazi regime constituted but a small part of a speech in which I attempted to explain frankly and honestly the attitude which I proposed to adopt toward the German Government and the Nazi party, since it was the latter which actually governed Germany. Its whole theme was the necessity for the peaceful negotiation of outstanding problems. Provided that line was adopted, all would, I said, be well; and I told my listeners that I could assure them that the reproach, which had been repeatedly made to me, to the effect that Britain was attempting to hem Germany in was untrue. I reminded them that, on presenting my letters of credence to the Reich Chancellor, I had said to Hitler that I was convinced that there was no question between our two countries which could not be solved by peaceful good will and mutual co-operation. I observed that those words came from the bottom of my heart and I concluded as follows: "Guarantee us peace and peaceful evolution in Europe, and Germany will find that she has no more sincere and, I believe, more useful friend in the world than Great Britain." That was in fact the whole basis of my policy.

The sentence which gave most offense to the left wing and others in England was that in which I remarked that it would be better if people in England laid less stress on the Nazi dictatorship and paid more attention to the great social experiment which was being tried out in Germany. I said that, if they did so, they might learn some useful lessons; and I regretted that too much concentration on those trees which appeared misshapen in English eyes rendered us insufficiently appreciative of the forest as a whole. One member of Parliament's comment thereon in the House of Commons was to the effect that "our old democracy has nothing to learn from Nazism." A laudably British sentiment, which might have been applied to Stalin's brand of Russian Communism as well as to German Nazism; nevertheless, one must pray that those who are responsible for the conduct of the war against Nazi Germany will not be guilty of the same fatuity. There are "sermons in stones and good in everything"; and there are, in fact, many things in the Nazi organization and social institutions, as distinct from its rabid nationalism and ideology, which we might study and adapt to our own use with great profit both to the health and happiness of our own nation and old democracy.

To my own countrymen I would, for instance, particularly recommend the labor camps. Between the age of seventeen and nineteen every German boy, rich or poor, the son of a laborer or of a former reigning prince, is obliged to spend six months in a labor camp, building roads, draining marshland, felling trees, or doing whatever other manual labor may be required in his area. In my humble opinion these camps serve none but useful purposes. In them not only are there no class distinctions, but on the contrary an opportunity for better understanding between the classes. Therein one learns the pleasure of hard work and the dignity of labor, as well as the benefits of discipline; moreover, they vastly improve the physique of the nation. The average weight which a German boy puts on during those six months is thirteen German pounds or a little over fourteen of our pounds of bone and muscle.

Few people in the twentieth century would deny that, with all its horrors and in spite of the ills of the Napoleonic epoch, the French Revolution left behind it theories and systems which were of lasting benefit to mankind. National Socialism is no less a revolution; and, however odious its ideology may today appear to most of us, just as did the French Revolution to our forebears at the end of the eighteenth century, it would be foolish to assume either that there is nothing to be learned from it, or that it will vanish in all its forms "unwept, unhonored and unsung" from this earth. Others have described with greater authority and competence the utility and beneficial nature of many of the institutions, such as, among others, the Strength through Joy movement, developed by the "socialist" rather than the "national" part of National Socialism. I do not propose to comment here on this. But it would be utterly unjust not to realize that great numbers of those who adhered to and worked for Hitler and the Nazi regime were honest idealists, whose sole aim was to serve Germany, to improve the lot of her people, and to add to their happiness. Hitler himself may well have been such an idealist at the start. Later he undoubtedly used this idealism as a cloak to justify the continued existence of the regime and of its leaders. But there were others who were true to their principles, and I left Germany with feelings of high regard for men like Dr. Gurtner, the Minister of Justice; Graf Schwerin von Krosigk, the Minister of Finance; Dr. Lammers, the head of the Reichschancery; as well as for many

The Background of My Mission

others in various walks of official life in Germany. Of all the qualities of the German race its capacity for organization is outstanding, and Germany owes much to the astounding organizing ability of men like Field Marshal Goering; Dr. Frick, the Minister of the Interior; Dr. Todt, the Director of Roads and Construction; Herr Hierl, the head of the Labor Service Administration; as well as to the soldiers, sailors, and airmen who built up the machine and restored Germany to her present formidable position. Most of us would have been proud to do for our own country what these and others like them did for theirs. It is not the machine which one must blame, but the uses to which it was put and the mind behind it.

Far be it from me to criticize those I have mentioned and many others like them. The mistake which was too easily made abroad was to condemn everything that was Nazi just because its ideology was contrary to ours and because some of its principles and many of its practices were utterly and inexcusably cruel and horrible. Ideological hatreds can be as dangerous to the peace of mankind as the ambitions of a dictator. Both involve the loss of sanity of judgment and of sense of proportion. The result at home was too much criticism and too little constructiveness in respect to Nazi Germany. If Central Europe were to settle down to peace, something more than criticism was essential.

It is probably true to say that, whatever attitude we had adopted toward Hitler and the Nazi gangsters, the result today would have been the same. Nevertheless, throughout those years from 1933 to 1938 we were not, in my opinion, always fair to Germany; and by being unfair we weakened our own case and merely strengthened that of the Nazis. The British tendency to self-righteousness played too big a part in our judgments, and Nazi methods blinded us sometimes to the arguable aspects of some of their contentions. We were too apt to make realities out of wishes and facts out of phrases. There can be no change of heart in Germany unless it comes from within; and we shall never inculcate true democratic ideas in the German people or persuade them to realize the higher responsibilities attached to force and strength, unless and until we ourselves treat Germany with strict impartiality and fairness.

One has heard much since the beginning of the war about there being or not being two Germanys: one, kindly, studious, and pacific; and the other, cruel, militarist, and aggressive. In wartime there can only be one Germany, which has to be fought and defeated. The innocent and the guilty have to suffer alike. Yet that does not alter the fact that there are two Germanys, and the outlook for the future would indeed be sad and hopeless if it were not so. Granted that the passive majority of decent Germans allow themselves today to be governed by a brutal and unscrupulous minority. Granted also that German history tends to show that this has generally been the case. Granted that Hitler is merely a typical example of an attitude of mind which has caused war after war. For it is, of course, the case that, in the last seventy years or so, Germany has initiated or been principally responsible for five wars; against Denmark and Austria in the eighteen sixties, against France in 1870, the war of 1914, and the present one. It is consequently argued that the passive majority always joyfully and willingly follows whither the aggressive minority leads and that it will always be the same. To my mind this argument is erroneous. It is equivalent to asserting that, because the Germans are sheep (and Hitler in *Mein Kampf* himself so describes the masses of the German people), therefore, they are goats. The wars of the last eighty years may yet prove to have been the evolutionary birth pains of German unity. Fearful thinkers may regard German unity as a consummation to be resisted to the last. A grave danger it certainly is, since no one can deny the German's tendency to be a bully when he is strong. Yet can evolution ever be more than retarded, and will not the price be too high if we persist in opposing that unity just because it is a hypothetical danger? Should not our object rather be to educate Germany politically up to a truer conception of civilization? We cannot do this unless there are in fact two Germanys. We have to help the sheep, if they are not always to follow the goats. Maybe this will never be possible unless we can first prove to the sheep, by the completeness of their defeat, that butting does not pay.

One cannot, however, be unfair in one's strictures on one branch of the Nazi system, and that is the Gestapo (Geheimstaatspolizei), or secret state police, under the command of Herr Himmler.

Himmler was for me the most enigmatical and elusive of all the Nazi leaders. Instinctively I distrusted him from the beginning more than any of the others. Yet, when one did meet and talk to him, it was scarcely possible to believe that this mild-looking and bespectacled young man, with his somewhat deprecatory manner and the appearance of a provincial schoolmaster, could be the tyrant directly responsible for the persecution of the so-called enemies of the state. Yet so it was, though it was often said that in police matters he was much under the influence of his right-hand man and second-in-command, Reinhard Heydrich, a notoriously unscrupulous and brutal gangster.

Born in Munich in 1900 and thus too young to have fought in the last war, Himmler was, nevertheless, one of the earliest adherents of the Hitler movement. He was the founder of the S.S., which was originally formed in 1922 as a small but specially trustworthy bodyguard for Hitler.

Up to 1933 he remained merely as chief of the S.S. and of the new Bavarian political police. He never advertised and rarely made political speeches. But, like a mole, he worked unceasingly underground; and his galleries were burrowed under the whole fabric of the German state. By 1936 he had succeeded not only in largely increasing the numbers of the S.S. but in getting under his own sole command the whole of the police forces of the Reich. It required a sharp struggle between him and Goering, who had hitherto controlled the Prussian police, before he could achieve this; but it was Himmler and not the Field Marshal who emerged victorious from it. Thereafter the power of the Gestapo silently and unobtrusively increased, until at the end there was no more powerful man in Germany under Hitler than Himmler.

Endowed with considerable moral and physical courage, the personal impression he gave me was one of desperate ambition and fanatical ruthlessness, but also of great efficiency. He was supposed to live simply, but he had a luxurious villa at Tegernsee in his native Bavaria, with extensive gardens and a private road, and surrounded by the barracks of his own blackshirted bodyguard. In the confusion of the private jealousies which were rife among the more powerful followers of the Führer, it was difficult at times to be sure of the various combinations, which were not always static. But Himmler and Ribbentrop were definitely allies: and a thoroughly mischievous combination they were, though, of the two, Himmler, in view of his undoubted ability, natural fanaticism, and greater intelligence was the more sinister figure.

The Gestapo was and is in all its forms and in all its aspects by far the most loathsome and detestable part of the Nazi regime. I do not need to refer to the brutalities of the concentration camps at Dachau or at Buchenwald, the two most notorious of them, and elsewhere. They have formed the subject of a White Paper published by His Majesty's Government after the outbreak of war; and this nauseating aspect of political hooliganism and barbarous sadism can be left to the judgment of civilized opinion. I once did my best to persuade Goering to use his influence with a view to their abolition. His answer was typical. After listening to all I had to say, he got up without a word and went to a bookcase from which he took a volume of the *German Encyclopaedia*. Opening it at *Konzentratinslager* (concentration camps) he read out, "First used by the British, in the South African War." He was pleased with his own retort; but the truth of the matter was that, though it was he who had originally formed these camps when he was Minister of Police for Prussia, he had no longer anything to do with them. They were entirely under the control of Himmler.

Not even in the days of Abdul Hamid in Constantinople was the horrible system of spying and denunciation carried to greater extremes than in Berlin and throughout Germany. One of Dr. Goebbels' propaganda films showed as its "hero" a small German boy who denounced his father and mother to their death at the hands of the Gestapo. The pogrom of the Jews in November, 1938, was entirely organized by Himmler's own policemen disguised as hooligans. The imprisonments and brutalities in Austria after March, 1938, were the work of the secret police. When Goering went to Vienna at the end of that month, he released several thousand of these unfortunates, among them one or two whom I had specially recommended to him on the ground that loyalty to their Emperor was a virtue in itself and could not be regarded as a crime. As soon as the Field Marshal returned to Berlin, the Gestapo, which had full and separate powers, lost no time in reincarcerating them. What the Czechs and Poles are suffering today is mainly the work of Himmler's Gestapo and blackshirts. One might give examples of their bestiality ad infinitum.

The Gestapo did more real harm to Germany's and the Nazi's reputation than anything else; and throughout my time in Germany I never ceased to inveigh against it to all who would listen to me. I remember that, at the time of the Munich Conference, when it had been decided that the Sudeten Lands should be progressively occupied by the German forces, I begged General Keitel to do his utmost to secure that the occupation was carried out, to the exclusion of the Gestapo, solely by the German soldiers, whose conduct as proved during the "rape" of Austria was always exemplary.

If I were entitled to apportion the blame for the tragic and ghastly war we have now entered, I should do so as follows: firstly, the overweening ambition and ever growing megalomania of Hitler; secondly, the self-interested and pernicious

The Background of My Mission

advice of Herr von Ribbentrop and of the small clique of Nazi veterans and gangsters, of whose names the world has never heard, who fought with Hitler in the streets and on the barricades and to whom, for their services in the struggle for power, were given many of the plums of victory such as the jobs of Reichstag Deputies, Gauleiters, etc.; and thirdly, Himmler and his blackshirted S.S. and secret police.

The vicious oppression of the Gestapo, the bestialities of the prisons and concentration camps, the degradation of the system of spying and denunciation not only constituted for me by far the most repugnant feature of the Nazi regime, but also represented for me one of the most unaccountable sides of the German character. Whatever his faults may be, the Anglo-Saxon is, without any doubt whatsoever, the kindliest creature in the world. To one who has lived abroad as much as I have, this is particularly apparent. Each time that I return to England and meet the first porter at Dover I am struck by this immediately noticeable characteristic. Even in his civil wars, unless it be for the brief episode of Judge Jeffries after Sedgemoor, the Englishman has never indulged in extensive persecution or torture for torture's sake. The streak of sadism in his Teuton cousin is the more inexplicable for that reason; for the German individual in normal life is as kindly as the Englishman, and his love for children and animals no less natural and sincere. But, put him in any abnormal position of authority, and in the majority of cases he will at once abuse it. Even in the old German Army, the N.C.O. bullied the private and the lieutenant the N.C.O. and so on. Perhaps it is the only language which the German thoroughly understands. I have endeavored earlier in this history to find some explanation for this in the very considerable amount of Slav blood which flows in the German veins. The mixture is probably a bad one; yet it cannot do more than account partially for this distressing and distinctive trait. A Gestapo would be inconceivable in England; why should the German nation, accustomed to submission and amenable to discipline though it is, have endured its methods and its cruelties if it did not itself accept such methods as natural, and consequently regard them with an indifference almost amounting to tolerance, if not approval?

The Gestapo will pass away in time; but what, having regard to the future, saddened me still more, as well as filled me with apprehension, was the education of the German youth. I am no educational expert, but roughly the education of the average German boy proceeds along the following course: At six he goes to the elementary, or day, school and at seven he joins the Jungvolk, or junior branch of the Hitler Jugend (Youth). Much of the training in the Jungvolk corresponds to that of our boy scouts, but he also gets there political lectures on National-Socialist lines (i.e. on the doctrines of racial superiority and national self-sufficiency) as well as training in target shooting. The musket is, in fact, put on his shoulder at the age of seven. At the age of fourteen and until eighteen it is compulsory for boys to join the Hitler Jugend itself, in which this politico-military education is intensified. At eighteen he does his six months' labor service, and between the ages of eighteen and twenty (i.e. after his labor service) he does his two years' military service. Only after the latter does he go to the university and while there is obliged to belong to the National-Socialist student organization. There are, of course, various arrangements for special-

The Background of My Mission

ized training which need not be mentioned here, since I am restricting myself to the life of the average German boy. Whatever his subsequent occupation in life and if he is not already in permanent military employment, he then joins one of the para-military formations such as the S.S. or the S.A.

The S.A. (Sturmabteilung, or storm detachment) was the brownshirted army, which had won Hitler's struggle for power for him and made him Chancellor and Führer of Germany. Captain Roehm had been its leader until, suspecting him of intriguing to seize supreme power for himself, Hitler had had him murdered in the "blood bath" of June, 1934. Thereafter the brown army, between three and four million strong, fell from grace and was reduced to a kind of party militia. Its position was taken by the blackshirted S.S. (Schutzstaffel, or protection squad) who formed Hitler's special Praetorian Guard. The latter, much smaller in numbers than the S.A. (some hundreds of thousands instead of millions), were a select body of younger, picked, and highly trained men. Part of them constituted Hitler's personal bodyguard, or household troops; some were later formed into military divisions, at least as well equipped as the Regular Army, but outside the command of the General Staff; and others were members of the Gestapo, or secret police. I refer to the S.S. sometimes in this narrative as "Blackshirts" but they might equally well have been called "Black Guards" written either as one word or two. There was considerable ill feeling between them and the brownshirts, whose favor with Hitler they had usurped and whom they treated with no little contempt. What the Regular Army thought of the S.S. I do not know. But they were a very essential part of the

Failure of a Mission

Nazi party stranglehold on the mass of the German people; and their chief was Heinrich Himmler, with the notorious Heydrich as his second-in-command. They constituted an essential ingredient of Hitler's internal technique of "divide and rule." It suited him to be surrounded by jealousies, with himself as sole arbiter of the quarrels of his followers. He could always play one off against the other, individually or corporately, and so rule all.

As a member of either S.S. or S.A. every German male is liable to be called up at any moment for special military service or any other duty and undergoes, till he is well past the age of fifty, refresher or other courses. That is what I mean later in this record when I describe Germany, on my arrival at Berlin, as being militarized from the cradle to the grave.

But even worse than this dangerous infusion of militaristic spirit, which has at least the redeeming virtues of discipline and obedience, so undeniably salutary to the young, is the politico-ideological poison which has no redeeming feature and with which the youth of the nation is being infected at its most malleable and impressionable stage. It is taught by means of a suppression of all real freedom and independence of thoughts, unparalleled in the history of the civilized world. "Brute force" as Hitler writes in *Mein Kampf* "can alone insure the survival of the race," and the educational values of Germany today are rated in the following order:

1. Race, i.e. the superiority of the Germanic, with its mission to dominate the world.
2. Character, i.e. political reliability in strict accordance with Nazi doctrines.

The Background of My Mission

3. Body, i.e. physical fitness.
4. Knowledge.

Along these few rigidly prescribed lines the mind of German youth since 1933 has been and is being intensively trained, and the reflection was one which made me wonder whether in Germany's own, as well as Europe's ultimate interests, it were not better that war should have come after six years of it rather than after perhaps twenty-six. Even so, maybe it will take a whole generation to eradicate the evil which has been wrought in this respect by Hitler, himself childless.

No dictator can ever feel that his position is permanently assured; and, apart from his army, it was on the Hitler Youth, his policemen, and his old revolutionaries that Hitler counted to keep himself in power. If he went, the last two categories would fall with him; they owed everything to him, and they could be relied upon to commit every crime in the calendar to insure that he did not fall. But, however deplorable these aspects of Nazism might be, internal oppression, which was the German nation's own affair, was distinct for me from external aggression, which was a British concern; and, when I first went to Berlin, I felt that it was unjust and impolitic finally to condemn a whole system because of certain of its more obvious vices. Moreover, I believed that there was no real prospect of stability either in Germany or in Europe generally until the grievances arising out of the Versailles Treaty—which had created Hitler—had been rectified so far as the Germans were concerned. This done, I trusted that Hitler and the reasons for his existence and the methods of his regime would disappear. But in the meantime I thought that the right policy was to carry conciliation to its utmost point before abandoning hope of agreement. That has always been the traditional policy of England; and, if Hitler had had better advisers, he would have realized that its basis was strength and moral justice and not national decadence and weakness, which Ribbentrop persuaded him to believe that it was. Therefore, I was resolved to err, if anything, on the side of impartiality, to try to see the good side of the Nazi regime, if there was one, and to believe in Hitler's word until he proved himself by his deeds to be a perjurer and a breaker of faith. The patient was abnormal, and I did not believe in continuing the treatment which had produced the disease. Peace was my big objective, and my influence with the Germans would be nil if I prejudged the Nazis from the start. In a sense my role, as I saw it, was to be the reverse of that of Balaam. I did not go to Berlin to curse, but, where possible, to bless. That was the background of my beginnings.

CHAPTER III. ARRIVAL IN BERLIN

I ARRIVED at Berlin on April 30th, 1937. May 1st is cele-brated as the great labor holiday in Germany and largely de-voted to speech making. It furnished me with my first oppor-tunity to see Hitler and hear him speak in person. Since I had not yet presented my letters of credence, I went on that day quite unofficially first to the German Opera House and afterward to the Lustgarten. I was accompanied by the First Secretary of His Majesty's Embassy, Mr. Kirkpatrick. What I would have done without Ivone Kirkpatrick during my first eighteen months, after which he was transferred to the F.O., does not bear thinking about. He had then been some six years at Ber-lin and knew everybody and everything. Extremely able and intelligent, he had in addition a kind of puckish Irish humor which made his counsel and experience as diverting as they were, I hope, profitable to me. Nor was I less fortunate in this respect during my last eight months with his successor, Adrian Holman. The latter had not, of course, Kirkpatrick's experi-ence of Germany; but he served me well and truly. He came and lived in the Embassy at the end, and during the last ten days or so before the outbreak of war he cannot have had many hours' sleep. Altogether I was very lucky as regards my staff, from the top to the bottom of it. They were, moreover, a happy family among themselves. I never heard a grumble and never had cause to grumble myself. I always had that very satisfactory feeling that my staff was always trying to do its best and to save me personally from all minor worries.

At the Opera House, where I was given a place apart from the other heads of missions, though Hitler was present, it was Dr. Goebbels who spoke. The subject was art and literature, and I must admit that I was charmed both by the natural fluency of his manner of speaking and his extremely agreeable voice. As politics did not enter into his subject, it was free from the venom, casuistry, and lies which were the normal feature of his usual propagandist outpourings. At the Lustgarten, after an introductory speech by Dr. Ley, it was Hitler himself who addressed the packed crowd drawn up in organized formation before him. His speech contained a scathing reference or so to the effete democracies, particularly Britain, against whom there was as usual a press campaign raging at the time; but in the main it was directed against Jewish influences in Russia. In speaking about Germany he used one phrase which stuck in my mind. It was that "no people could escape its own destiny," and referred to the necessity for the German people to put up with hardship in order to make itself independent of other nations and to fight, if need be, in eastern Europe in order to secure more *Lebensraum*, or space for development. Germany's sorrows, though she greatly exaggerates them, are not altogether of her own making. Her geographical position has had a good deal to do with their creation; and one of the most obvious but often least appreciated truths in the world is that foreign pol-

Arrival in Berlin

icy is to a greater extent governed by geography than anything else.

I was at the time, however, more interested in the individual
and in the psychology of the crowd than in the actual words
spoken. I found, as I had in listening to his speeches on the
radio when I was British Minister at Belgrade, his voice harsh
and unsympathetic. But he had the gift of oratorical exhorta-
tion, and the people seemed to appreciate what he said. Yet
it was a lovely day; and I could but feel that the crowd would
have preferred to be amusing itself elsewhere rather than
standing, packed like disciplined sardines, listening to the
kind of speech that they must have heard often enough, and
shouting their "Heils" or their "Pfuis" whenever Hitler
raised his voice rather higher than usual or paused to mark
his point in his flow of oratory. It was impossible, indeed,
not to wonder on that first occasion and up to the last
wherein the greatness of Hitler lay, by what means he had
succeeded in imposing himself as the undisputed leader of a
great people, and what was the—to me—hidden source of his
influence over his followers and of their complete subservi-
ence to him. To convince oneself of his greatness, one had
to remember his actual deeds and judge by facts. Of the
facts themselves there was no doubt. He had restored to
Germany her self-respect and re-created orderliness out of
the chaos and distress which had followed her defeat in 1918.
It is true that the price that the Germans had had to pay was
a heavy one; namely, complete loss of personal liberty, of independent thought, and of free speech. All were obliged to
think, speak, and act as they were told to do or suffer exile
or persecution. The rails of National Socialism were laid in a

straight line, and any deviation from them met with instant punishment. Yet some sort of an operation had been necessary. In 1933, 10 per cent, over 6,000,000 men, of the population of Germany were out of work. Within 4 years the number of unemployed had been reduced to an infinitesimal figure, and by 1939 there was a labor shortage estimated at 2,000,000. That in itself, however much one may attribute it to war production, was no mean achievement. To the wheels of Hitler's chariot were, in fact, harnessed the amazing power of organization, thoroughness, and discipline of the German nation. Nor can it be denied that the rebirth of that nation was due to Hitler's own personal inspiration. For the fact remains that he is the living example of one of those almost incomprehensible leaders who appear from time to time on earth "to fashion the destiny of a race, for its weal or its woe, or to crucify the world by a sudden revelation of violence and power." He was abnormal, but so after 1918 was the whole German nation.

National Socialism is a revolution; and, if, apart from his demagogic faculties, Hitler had one quality which placed him in an unassailable position above the rest of his fellow revolutionaries, it was his faith. Faith in Germany, faith in his mission for Germany, and, alas, increasingly arrogant faith in himself and in his own greatness. Faith and will power. I once watched Hitler review his black- and brownshirted army. The march past lasted for four hours, and practically throughout he remained with his right arm stretched out at the Nazi salute. I asked him afterward how he managed to do it. His reply was "will power"—and I wondered how much of it was artificially cultivated. He was no such ad-

ministrator as is Signor Mussolini—I doubt if he either cared
or knew very much about the details of the machine which
functioned in his name. But he set its course, put it in motion, or stopped it according to his own plan. During my
first year in Germany I constantly asked those in closest
touch with Hitler of what his chief quality consisted. I was
told almost unanimously, in his *fingerspitzgefühl* (tip of the
finger feeling), that is to say, his sense of opportunity, allied
with clearness of mind and decision of purpose. The typical
example which was quoted of this was his decision to re-
occupy the Rhineland in 1936, which was taken contrary
to the warning of his general staff and of all his closest advisers. Germany was at that time not militarily strong enough
to disregard a French veto; and his followers shrank from
an act which would, they believed, be forcibly opposed by
the Western Powers. Hitler's instinct told him that the latter
would accept an accomplished fact, and he disregarded all
warnings to the contrary. The event proved him right and
greatly reinforced his prestige, not only among his own immediate supporters but throughout Germany as a whole.
Incidentally, it was probably the last opportunity when it
would still have been possible for Britain and France to have
said "no" to the Dictator without being obliged to go to war
to enforce that "no."

Be that as it may, Hitler, whatever the external impression
which he may give and whatever may be one's judgment of
him based, as mine was, on a superficial personal acquaintance, is, or at least began by being, a visionary of genius and
a man who was able to tell the German people what it was
that they wanted. So long as he procured it for them with-

out war, his word was absolute and their confidence in him unshaken. The first shock to their belief in his infallibility came in September, 1938, when he led them to the abyss of war over the Sudeten German question. Many Germans must then have asked themselves whether Hitler by that time was still thinking of Germany or only of himself, his party, and his personal ambitions. They may be thinking it still more today. But by this time the shackles of the Nazi organization and regime are so riveted on the whole country that what the German people themselves may feel or want is a matter of indifference to a system which must go forward or end, to individuals who must remain in power or become nobodies again, and to a leader whose ambitions have now become a form of hysterical megalomania. *Sic volo sic jubeo* is now Hitler's only creed. And he has behind him the entire might of the German Army, which has taken the oath of loyalty to him, as well as the complete organization of the party, which owes its very existence to him, and the wholehearted enthusiasm of the entire credulous youth of the country, which has been taught to worship force and Hitler. The German people collectively are but grist for the mill, and as one of them whom I met by chance after war had been declared said to me, *"Wir sind zu klein, wir können nichts machen"* (We are too small, we can do nothing).

It will always be a matter of regret to me that I was never able to study Hitler in private life, which might have given me the chance to see him under normal conditions and to talk to him as man to man. Except for a few brief words at chance meetings I never met him except upon official and invariably disagreeable business. He never attended informal

34

parties at which diplomatists might be present; and, when friends of mine did try to arrange it, he always got out of meeting me in such a manner on the ground of precedent. Up to a period in his career he was accessible to foreigners, to whom he readily accorded interviews; but he gradually became less so; and he had apparently a rooted aversion to private contacts with diplomatists, whom, as a category, he distrusted. The greater one becomes the more one is obliged to live on a pedestal lest, if one descends from it, one loses, through commerce with ordinary people, the godlike attributions of greatness. No man is a hero to his valet, and Hitler may have taken that saying to heart. He was a true demagogue, and crowds stimulated him, but social life of any sort bored him. He liked the company of his intimate friends, whom he could harangue to his heart's delight; but he always looked self-conscious when he had to entertain the diplomatic corps, which happened normally three times a year: at his New Year's reception, at his annual dinner to the heads of missions, and at the tea party which he gave for them in September during the party rally at Nuremberg.

I was once asked by a German acquaintance who must, in view of his former official position, have had many talks with him whether I ever managed during my interviews with Hitler to get a word in edgeways. It was a curious observation, suggesting as it did that he himself never had. That was, however, not my experience. He may not have heeded what I said; and he may, like Ribbentrop, only have been thinking what he himself was going to say next; but he always seemed ready to listen, nor did he speechify to any unendurable extent. I myself once made him a little speech which lasted for five or ten minutes. His reply lasted three times as long; and thereafter, for obvious reasons, I avoided making speeches myself. If I thought his own were getting too long and that he was becoming carried away by his own oratory, I interrupted him; nor did he ever seem to be offended thereby.

My impression was that his emotional outbursts were not spontaneous but that he deliberately worked himself up into a state of excitement. But it may have become second nature with him after all the impassioned orations which he had had to make during the years of his struggle for power. Or he may have thought that, since demagogical eloquence swayed the masses, it must have a similar effect on the individual. Anyway, with his own people he seems to have claimed the monopoly of the talking, though he probably was attentive enough if he had anything which he wished to learn from them. But contradiction was insupportable to him; and, if anyone attempted it, as General von Fritsch did in January, 1938, he was dismissed. I never heard of his ever doing a generous action. On the other hand one of his most marked characteristics was sheer vindictiveness, and his resentments were enduring and intensely disagreeable for anyone on whom it was in his power to exercise them. I am not surprised that his followers were afraid of him. They had plenty of examples of his capacity for revenge to intimidate them.

His defect in this respect was his tragedy, as it is necessarily that of any dictator. No man of independent mind can long tolerate the lack of all freedom of utterance. Unable to express views which may be contrary to those of their master, the best men leave him one by one. His entourage steadily and inexorably deteriorates, until at the end he is surrounded by mere yes-men, whose flattery and acquiescence are alone endurable to him. That, too, was Hitler's fate during the last year which I spent in Berlin.

He was always urging his fellow countrymen to forget their inferiority complex, but he was subject to it himself. Both on this account and because of his demagogue's nature he always had to have applause. If it was not the crowd's, it had to be that of the coterie of his intimate friends, particularly of his old street fighters of the Brown House at Munich. At the same time his tastes were excessively simple. He drank no wine, he did not smoke, and he ate no meat. He was a bad sleeper, especially at Berlin, which was one reason why he spent as little time as possible in the capital. He got up late and disliked working till after luncheon, but he would also go to bed late and would sit up talking till all hours of the night. He liked to relax after dinner in the company of pretty and ornamental young women.

Beautiful scenery appealed to him in the same way, and his real home was the Berghof at Berchtesgaden on the top of a mountain with a magnificent view looking over to Salzburg and the lovely scenery of his native Austria. He kept no particular state there, and on the two occasions on which I visited him there, there was little evidence of any excessive precautions for his safety. Yet he was very strictly guarded; and the necessity for his protection was one of the holds which Himmler, as head of his secret police, had over him. The path to him was, however, made easy for an ambassador, who might be counted upon not to have a revolver or a bomb concealed upon his person. For others, if there was any doubt whatsoever, it would probably have been made much more searching and difficult. It was part of the show to give the impression of a beloved ruler, unafraid and reliant on the devotion of his people. But in the forest which surrounded the villa (Berghof) stood the barracks of his special bodyguard of blackshirts; and its trees and bushes probably concealed numbers of highly alert and expert gunmen. He had, withal, another bolthole in the form of an eyrie on the summit of a yet higher mountain peak. It could only be reached by a road built for some miles out of the solid rock, through bronze doors let into the mountain side, and by an elevator tunneled in the mountain itself. It was said to be guarded on all sides by machine guns, but I never saw it myself and can only write from hearsay.

Hitler always wore a simple brown tunic without any decorations except the Iron Cross of the second class, which he had won in the great war. He was very unlike Goering in this respect; yet, in a sense, both extremes appealed to the Germans. They might make fun of but they liked Goering's unabashed display of show and medals. At the same time Hitler's simplicity was one of the sheet anchors of his hold on the people. His followers built themselves villas and gardens and acquired estates and other private belongings by means which were suspected of being of doubtful honesty; and, except in Goering's case, the people were indignant and resentful. The comparison between the other Nazi leaders and Hitler in this respect was all the more flattering to the latter and was appreciated by the mass of the nation accordingly. The others may have provided for themselves nest eggs abroad, but Hitler would certainly not have done so unless it were in the form of the legitimate royalties which he must have drawn from the sale of *Mein Kampf* in the United States or elsewhere.

Before an ambassador or a minister has presented his letters of credence to the head of the state to which he is accredited, his position is an unofficial one, not only as regards the functionaries of that state, but also as regards his diplomatic colleagues, with whom he is not supposed to have any relations until after the presentation of his credentials. The coronation of King George VI was to take place on May 12th, and preparations had been made for a service in the English Church for that occasion. My South African colleague, with whom I was on terms of the closest and friendliest co-operation throughout the whole of my residence at Berlin and whose balanced and sound judgment I always highly valued, had announced his intention of attending it.

Contrary to precedent I had called on my United States colleague shortly after my arrival; and, when I also asked him whether he would care to come, he telephoned to say that he would be glad to do so.

Incidentally, I would mention here that Mr. Dodd went on leave in the summer and never returned to his post, having disagreed with the policy of his government in authorizing the American representative to attend the Nuremberg rally in September. He was succeeded as American Ambassador by Mr. Hugh Wilson. The latter was, unlike Mr. Dodd, a diplomatist by career. He had been for some years American observer at Geneva. He must have served his government well in that capacity, for I have seldom met his equal for keen observation and sound judgment. I always kept in the closest touch with him, and his appreciations of the situation were always extremely useful to me. He was withdrawn from Berlin after the Jewish persecutions of November, 1938. He was on the point of coming back to his post when the occupation of Prague in March, 1939, finally put an end to all idea of his return. I missed him greatly during that and the succeeding crisis.

I also made an exception as regards official calls in the case of Field Marshal Blomberg, who had been selected by Hitler to represent Germany at the Coronation in London, together with Admiral Schultze and General Stumpff. I called on him at the Ministry for War and invited him and his fellow delegates to lunch with me before their departure, which they did. I was particularly impressed by the Field Marshal. A man of fifty-eight, tall and soldierly and good looking, he was typical of the old German Army; and no better selection could have been made for the task of representing Germany at the Coronation. He was a fervent admirer of Hitler, whose praises he was never tired of singing. He once said to me that if Hitler ordered him and his army to march the next day to the North Pole they would do it without a moment's hesitation. It was related that Hitler had a similar affection for the Field Marshal, and had more than once stated that if Blomberg deserted him he would throw himself from the window. In the end Blomberg, if not deserting him, did act contrary to his wishes. Whereupon it was not Hitler who threw himself from the window, but Blomberg who was thrown onto the rubbish heap. But that was to come some ten months later, and at the time Blomberg was perhaps Hitler's closest friend and adviser.

Arrival in Berlin

Poor Blomberg! He was the first German whom I entertained at His Majesty's Embassy, and he was one of the first to invite me to his house. It was a man's party, and with the exception of Neurath and myself all the others were soldiers or airmen. The regime might be Nazi; but the senior commanders of the Navy, Army, and Air Force were officers of the last war; and I often wondered what they felt about their political leaders. Some, of course, saw in enthusiastic adherence to the party doctrines the steppingstone to promotion, and all must have recognized the greatness of Hitler's achievement in restoring the German Army to its former great position. But there must have been a good deal of heartburning and irritation over some of the Nazi peculiarities and interference in military matters. Goering was also at that dinner; and I recall that, when he, Blomberg, and Neurath were talking to me after it, one of them asked me what I did when anyone gave the Nazi salute or said "Heil Hitler" to me. For once I happened to be quick on the uptake. "I bring," I replied, "my right hand, with fingers closed and palm to the front, to a position one inch above the right eyebrow, click my heels, and say 'Rule Britannia.'" They all laughed; but, as a matter of fact, nobody except an occasional cloakroom attendant and Miss Unity Mitford ever did greet me with "Heil Hitler." And when Miss Mitford did it, in the middle of a big crowd at Nuremberg, I was so surprised and dumbfounded that I forgot "Rule Britannia" and said nothing at all.

On the day before the Coronation I was received by Hitler and presented my letters of credence. As it happened the disaster to the airship *Hindenburg* had occurred just before my audience; there were rumors of foul play; and Hitler was in an excited mental state on the subject. It was always my fate to see him when he was under the stress of some emotion or other. We read to each other friendly little set speeches, but he showed little interest until I expressed my condolence at the loss of his airship and of a number of German lives. He then invited me into another room to sit down, and told me that there had been a number of warning letters before the departure of the *Hindenburg*, and that the whole airship had been searched from stem to stern before she left on her last journey. His attitude toward me was quite friendly, but I was left again wondering wherein lay the secret of his hold over Germany.

Many Germans, women in particular, used to descant to me upon the radiance of his expression and his remarkable eyes. When I looked into the latter, they were generally hot and angry. That was possibly my misfortune, since I only saw him on official occasions; but I must confess that, in spite of his achievements, which no one could belittle, he never on that first occasion or later gave me any impression of greatness. He was a spellbinder for his own people. That is self-evident, nor was there any doubt about his capacity to charm, if he set himself out to do so. It was part of his stock in trade, and I was more than once the spectator of its efficiency. But he never exerted it in my case, and I consequently never experienced it. In his reasonable moods I was often disconcerted by the sanity and logic of his arguments; but, when he became excitable, which was the mood

which most influenced his countrymen, I had but one inclination, which was to beg him to calm down. He had considerable natural dignity and was invariably courteous; but
to the last I continued to ask myself how he had risen to
what he was and how he maintained his ascendance over the
German people. The answer to the second question lies, in
my opinion, in the fact that, firstly, the Germans like to be
governed by an autocratic ruler and that, secondly, the party,
having got its leader, cannot afford now to change him. To
avoid its own destruction it is obliged to keep him there. No
one realizes this more than Himmler.

The Minister for Foreign Affairs, Baron von Neurath, and
the Minister for Justice were present at my audience, together with Hitler's celebrated interpreter, Dr. Schmidt. The
latter was invariably in attendance when Hitler received foreign diplomats or statesmen; and, if he is ever able to publish
his memoirs, they might throw an interesting light on many
problems. So far as I personally was concerned, I always
spoke in German direct to Hitler; and Dr. Schmidt's services
as an interpreter were never required. He always, however,
took copious notes, which I can imagine were exceedingly
useful as records to his master. On one occasion he was allowed to furnish me with an expurgated copy of them, and,
when Lord Halifax saw Hitler that autumn, he, also, was
given Schmidt's written account of their conversation. But
that was in Baron von Neurath's time as Minister for Foreign
Affairs. When Herr von Ribbentrop succeeded him in that
post, this courtesy was no longer tolerated.

Baron von Neurath was an astute and experienced Swabian
who had been Ambassador in Rome and in London before

becoming Minister for Foreign Affairs. Among the Germans, the Swabians enjoy a reputation for economy and dourness, similar to that of the Scots among the English. He and his wife had been extremely popular in England, and I liked them both immensely. His charming daughter was the wife of the son of the veteran Field Marshal von Mackensen. The son worked under his father-in-law as Secretary of State, which is the equivalent of our Permanent Undersecretary for Foreign Affairs. The political director of the Ministry was Baron von Weizsäcker, who had served as a naval officer in the war. There is no finer type than the hard-headed, intensely German but, at the same time, absolutely honest and honorable German official. Of such was Weizsäcker, and he succeeded Mackensen about a year later as Secretary of State under Ribbentrop. With all of these my relations were excellent, and the Ministry itself a happy and united department. It was to change later when it came under the direction of Herr von Ribbentrop, but at that time my diplomatic colleagues and I were exceedingly fortunate. Baron von Neurath himself was a survivor of the Hindenburg regime and not yet a member of the Nazi party. He became one later, but at that time his position was somewhat anomalous, and one could not always be certain that he was fully cognizant of the views of Hitler and the inner council of the party. There had even been at one time three kinds of ministries for foreign affairs in existence at the same time in Berlin: Herr Rosenberg's, Herr von Ribbentrop's, and the official Ministry in the Wilhelmstrasse. The former's activities had ceased before my arrival, but that of Herr von Ribbentrop, Hitler's Ambassador at Large, still functioned to some

Arrival in Berlin

extent and must have constituted a considerable handicap to the official department.

After I had presented my letters of credence, there was still another ceremony to be performed before I could be regarded as definitely installed. Berlin is one of those capitals in which the head of a foreign mission has, on first arrival, to undergo what is known in diplomatic language as a *ricevimento*, or, in plain English, an official reception. Though not a universal custom—it is not, for instance, followed in London or Paris—it is a practical and useful one. When he first arrives an ambassador is technically regarded as knowing nobody. In order to overcome this initial handicap, the head of the protocol or master of ceremonies at the ministry for foreign affairs issues, on the ambassador's behalf and, naturally, at the latter's expense, invitations to the diplomatic corps and all the higher government officials to attend a party at the embassy on a day and at a time agreed upon with the ambassador. In this manner the newcomer gets to know at once everybody with whom he may later come into contact.

After my audience with the Reichschancellor I was accordingly asked to fix a date for my *ricevimento*. Being mostly Scot by origin, I selected June 10th. Abroad the King's birthday is celebrated on June 9th. It is an occasion for patriotic and loyal demonstrations, and I had decided to invite on that day all the British residents in Berlin to tea at the Embassy. There would, it seemed to me, be a certain economy in flowers and in other respects if the official reception were to take place the day after. It was consequently so arranged, but what I had not foreseen was that in 1937 June 9th and

45

10th were to be the two hottest days of the year in Berlin. Consequently what I gained in flowers—and even so a good many of them wilted and had after all to be replaced—I, so to speak, lost in drinks, which were in unusual request on both occasions.

The British Embassy in Berlin is a dignified house with a large frontage in the Wilhelmstrasse, or Downing Street on a larger scale of Berlin. Except for the Embassy it consists almost entirely of Government offices, including the Reichschancery, or Chancellor's official residence, as well as the Ministry for Foreign Affairs, etc. (When I left Berlin Bismarck's old palace there was being completely renovated in order to house Ribbentrop.)

The Embassy itself had been built in the early seventies by a German, who had made a large fortune out of railway construction. He went bankrupt shortly after, whereupon the house was acquired by the British Government. In those early days it had a large garden at the back, running up to the street which forms one side of the Tiergarten. For some reason or another, which may either have been cupidity on the part of those de facto rulers of Britain, the officials of His Majesty's Treasury, or the difficulty of refusing a direct appeal made to the Ambassador of the moment, Sir Frank Lascelles, by the reigning Emperor, the garden was eventually sold in order to provide a site for the Adlon Hotel, which Wilhelm II wished to make into the superhotel of Berlin. Possibly it was a combination of both these considerations; but, whatever the reason, the result was a catastrophe from the point of view of the amenity of the Embassy itself. Shut off on the south from the sunlight by the great edifice of the Adlon and sullied by the smoke from the hotel's vast kitchen chimney, the house was always dark and always dirty.

In addition the railway magnate's idea as to internal comfort in the eighteen seventies were somewhat rudimentary. His main object seemed to have been to waste space instead of to use it. Large though the house was, the total number of bedrooms was only about half a dozen; and my predecessor, who was a married man with a family, can barely have had more than one guest room available for visitors. It is true that there had originally been more rooms; but a number of them had, in course of time, been expropriated and allotted to the Chancery, the offices for which were also situated in the Embassy building. Even with these additions the Chancery accommodation was inadequate and unhygienic.

Those who imagine that the diplomatic secretaries and the personnel of His Majesty's Embassies abroad work in the utmost luxury and comfort are under a grave misconception. Since the war the work of His Majesty's Missions abroad has increased out of all comparison with prewar days; and, though the increase in the size of the staffs has been correspondingly great, it has not always been possible to find the extra space required. This was particularly the case in Berlin, in many respects the postwar Cinderella of our missions abroad. The fact was recognized at home, and I had been authorized to put forward suggestions with a view to the acquisition of a new Embassy building. From a sentimental point of view it would have been sad to leave the historic building in the Wilhelmstrasse, but from the point of view of work it was essential. As it was, the Embassy only provided offices for the diplomatic staff and the Financial Adviser. The Commercial Secretariat, the offices of the Naval, Military, and Air Attachés, the Passport Offices, and the Consulate General were all situated in a building about a kilometer away, an arrangement which was highly inconvenient and prejudicial to the competency of the work of the Embassy.

In these days economics in particular cannot be separated from politics; and the closest co-operation is necessary if the work is to be carried out rapidly and efficiently, more especially when, as in Berlin, the telephone can only be used as contact in respect of matters of an entirely nonconfidential character. My idea, therefore, was to exchange the Embassy, which the German Government would have been glad to use for government offices, for some large site on a corner of one of Hitler's new thoroughfares. Thereon we might have built an embassy suitable for all modern requirements, both to hold offices for the whole staff without exception and to serve as a private residence for the Ambassador. I spoke both to Goering and Ribbentrop of this plan and asked them to let Hitler know that I contemplated it. I suggested that they might inform him that I meant one day to talk to him about it and hoped it would form part of a general understanding with Germany. In the event, however, conditions were never peaceful or hopeful enough for me to raise the question, as I should have liked to do, with Hitler himself.

Inconvenient though the Embassy was from the point of view of personal accommodation and public efficiency, the reception rooms on the ground floor were, on the other hand, well suited for large entertainments. About a thousand British subjects, out of about fifteen hundred established altogether in Berlin, attended my tea party on the King's birthday; and one might hardly have noticed that they were there. This was partially due to the fact that they were all crowded into two rooms, the dining room, where the refreshments were, and the ballroom, where there was a cinema of the Coronation in colors, which had very kindly been lent to me by Fox Films. The ballroom held over three hundred people, and the film lasted for about forty minutes. I gave it three times that hot afternoon, and thus everybody was able to see it. Those who were not in the ballroom spent their time in the dining room. My very competent German butler said to me afterward that he always knew that Germans ate a lot, but he had never seen people eat so much as those loyal subjects of His Britannic Majesty. The British colony in Berlin was an extremely poor one, and I do not think that any party which I ever gave provided me with greater pleasure than that one.

About seven hundred Nazi functionaries and diplomats attended the official reception the following day. The amount of food eaten was much less on that occasion, but the cinema, of which I again gave two performances, was almost equally appreciated. I was very grateful to Fox Films. The captions, being American, were excellent propaganda and better than they would have been if the film had been British. I was hopeful that what they saw and heard about the British Monarchy and Empire might be instructive and salutary for the Nazi officials, few of whom had ever been in London. It may have been; but, if so, they soon forgot it. It is, however, only just to say that the German controlled press, in reporting on the Coronation, abandoned for once its anti-British attitude and described the various ceremonies and proceedings during the Coronation week with absolute fairness and no little sympathy.

CHAPTER IV

THE BACKGROUND OF
GERMANY IN MAY, 1937

BEFORE proceeding with the relation of actual events, I would like, in this chapter, to describe, as briefly as I can, the position in Germany as I found it on taking up my post there on May 1st, 1937.

Hitler had been in power for over four years and during that period had achieved gigantic progress in the military, industrial, and moral reorganization of Germany. It was patent that she could no longer be coerced except by the actual use of force.

The Saar territory had been recovered in 1935 by means of an overwhelming plebiscite in favor of the Reich; and the Rhineland had been occupied and remilitarized in March, 1936. All the internal disabilities imposed on the Germany of the peace treaties had thus, to all intents and purposes, been liquidated; and the vast preparations for the achievement of the next step, the unity of Greater Germany, i.e. Austria, the Sudeten Lands, Memel, and Danzig, were in full swing. Military preparedness was the keynote of Nazi policy. The Army and Air Force were being rapidly expanded, air defense on a large scale was being developed, compulsory military service had been extended from one to two years, the Labor Service Corps had been greatly increased, and the whole youth of the country was in process of being incorporated in the Hitler Youth.

Germany, as I wrote in one of my earlier dispatches, was being militarized from the cradle to the grave. The writing was thus on the wall for all to read. The only real question was whether it was intended to use this German might as backing for the attainment of not illegitimate aims or for the prosecuting of illegitimate ambitions. The "I told you so's" will say that there never was any doubt on the subject. That may be so; but, nevertheless, the contrary had first to be proved.

The Ministry of Economics was being filled with soldiers, and in fact the whole economy of the country was being harnessed to the military machine. The slogans of the Nazi party were still "Purity of Race" and "Guns instead of butter"; and all industrial considerations were being subordinated to the Four Years' Plan, or in other words, to the necessity of rendering Germany independent of supplies from abroad. The Nazi system was calculated, better perhaps than any other could have been, to weld the German people into an efficient war machine; and to the appreciation of this fact may possibly be attributed the tolerance shown by the Army to a party whose political activities it must often have found irritating and embarrassing, as well as subversive of discipline.

While the steady forging of the Siegfried sword was the most obviously alarming symptom of the situation from the point of view of the outside world, the rise in the cost of living, the downward trend in the standard of life, the exactions of the party, and the restrictions on individual liberty were a heavy burden on the people and the cause of consid-

erable internal dissatisfaction. Many Germans have, in conversation with me, attributed Hitler's dynamic impatience to
his alleged conviction, to which he himself frequently alluded,
that his life was not destined to be a long one. He was so full
of tricks that I often wondered whether that assertion was
not one of them. It seems to me at least as likely that Hitler
suspected that his own people might not submit indefinitely
to the hardships imposed upon them by the regime. He had,
therefore, to excuse his own impatience and to act quickly,
if the economic situation were not to break or the people to
become too dissatisfied before he had had time to perfect the
military machine which was necessary for the execution of
his long-term plans and the satisfaction of his far-reaching
ambitions. It was for him a race between the readiness of his
army and the possible collapse of German economy.

On the other hand, Germany's growing military strength
had enabled her to take a more independent line in foreign
affairs than she had hitherto done; and the political situation
in Europe had, in the year preceding my arrival, greatly
changed, to Germany's advantage. By 1937, there was no
longer any risk of foreign intervention in Germany's internal
affairs. The Berlin-Rome Axis had been invented; and the unity
of Italo-German interests was to be affirmed a few months
later in September, when Signor Mussolini officially visited
Berlin. The Axis served the immediate interests of Italy during the period of sanctions against her and in view of the
support which she was giving to the Franco party in Spain;
but its ultimate benefits were of far greater value to Germany
than to Italy. Among other things it removed for the former
the most dangerous obstacle to Nazi intrigues in Austria and

the actual stumbling block which had caused them to fail at the time of the Dolfuss murder in 1934.

The Nazi party and the press were still hard at work at that time beating the anti-Bolshevist drum, mainly for purposes of internal consumption but also with a view to making the outside world believe that Germany was the sole bulwark against universal communism. The opportunity offered by Japan's bad relations with Russia had been seized in the preceding year to sign the German-Japanese agreement. This so-called anti-communist but equally anti-democratic front was to become a triangular one toward the end of 1937, when Italy joined it. The ten-year German-Polish agreement had been signed in 1934, and thus, by 1937, Germany, so far from being friendless in the world, as she was so apt in self-commiseration to depict herself to be, had greatly fortified her political situation. The success of Nazism was attracting many sympathizers abroad, particularly in Hungary with irredenta of her own, but also in other European countries, as well as overseas. The *Auslandsdeutschen*, or Germans living in foreign countries, were busily organizing themselves abroad in support of the movement in the fatherland and as an advance guard for political invasion by that fatherland.

It was the heyday of the movement and of Hitler himself. Though there might be restiveness in Germany itself at the exactions of the party and the recurring food shortages, the Germans are a docile, credulous, and disciplined people who like being governed; and they comforted themselves with the assurance that Hitler had the knack of getting everything he wanted without war. Above all, the malleable German youth were enthusiastic over a movement which appealed so strongly to the young and were being taught to accord to Hitler the attributions of something very near akin to God. When people lightly talk of the German nation's overthrowing its present rulers, it must be borne in mind that for nearly seven years the whole of the German youth has been taught the cult of force and power and that they are Hitler's most devoted adherents in its worship.

To an objective observer there was something almost fascinating in the skill with which Hitler was moving the pieces on his chessboard. None of his political maneuvers were really to the liking of his people, who cared little for either Italians or Japanese; but each of these in turn served his purpose at the time. He needed peaceful and good relations with his neighbors while he matured his plans for their destruction; and in the pause which these alliances afforded him he quietly transformed Germany into one vast military camp for that purpose. The pact with Japan was useful not only to contain Russia but also in order to embarrass the Western Powers and to distract their attention in the Far East. The fact that Hitler could count on Italy's neutrality in 1936 had enabled him to risk the occupation of the Rhineland in March of that year. The new Berlin-Rome Axis was not only a general set-off to the Anglo-French entente but was also destined to make the Vienna coup in 1938 comparatively easy. So long as all these friendships were valuable to him, he was profuse in the warmth of his utterances about them; and a study of his speeches on this subject would make interesting reading. Once they had served their purpose they were, however, discarded as if they had never been.

Failure of a Mission

In the midst of one of his tirades against the Poles in August, 1939, I interrupted Hitler to observe that he seemed to forget how useful the agreement with Pilsudski had been to him in 1934. Hitler's answer was that it had never been of any use whatsoever and that it had merely made him unpopular with his own people. He had a phenomenal capacity for self-deception, and was able to forget everything which he had ever said or done in the past, if it no longer suited his present or future purpose to remember it. In the same manner, Japan was thrown aside like a squeezed lemon just as soon as Hitler concluded that the U.S.S.R. would suit his immediate purpose better than Japan.

Hitler's Germany showed no regard for any of her friends; the Führer never took the trouble even to warn Signor Mussolini in advance of his plans; and I am confident that, if the British Government had been prepared to accept the German proposals of August 25th, 1939, Hitler would have lost no time in finding some excuse for scrapping the Moscow agreement which he had signed a few days before.

Verbal or written engagements had absolutely no meaning for him once they ceased to contribute to the greater glory of Adolf Hitler and of Germany. They were merely provisional documents to be torn up whenever it suited him; whereupon he would then offer another agreement in exchange. As I have said earlier, I am ready to believe that Hitler started by working sincerely for Germany. Later, he began to confound Germany with himself; and at the end Adolf Hitler was, I fancy, the sole consideration.

Briefly recapitulated, the position in May, 1937, when I

reached Berlin, was accordingly as follows: All power was concentrated in the hands of Hitler. There was control of the press but not of the budget; no rival parties were tolerated, and every official was his nominee, removable at his will. While the economic and financial position of Germany was showing signs of deterioration, her military strength in material and man power was vastly and rapidly increasing; and her foreign alliances were being consolidated and exploited. Europe was being soothed by repeated assertions that nothing was further from Hitler's mind than any thought of revolutionary or territorial conquests. Respect for other nationalities was still the declared principle of Nazism, which was sometimes euphemistically described as the form of democracy most appropriate to Germany. It was a period of comparative calm; but, as far as Germany was concerned, of concentrated preparation.

The two main political questions were the civil war in Spain and the future of Austria. Germany was still being represented abroad as the barrier to Bolshevism, and communism was still serving as the justification for much internal oppression. But Britain, to judge from the German press, was public enemy No. 1. The campaign for the return of the German colonies had been revived in 1936 and was still intermittently but consistently prominent; but the chief grievance was Britain's dog-in-the-manger attitude toward Germany's rightful place in the sun and her claims to *Lebensraum*, or living space, in Central and Eastern Europe. As Goering said to me on the occasion of my first visit to him, "Germany cannot pick one flower without England's saying to her, '*Es ist verboten*' (It is forbidden)." It was useless to discuss that misused word *Lebensraum* with the Nazis. They could or would not see that "living room" was only justifiable, if it implied the strengthening of economic relations by legitimate means, but was unjustifiable if it signified political domination by means of military or economic pressure. To them it only meant the latter.

As for the claim for the return of the German colonies, it was quite obvious that it was merely being exploited momentarily for propaganda purposes, partly to keep the claim alive for use later, when Germany's aspirations in Europe—a prior consideration—had been achieved and digested; partly to make the German people believe that it was the want of colonies and not excessive rearmament which was causing the lack of butter and other comforts. When Goering outlined to me in October of that year an Anglo-German understanding of mutual guarantee in two clauses, I asked him what he would suggest about colonies. His answer was that colonies did not matter. When I spoke to Hitler about colonies in March, 1938, his attitude was that the time had not come for discussion about them. They might wait, he said, four, six, or ten years. It is true that the press campaign was to some extent aggravated by articles and letters in the British newspapers arguing that Germany had never made any use of her colonies before the war, that they had never provided her with more than 1 to 3 per cent of her foreign imports, and that in general they were a quite unnecessary luxury for her. At my first interview with Dr. Goebbels, shortly after my arrival, he talked about Germany's having been robbed of her colonies. I told him that "robbed" was an entirely incorrect term, since she had lost them as the result of defeat in war. Goebbels' reply was that that was an argument which he could understand; but what irritated him and all Germans was the sanctimonious and hypocritical arguments put forward in England to prove that colonies were merely a luxury and of no real value to anybody. There was some truth in this retort.

I have the greatest respect for the power and freedom of that "chartered libertine" the British press. I must, however, reluctantly but in all honesty record that it handicapped my attempts in 1937 and 1938 to contribute to the improvement of Anglo-German relations, and thereby to the preservation of peace. Experience has proved that those attempts were foredoomed to failure, but they might not have been. In a letter of Lord Baldwin's, which was published in *The Times* last November, he observed that the "weakness of democracy is a certain proneness to short views, hastily formed and vigorously asserted on an inadequate basis of reflection and knowledge." Lord Baldwin has the knack of hitting the nail on the head. However justifiable the majority of the press criticisms undoubtedly were at this time, they were also sometimes biased and unfair. It would not have mattered so much had Hitler been a normal individual, but he was unreasonably sensitive to newspaper and especially British newspaper criticism and quite unable to distinguish values, or to appreciate the difference between, say, the *Manchester Guardian* and the more sensational journals. It did not help me in my diplomatic task if Hitler's back was being constantly rubbed up the wrong way by press criticisms, and I consequently tried on various occasions to persuade those

responsible for submitting to Hitler the British press cut-
tings (which had of course first to be translated) to put some
of them in the wastepaper basket before ever they reached
him. But I never succeeded, at any rate for any length of
time, and always suspected that certain members of his anti-
British extremist entourage took special pleasure in seeing that
he missed nothing which might inflame his facile resentments.

While the British press comments might be tiresome or even
unjust, reflecting as they sometimes did the views of irre-
sponsible individuals and the battle of internal party politics,
the German officially controlled press was, on the other hand,
utterly despicable. No lie, however great and obvious, was
too much for the *Völkischer Beobachter* or the *Angriff* and
suchlike purely party organs or for the *Stuermer*, the notorious
great anti-Jew newspaper edited by Dr. Streicher at Nuremberg. Common vituperation and abuse were their main stock
in trade. They were not newspapers but emetics; and, when
they were really on the warpath, as during the Czech and
the Polish crises, it was impossible to read them without
actually feeling sick. It made me sad to think of German youth
being educated on such utter trash and on such complete
misrepresentations of the truth.

Alone among the Berlin newspapers, the *Deutsche All-
gemeine Zeitung* attempted to preserve some, at least, of the
decencies of normal journalism, as did also to some extent the
Börse Zeitung, which was the organ of the Ministry for Foreign Affairs, though it was always ill-tempered and dete-
riorated after Ribbentrop took charge of that Department.
But the best and fairest newspaper in Germany was the
Frankfurter Zeitung, and I often wondered how it managed

among so much censorship and corruption to preserve its last vestiges of independence. Personally, I used to see regularly three morning newspapers and two evening editions. But, as the wife of a Nazi official once said to me, "What on earth do you do that for? If you read one, you have read the lot."

CHAPTER V. ATTEMPTS TO IMPROVE
ANGLO-GERMAN RELATIONS

I HAD been just one month at Berlin when I was instructed by His Majesty's Government to make the first of what was destined to be a series of definite and considered attempts by Mr. Chamberlain (who had now succeeded Lord Baldwin as Prime Minister) to improve Anglo-German relations. It consisted in an invitation to Baron von Neurath to come to London at an early date to discuss, primarily, naval control in Spain, in which Germany had ceased to participate after the attack on the pocket battleship *Deutschland* by Spanish Government bombers at Iviza, but also in general to review the whole external political situation. I recollect the hesitation on Neurath's part when I first put forward the suggestion to him. He was in fact conversant—as I was not—with the inner difficulties of such a proposal. However, he said he would consult Hitler, though the visit could not, he pointed out, take place till after his return, namely, June 20th, from a tour of the Balkan capitals which had already been arranged for him. Nevertheless, in spite of this and some other minor difficulties, the invitation was eventually accepted, and announced to take place between the twenty-third and twenty-eighth of that month.

My satisfaction at this apparent success was short-lived, and was typical of the malignant fate which seemed to dog all our efforts to open the door to Anglo-German discussions. At first I was inclined to attribute this to ill chance, and it was not until later that I realized it was by design. On June 19th it was officially announced in Berlin that following the bombing of the *Deutschland* an unsuccessful torpedo attack had been made on the German cruiser *Leipzig* off Oran; and on the following day I received a brief private letter from Neurath telling me that his visit to London could not now take place. The twentieth of June was a Sunday, and I spent all the morning and the afternoon in trying to find the Minister for Foreign Affairs. He had, I think, regarded discretion as the better part of valor and disappeared into the country, destination unknown. I managed, however, to get hold of him late in the evening and went to see him at his private house in the garden of the Ministry for Foreign Affairs. I told him that the *Leipzig* incident in itself only rendered his visit to London still more desirable, that I could not take his refusal to go there as a final answer without having first seen the Chancellor myself and put the case to him. Baron von Neurath was good enough to arrange this for me, and I had an interview with him and Hitler on the following morning.

Hitler had just come back from Wilhelmshaven, whither the *Deutschland* had returned to bury the thirty-odd sailors who had been killed in the bomb attack at Iviza. He was, as in the case of my first meeting with him after the *Hindenburg* disaster, in the emotional state into which he worked himself at the sight or report of any dead Germans. He refused to listen to any of my very logical arguments and persisted in the standpoint that he could not at such a moment permit his

Foreign Minister to leave Germany. His attitude was so utterly unreasonable that I was at a loss to explain it even to myself. In the light of a better acquaintance later with the inner facts, I derived the conclusion that the *Leipzig* incident —the truth of which was never even verified—had merely served as a pretext for going back on an acceptance which had never really appealed to Hitler himself, but still less to his Ambassador in London, Herr von Ribbentrop. The latter, in addition to his London post, was Ambassador at Large, and felt that Neurath's visit was detrimental to his own prestige and wounding to his personal vanity. He had the fatal defect of always looking for offense, and of having, in consequence, a perpetual "chip on his shoulder." I feel sure that he did his utmost from the outset to dissuade his master from agreeing to the course proposed by His Majesty's Government, and the *Leipzig* story enabled him to win his case. The notorious failure of his mission to London was already rankling, and it was intolerable that another should come and show up the personal cause of that failure. History will assuredly attribute a large share of the blame for September, 1939, to Ribbentrop; and his successful intrigue against Neurath's visit to London was neither the first nor unfortunately the last instance of his sinister influence on the policy of his Führer. It was a disheartening beginning for myself, and the abrupt manner in which the visit was cancelled by the German Government was not encouraging for His Majesty's Government. In accordance with the rules of ordinary civility, it would have been proper for the German Government, as soon as the excitement over the *Leipzig* incident had died down, themselves to suggest a later date for the visit. They did not, however, do so; and it was left to Mr. Chamberlain to take the initiative again and to make a second attempt, later in the year, to establish contact by sending Lord Halifax to Berlin.

As I have related earlier, the first of my purely personal efforts to improve relations with the Nazi rulers of Germany had been the speech which I had made at the dinner given to me in May by the Deutsch Englische Gesellschaft. My second was my attendance at the Nuremberg party rally in September. No British, French, or U. S. Ambassador had hitherto gone to Nuremberg, on the ground that as a party day it could not be regarded as a purely official meeting. For the first time my French colleague, M. François-Poncet; the U. S. Chargé d'Affaires, Mr. Gilbert; and myself were authorized in 1937 by our respective governments to attend the rally, albeit our presence there was limited to two days.

Nobody who has not witnessed the various displays given at Nuremberg during the week's rally or been subjected to the atmosphere thereat can be said to be fully acquainted with the Nazi movement in Germany. It was an extremely necessary and useful experience, and not a single moment of my time during the two days I was there was left unoccupied. In addition to attending a review of the party leaders, 140,000 in number and representing at that time over 2,000,000 members of the party (a year later again at Nuremberg Hitler was to tell me himself that there were well over 3,000,000 party officials); a rally of the Hitler Youth, 48,000 strong, with 5,000 girls; at a supper party in Herr Himmler's S.S. camp of 25,000 blackshirts, I had talks with Hitler himself,

Neurath, Goering, and Goebbels, as well as a number of other less important personages.

The displays themselves were most impressive. That of the party leaders (or heads of the party organizations in the towns and villages throughout the country) took place in the evening at 8 P.M. in the stadium, or Zeppelinfeld. Dressed in their brown shirts these 140,000 men were drawn up in six great columns with passages between them, mostly in the stadium itself, but filling also all the tiers of seats surrounding the stadium and facing the elevated platform reserved for the Chancellor, his ministers, and his guards, the massed bands, official guests, and other spectators. Hitler himself arrived at the far entrance of the stadium, some 400 yards from the platform and, accompanied by several hundred of his followers, marched on foot up the central passage to his appointed place. His arrival was theatrically notified by the sudden turning into the air of the 300 or more searchlights with which the stadium was surrounded. The blue-tinged light from these met thousands of feet up in the air at the top to make a kind of square roof, to which a chance cloud gave added realism. The effect, which was both solemn and beautiful, was like being inside a cathedral of ice. At the word of command the standard bearers then advanced from out of sight at the far end, up the main lane and over the further tiers and up the four side lanes. A certain proportion of these standards had electric lights on their shafts, and the spectacle of these five rivers of red and gold rippling forward under the dome of blue light, in complete silence, through the massed formations of brownshirts, was indescribably picturesque. I had spent six years in St. Petersburg before the war in the best days of the old Russian ballet, but in grandiose beauty I have never seen a ballet to compare with it. The German, who has a highly developed herd instinct, is perfectly happy when he is wearing a uniform, marching in step, and singing in chorus; and the Nazi revolution has certainly known how to appeal to these instincts in his nature. As a display of aggregate strength it was ominous; as a triumph of mass organization combined with beauty it was superb.

The review of the Hitler Youth was no less an object lesson from an observer's point of view. Standards, music, and singing again played a big part in the performance, and the fervor of youth was much in evidence. The speeches on that occasion were made by Hitler, Hess, and Baldur von Shirach, the leader of the Hitler Youth.

Rudolph Hess was the Führer's deputy, appointed to represent him whenever or wherever he could not himself attend any function. In a sense he seemed to me to be a sort of adopted son to Hitler, and on the outbreak of war he was named as second after Goering in the order of succession to the leadership of the German nation. In less troublous times he might well have been named first, but his authority with the Army would scarcely have been great enough in wartime to hold the balance between the soldiers and the Nazi party. Hess, who was born in 1896, belonged to a merchant family established at Alexandria. Educated in Germany, he served in the last war, first in the infantry but later in the flying corps. Up to 1935 flying remained his hobby, and he actually won an important civil contest while a Cabinet Minister. After that Hitler forbade his risking his life by any further excursions in the air.

Failure of a Mission

Hess was one of Hitler's first collaborators and friends; and his membership in the party, as I have mentioned elsewhere, began in the early twenties. He took part in the Munich Putsch in November, 1923, was condemned after it to imprisonment, and shared Hitler's confinement in the fortress of Landsberg. When Hitler took office in 1933, he was given Cabinet rank as a Minister without Portfolio.

Tall and dark, with beetling eyebrows, a famous smile, and ingratiating manners. Hess was perhaps the most attractive looking of the leading Nazis. He was not inclined to be talkative and in conversation did not convey the impression of great ability. But people who know him best would have agreed that first impressions—and I never got further with him than that—were deceptive; and he certainly wielded more influence than people generally believed in Germany. I should have summed him up as aloof and inscrutable, with a strong fanatical streak which would be produced whenever the occasion required it.

That day, however, it was von Shirach's speech which, in spite of its painfully adulatory references to the Führer, impressed me most, though it was quite short, as befitting a wet morning on which it must have been most unpleasant for the boys, who had come from some distance, to stand in the rain. One part of Baldur von Shirach's speech surprised me when, addressing the boys, he said: "I do not know if you are Protestants or Catholics; but that you believe in God, that I do know." I had been under the impression that all reference to religion was discouraged among the Hitler Youth, and this seemed to me to refute that imputation. Theoretically, however, in spite of the revolt against the sacred

68

books of the Jews, religion was free to the Hitler Youth; but, where and whenever it was possible to do so, it was in practice discouraged by various effective methods. The God of the Hohenzollerns had not saved Germany from defeat in 1918; and, though God might still be worshiped, it must be a purely German one, to whom Hitler was so closely allied as to be barely distinguishable from the Deity Himself.

Hitler in his speeches constantly referred to the Almighty. He was not an atheist, but merely pro-Hitler and anti-Christian. In the course of one of my interviews with him we touched upon the subject of religion. He was at the moment incensed against certain English bishops for supporting the case of Pastor Niemoller. He would not, he shouted, brook any further interference by English churchmen in the religious affairs of Germany. It was their meddling, he said, which had caused him to give orders for Niemoller to be put in a concentration camp after he had been set at liberty by the tribunal which had tried him for, and to all intents and purposes acquitted him of, sedition against the Nazi state. If, he continued, any English bishops tried to come to Germany they would be turned back at the frontier; and he concluded with the astounding statement that "nowhere was religion freer than in Germany." It was the sort of remark to which I never was able to find an answer, nor would it have served any purpose if I had. His own National-Socialist religion, as he conceived it, with its German God was free, and that was what he meant and all he cared for. Furthermore, he could always make himself believe whatever he said. It was this kind of attitude which made ordinary conversation and argument with him and his imitator, Ribbentrop, so extraordinarily difficult and unsatisfactory.

The supper in a great tent in Herr Himmler's S.S. police camp at Nuremberg was equally instructive in another sense. During supper a number of songs were sung by a chorus of blackshirts, and after it there was a tattoo for the lowering of the Swastika camp flag. The music as well as the bearing and drill of the special color party was exceptionally good. The S.S. played a big part in ruling Germany for Hitler, and they were picked men of powerful physique. "But," as I wrote at the time, "the camp in the darkness, dimly lit by flares, with the black uniform in the silent background and the skull and crossbones on the drums and trumpets lent to the scene a sinister and menacing impression." I felt, indeed, as if I were back in the days of Wallenstein and the Thirty Years' War in the seventeenth century.

But, quite apart from the obvious menace of these various militaristic or para-military spectacles, Nuremberg gave me at the time the following chief impressions: Firstly, judging from the reports of the previous rallies, of a calmer atmosphere than heretofore, resulting partly from a growing sense of strength and self-confidence, but partly also from an increasing feeling of boredom; secondly, and deriving from the first, of a growing hope that Nazism might be entering upon a quieter phase; thirdly, as drawn from my conversation with the Nazi leaders, of the possibility of a better understanding between Britain and Germany; fourthly, of an increasing adulation of Hitler amounting almost to idolatry; and fifthly, of superlative organization.

Attempts to Improve Relations

As I have said before, I spent but two days at Nuremberg; and the atmosphere, however illuminating and instructive in respect of Nazism itself in a concentrated form, may have been scarcely that best suited to obtain a true picture of Germany as a whole, of her apprehension and discontents as distinct from the enthusiasm and chauvinism of the Nazi party there forgathered. Yet the Nazi party was Germany; and it was merely wishful thinking to imagine anything to the contrary.

Herr Hitler was more friendly to me personally on that occasion than on any of the others on which I saw him. He was undoubtedly pleased at the attendance for the first time of the British, French, and American representatives; and he indicated that he attributed this innovation to my initiative. I took the opportunity to tell him that the invitation to Baron von Neurath to visit London remained open if he cared to avail himself of it. In this respect, however, he was at once, and typically, less forthcoming. He said that he feared lest such a visit should give rise to exaggerated hopes, and observed that a preliminary requisite to such a visit should be a change in the attitude of the British press toward, and a juster appreciation in England of, Nazism.

As it happened, I had had a long talk with Dr. Goebbels at lunch that day on the subject of our respective presses; and I told Hitler so. There was nothing very new in that talk, and up to the last the press problem remained insoluble, but Goebbels had been friendly and sensible. The "little doctor" was probably the most intelligent, from a purely brain point of view, of all the Nazi leaders. He never speechified; he always saw and stuck to the point; he was an able debater and, in private conversation, astonishingly fair-minded and reasonable. Personally, whenever I had the chance, I found pleasure in talking to him. In appearance and in character he was a typical little Irish agitator, and was, in fact, probably of Celtic origin. He came from the Rhineland and had been educated in a Jesuit school. He was a slip of a man; but, in spite of his slight deformity, he had given proof of great courage when he fought the communists in Berlin and won the capital for Hitler and Nazism. When, however, he was on a public platform or had a pen in his hand no gall was too bitter and no lie too blatant for him.

Baron von Neurath, whom I saw the following day, was more forthcoming than Hitler. He told me that he found his Führer less resentful and more anxious for an understanding with Britain than he had been for a long time past. He did not, however, encourage me to think that Hitler would reopen the question of his visit to London. I remember that I asked him, in the course of conversation, what were Germany's ultimate aims. His reply was: "Austria is the first and last of our aims; the Sudeten German problem is a matter for compromise and can be settled amicably, provided the Czechs leave the Russian orbit and give true equality to their German subjects."

Such a statement was, as I was to discover, a characteristic example both of the half-truths indulged in whenever it was necessary to define German policy and of the deceptive nature of German assurances in general; i.e. readiness to admit an obvious objective, coupled with a positive declaration that nothing more thereafter was aimed at. It was so far true that Austria was in fact Hitler's immediate objective. Of that there was no shadow of doubt, and in commenting on the greater calmness of the 1937 party rally, I had reported, "Germany today feels that she can not only afford to wait, but by waiting will be yet stronger and more sure of her goal. And the big goal is German unity. Of that let there be no mistake either; and if we intend definitely to oppose it, we should lose no time in asking ourselves the first and capital question 'How?'" It was already quite evident that it would be futile to say "no" to the Dictator without being prepared to go to war to enforce it.

The question of the Austrian *Anschluss* was also mentioned in a long conversation which I had with General Goering at this time. He insisted that it was inevitable; and he told me that a few days earlier he had seen Herr Guido Schmidt, the Austrian Minister for Foreign Affairs, and had bluntly told him that the sooner the Austrian Government accepted it as such, and without creating bad blood, the better it would be for all concerned. But the greater part of my interview with Goering on that occasion was on the subject of a request which I had made to him in July for a written statement of (a) Germany's concrete grievances against Britain in the matter of our alleged attempt to hem Germany in, and (b) her ultimate aims. Needless to say, I never received such a reply in writing, though Goering was always ready to talk and to express views "subject to Hitler's confirmation or consent." This time the General begged the question, as he had done in July, by saying that he would consult Hitler again and might be able to give me the answer I wanted if I came and shot a stag with him at Rominten, in East Prussia, during the first week of October—an invitation which I was delighted to accept.

As usual Goering was very outspoken and at times bellicose. Yet our many talks, in spite of complete frankness on both sides, were never conducted on any but mutually friendly lines. He suffered comparatively little from the personal resentments which so often inspired Hitler and Ribbentrop, and up to the last I was inclined to believe in the sincerity of his personal desire for peace and good relations with England. He laid stress on this at Nuremberg, though at the same time he added that, if the British Empire refused to collaborate with Germany, there would be nothing for the latter to do but to devote herself to the destruction of that Empire instead of to its maintenance. In that connection he mentioned to me, and was the first German to do so, the possibility of the Reich being compelled to revise the Anglo-German Naval Agreement. I told him then, and again some months later, that such a step would inevitably lead in the end once more to war with Britain. He regretfully admitted that this might be so and added that it was against his advice that Hitler had insisted, when he did, on the conclusion of that Agreement. Baron von Neurath once told me the same thing, the argument of both of them being that Hitler should have kept the Naval Agreement as a trump card up his sleeve for eventual use in a final bargain. They were both more honest in this respect than Hitler, since, from Goering's remark, I fancy that the contingency of repudiating that treaty was already in Hitler's mind; and, judging by subsequent experience, I can only conclude that he never intended to observe its terms longer than it suited him. It was difficult or even materially impossible for him to rebuild a navy at the same time that he was re-creating his immensely formidable military and air machine; and the sole object, in Hitler's mind, of the Naval Agreement was to disarm British opposition to his schemes in Central Europe until such time as they came to fruition and were realized. Thereafter it would be the turn of the British Empire. It is impossible today to draw any other conclusion. There is a passage in Rauschning's book, *The Revolution of Nihilism*,* which is illuminating in this respect, particularly in view of the writer's intimacy at one time with Hitler. He writes of the latter as follows:

He was ready to sign anything. He was ready to guarantee any frontier and to conclude a non-aggression pact with anyone. [According to Hitler himself] it was a simpleton's idea that expedients of this sort were not to be made use of, because the day might come when some formal agreement had to be broken. Every pact sworn to was broken or became out of date sooner or later. Anyone who was so fussy that he had to consult his own conscience about whether he could keep a pact, whatever the pact and whatever the situation, was a fool. He could conclude any pact and yet be ready to break it the next day in cold blood, if that was in the interests of the future Germany.

Such was Hitler's own profession of faith about the sanctity of treaties and his plighted word. *Verb. sap.* But at that time, it was still possible to hope for the best; and after a brief holiday at Belje in Yugoslavia, shooting stags in my old haunts at the invitation of the Prince Regent, I proceeded to Rominten to stay with Goering as he had suggested.

* New York: The Alliance Book Corporation.

OF all the big Nazi leaders, Hermann Goering was for me by far the most sympathetic. He may have been the man who was chiefly responsible for the firing of the Reichstag in 1933; and he certainly was the one to whom, as his most trusted adherent, Hitler confided the task of cleaning up Berlin at the time of the Roehm purge in 1934. In any crisis, as in war, he would be quite ruthless. He once said to me that the British whom he really admired were those he described as the pirates, such as Francis Drake; and he reproached us for having become too "debrutalized." He was, in fact, himself a typical and brutal buccaneer; but he had certain attractive qualities; and I must frankly say that I had a real personal liking for him.

He had the advantage of a better education than most of Hitler's entourage. His father had been the first Governor of German South West Africa and, according to Goering himself, an anglophile. At the time of the South African war Goering was a boy and had, in spite of his father's disapproval, been a violent partisan for the Boers. He still had somewhere, he once told me, a photograph of himself in a slouch hat inscribed "Hermann Goering, General der Buren" (General of the Boers). He had sent at the time all his small

76

savings, a gold piece or two which his aunts had given him, to the fund collected for the Boers in Germany. That was, he said, one of the things which in his life he most regretted, inasmuch as South Africa had, after all, come in on the side of Britain in the war of 1914. His own home in his youth had been a small house at Veldenstein, which he took me to see one afternoon during my second visit to Nuremberg, built amid the ruins of one of that series óf old castles perched upon the rocks of Franconia which had been constructed in the tenth and eleventh centuries against the Slav invaders of Germany. There he had been the daring leader of the village boys, and had fitted himself for the life of adventure which was afterward to be his fate.

In 1914 he had been an infantry officer but was soon transferred to the Air Force, where he became a pilot in the famous Richthofen Circus, which was so long a thorn in the side of the British Flying Corps. He was himself, I believe, credited with a number of air victories, and received the decoration, Order for Merit, which is the nearest German equivalent to our V.C. (About nine hundred such crosses were given in Germany during the World War of 1914-1918.) When we obtained the mastery of the air in 1918, and after Richthofen had been killed and two thirds of the circus shot down, Goering was the next in command, and gallantly led what was left of the squadron till the end of the war. When the Armistice came, he refused to hand over his airplanes to the Allies; and, filled with rage at defeat and disgust at the revolution in Germany, he retired to Sweden and took up a civil flying appointment there. While in Sweden he married a member of a well-known Swedish family and returned to Germany at the beginning of the Hitler movement. His membership number in the Nazi party was in the nineties. To be one of the first hundred members of it was a great distinction. Herr Hess, the Führer's deputy and second heir presumptive, is in the twenties; but most of the earlier partisans are comparatively obscure. They were to be found chiefly in the Brown House at Munich, and in posts such as Gauleiters or Reichstag members. Hitler's loyalty to his earliest adherents is notorious; but, however sympathetic as a quality in principle, it did not tend to raise the standard of Nazi administration. The characteristics of the street fighters and swashbucklers of the struggle for power against the communists were not such as to contribute to the decency of normal life. But Hitler clung to them and they to him; and, for all that they remained in the comparative shadows, I always felt that Amman and others of that ilk were a real power and influence behind the façade of the more respectable Reich Ministers, or official Cabinet. Some of the latter were merely figureheads destined to dupe the German public as much as the foreigner. Among his other artifices Hitler was, as all dictators must be, a master of showmanship and make-believe. As long as decent people like Baron von Neurath, Count von Krosigk, Dr. Gunther, Dr. Schacht, etc. were in office, the simpler German might perforce conclude that the whole regime was honest.

From the moment when he joined the Nazi party, Goering, as a fighting officer of the World War with a distinguished record, became one of its most active leaders and the so-called Paladin of the movement. He took part in the Munich Putsch

Goering

in 1923, when he was severely wounded. He escaped imprisonment and recovered from his injury thanks to the devotion and care of his wife, who died three years later. Her death was a sad blow for Goering, who was devoted to her; and his estate at the Schorfheida about forty miles north of Berlin was called after her, Karinhall, and contains a mausoleum in the grounds to her memory. Some ten years later Goering married again; this time a charming actress, Emma Sonnemann, by whom, to his immense delight, he had in 1938 a daughter Edda, who is the living image of her father, with the same blue eyes. I liked Frau Goering as much as her husband, and possibly for better moral reasons. Absolutely unaffected, she was all kindness and simplicity. The first time I met her was when she came with her husband to a big lunch at the Embassy to meet the Prime Minister of Canada, Mr. Mackenzie King, who was paying a visit to Berlin after the conclusion of the Imperial Conference in June, 1937. At the end of lunch there was a dish of cheese on pastry, which she refused on the ground that her doctor did not allow her to eat pastry. I suggested that it was a question of her excellent figure, and her reply was: "Oh, no. Hermann likes women who are fat." I apologized to her, saying that I was not trying to be personal, and that I thought it only right that women should consider their figures. Vanity was, in my opinion, I said, just as charming in women as it was repugnant in men.

It was possibly a tactless remark to make to her, as her husband's vanity, though harmless and childish, was notorious. But her only comment was, "Do you really think so? I approve of vanity in a man." She said it so simply and naturally that one could not have helped liking her; and the more I saw her, the more I did like her. Had she been politically minded, she and her baby could have been, and possibly were, a good influence in Goering's life.

I should like to express here my belief that the Field Marshal, if it had depended on him, would not have gambled on war as Hitler did in 1939. As will be related in due course, he came down decisively on the side of peace in September, 1938. He was rumored to have lost much of Hitler's favor on that account, and it is possible that if it had not been for his efforts in 1938 he would have played the same role in 1939. Once was an experience, but twice would have been regarded by Hitler as vice; and it was unfortunately all part of the Greek tragedy that Goering had his 1938 past behind him, and could not repeat it.

He was the absolute servant of his master, and I have never seen greater loyalty and devotion than his to Hitler. He was admittedly the second power in the land, and had always given me to understand that he was Hitler's natural successor as Führer. Seconds are often inclined to lay stress on their own importance. In all the very frank talks which I had with Goering, he never once spoke of himself or of the great part which he had played in the Nazi revolution. Everything had been done by Hitler, all the credit was Hitler's, every decision was Hitler's, and he himself was nothing. Inasmuch as the enumeration of the posts which Goering filled in the Nazi regime took about five minutes to read aloud, this self-effacement before his leader was all the more remarkable; and the more so, since, without Goering, Hitler would never have reached where he was. Hitler's brain might conceive the impossible, but Goering did it. The building up of the German

Goering

Air Force was in itself a striking achievement, and that of which Goering was probably, and legitimately, proudest. However vain he may have been in small ways and however much he loved pomp and uniforms and decorations, jewels and pictures, and the applause of his fellow men, he was quite without braggadocio over the big things which he had accomplished. He had, too, a Falstaffian sense of humor, and was said to have made a collection of the innumerable jokes which were made about his foibles by the Berliners. In this respect he was quite unlike Dr. Goebbels or Hitler himself. Any jokes against the latter were *lèse-majesté*, or treason if made at the expense of the regime; and at the beginning of 1939, a number of the comic turns in the Berlin theaters were prohibited by law under penalty of imprisonment in concentration camps. There was one irrepressible but very popular comic artist in Munich who spent his time in and out of the Dachau concentration camp.

Most of the stories about Goering were, however, good-natured and generally (like the following) made fun of his love for decorations with which to cover his extremely broad chest: "Hitler went one day to visit God. The Almighty said, 'I am always glad to see you, Adolf, but I wish you would stop that fellow Hermann from coming up here. Every time he comes he takes away another star.'" Another was about a motorist who ran into the Field Marshal's car on a dark night and was brought before the judge on a charge of reckless driving. He pleaded that it was not his fault but that of the Field Marshal, who, he said, had forgotten to dim his decorations. He was acquitted. Another popular story which went the round of Berlin at the time of the 1938 crisis

Failure of a Mission

referred to Goering's air force: "The English," said the Berliners, "have so many airplanes that the sky is black with them, and the French ones are so numerous that you can't see the sun for them. But when Hermann Goering presses the button, the birds themselves have got to walk." Some people say that the Germans have no sense of humor. That is certainly not true of the Berliners.

Nevertheless, behind all the ruthlessness and brutality which led Goering to shrink from nothing to obey an order or to achieve an end and behind his harmless vanity and love of display, there were agreeable qualities. However little compassion he may have had, like so many Germans, for his fellow men, he loved animals and children; and, before ever he had one of his own, the top floor at Karinhall contained a vast playroom fitted up with every mechanical toy dear to the heart of the modern child. Nothing used to give him greater pleasure than to go and play there with them. The toys might, it is true, include models of airplanes dropping heavy bombs which exploded on defenseless towns or villages; but, as he observed when I reproached him on the subject, it was not part of the Nazi conception of life to be excessively civilized or to teach squeamishness to the young. Failing children, he would romp with one of the baby lions, of which there was always one in the house until his daughter Edda arrived. Each lion, as soon as it was ten months old was presented to the Berlin zoo, where they were kept in one cage, into which Frau Goering, to the terror of the keepers, would sometimes go quite alone and play with them.

Goering was also a keen sportsman and a first-class shot with a rifle. His game laws for Germany were a model for the protection and improvement of animal life. All kinds of steel traps were, for instance, absolutely prohibited in Germany, where rabbits are not the scourge that they are in England. He had successfully introduced elk into the 100,000-acre estate at Karinhall in spite of the unfavorable advice of all his foresters. He was also endeavoring to reintroduce there not only the European bison but also the original wild horse, such as is represented on the old Greek friezes. Sportsmen all over the world should in fact be ready to recognize the services which he rendered to international sport in general; and his great hunting exhibition of 1937 was quite the finest ever held of its kind, and on a far larger scale even than that of Vienna in 1910.

In addition to being the builder and head of the German Air Force, the head of the Forestry Department and Game Warden for the Reich, the head of the State Opera House and various State Museums, Prime Minister of Prussia, and chief of a score of other activities, Goering was also supreme head of the Ministry of Economy, and Commissioner for the Four Years' Plan for making Germany economically independent of other countries. It was a curious combination for an air-force leader, but those who worked with him commented on his great ability to study files of documents and rows of figures and to extract everything which was essential out of them. He was, in fact, much more the able administrator of the Mussolini type than Hitler could ever be; and he owed his indisputable position as second-in-command chiefly to these organizing abilities. Hitler might turn to others in order to win approval of his foreign policy or of his other schemes, but Goering was indispensable when it came to action and administration. His loyalty and devotion could always be counted upon in any crisis, and his personal popularity with the public was an asset to the regime. So far as I was able to judge, none of the Nazi leaders except Goering had any sort of hold on the people; and some of them, such as Ribbentrop and Himmler, were cordially disliked and distrusted. The Germans may be docile but they are not altogether stupid.

In spite of his innumerable activities, Goering would always find time not only to see one if one proposed it but to give one an apparently unlimited amount of his time. He was a man to whom one could speak absolutely frankly. He neither easily took nor lightly gave offense and he was quick to seize the point at which one was driving. I do not flatter myself that in the long conversations which I had with him I ever modified his opinions, but he was always ready to listen and eager to learn. He was always, for instance, asking questions about England and English personalities, about whom he was very fully, though often incorrectly, informed, but in respect to whom he often also expressed shrewd judgments. Nor, except on the last occasion on which I ever saw him, did he ever make those long and tiresome oratorical speeches to which one had sometimes to listen from others. Brutal he was and "just as bad as the others" according to anti-Nazis, but away from politics he had many good points. I spent two hours in his company on August 31st last while the Polish Ambassador was seeing Ribbentrop and a few hours before the advance of the German Army into Polish territory and the dispatch of his airmen at dawn to bomb the Polish airdromes. At that moment the order for the aggression had not yet finally been signed by Hitler, and everything was believed to hang upon the nature of the interview between Lipski and Ribbentrop. Goering, though absolutely ready to press the button, still seemed at least half-hopeful of a peaceful issue. Incidentally, he gave me the most categorical assurances that, in the event of war with Britain, his airmen would not bomb anything except definitely military objectives. When I pointed out that, owing to the height and speed of modern aircraft, that would not prevent bombs, aimed supposedly at a military target, falling in residential London and that I would much object to being hit on the head by "any such present from Hermann Goering," his immediate answer was that, if that did happen, he would certainly send a special airplane to drop a wreath at my funeral. And, if it did happen, I have no doubt he would do so.

I have digressed at some length about Goering, but I knew him better than any of the other prominent Nazi leaders. One must, I suppose, judge a man by his friends. Thanks to his connection with Hitler, he has played a big part in European history, and one cannot touch pitch and keep one's hands clean. My own recollections of Goering will be of the man who intervened decisively in favor of peace in 1938, and would have done so again in 1939 if he had been as brave morally as he was physically; of the hospitable host and sportsman; and of a man with whom I spent many hours in friendly and honorable dispute and argument.

Rominten was my first experience of that hospitality. The house itself was a simple shooting box with a thatched roof, but fitted internally with every comfort. As far as I was aware, the household consisted solely of maids with one man-servant; and there was no ceremony of any kind. One of his Swedish brothers-in-law, Count Rosen, was the only other guest; and the rest of the party consisted of Oberstjäger-meister Scherping, Oberstjägermeister Menthe, and a young Air Officer A. D. C., von Brauschitsch, a son of the present German Commander in Chief.

Stag shooting in the dense forests of Europe is not like deer stalking in Scotland—the deer cannot be spied from a distance, and their whereabouts can only be discovered when they roar during the rutting season. A rutting stag has a regular pitch, in the neighborhood of which he is always to be found in the company of the hinds which he has succeeded in collecting. In the evening he comes out into some favorite clearing in the forest where the grass is sweetest, and the easiest way to shoot him is to wait at some suitable spot on its edge till he does so. *Hochstände* (literally highstands, or a sort of platform, or machaan, some twenty to thirty feet high) are sometimes erected at such spots; and all the sportsman has to do is to climb it and wait an hour or so before the stag usually appears with his harem to feed.

I had arrived early in the morning and at about 4 P.M. arrangements were made for me to go to such a place to shoot a big fourteen-pointer which was known to frequent it. Before starting off, Goering remarked that Englishmen, however good they might be with shotguns, were no good with a rifle. The week before, he said, he had invited an English sportsman to shoot a stag, and he had missed it three times! It was not an encouraging start and made me feel as if I had to defend the whole sporting honor of the British Isles, nor was my nervousness diminished when I found that I was to be accompanied by Scherping and Menthe as well as by the regular keeper on whose beat this particular stag lived. I could not help reflecting that my companions were all feeling rather contemptuous of a poor damned diplomat and a British one at that. Fortune was, however, with me on that occasion. We mounted the high stand, and after a wait of over an hour the stag and his harem appeared at quite a different place from that at which they were expected, and a good half mile away. There was nothing for it but to descend and attempt a stalk on more or less Scottish lines. That meant walking some distance, then a long crawl on hands and knees, and finally creeping all alone on the flat of my face till I reached a small knobbie about a hundred yards from the herd. When I got there, the stag was kindly standing broadside on; and I shot it through the heart. From that moment my reputation as a sportsman was secure. Goering was, I felt, delighted; and, when his people told him that I had had to crawl on my stomach (a rare event in a German forest), he remarked with a guffaw of laughter that that was the right way for diplomats to get about. Incidentally, I shot a second stag the next morning, again with one shot, and once more in the course of a stalk instead of a set "highstand," which always gives one the impression of shooting at a target. After that I was considered worthy to become, as I did later, an honorary member of the German *Jägerschaft*.

Nothing could have been pleasanter than my two days' visit to Rominten. There is no rabid nationalism in sport, or at any rate, in that kind of sport, nor socialism, either, in the midst of unspoiled nature, where all men are equal. From my host downward everyone was simple, unaffected, and extremely friendly. The weather was perfect, and I enjoyed it immensely. Each night, after supper, the stags killed in the course of the day were brought in and laid on the grass in front of the house. A bonfire of pine branches was lit beside them; a row of *Jägers*, or foresters, in their dark green uniforms, stood in the shadows behind them; and, after the Head Forester had read out the bag and the names of those who had killed it and had been answered in a few words of thanks by our host, the *hallali*, or death of the stag, was sounded on the horns of the *Jägers*. In the starlit night, in the depths of the great forest, with the notes of the horns echoing back from the tall fir trees in the distance, the effect was extremely beautiful.

I left Rominten with regret on the following morning. I had had one long political talk with Goering. Very shrewd and astute, as fat men so often are, his mind was simple and dealt only with essentials. His idea of an understanding between Great Britain and Germany was an agreement limited to two clauses. In the first, Germany would recognize the supreme position of Great Britain overseas and undertake to put all her resources at the disposal of the British Empire in case of need. By the second, Great Britain would recognize the predominant continental position of Germany in Europe, and undertake to do nothing to hinder her legitimate expansion. It was the theory of the free hand for Germany in Central and Eastern Europe, and in substance was identical with the last proposals handed to me by Hitler on August 25th two years later. Its very simplicity made it the more plausible, but it left out of all account not only the national conscience and international idealism of the Western Democracies, but also the methods and exaggerated pretensions of Nazism. With a Germany prepared to admit the equality of rights of others and to solve problems by negotiation instead of by force, a gentleman's agreement on such lines would have had much to recommend it. Any attempt to achieve it was bound to fail, as long as Hitler and his Nazi regime persisted in employing outside Germany the same methods which they had used to secure their position within Germany. In the name of the Führer and the party, it had crushed out all individual personality and freedom within the boundaries of the Reich; and, in the name of the superiority of German culture and of the transcendental rights of Germans over all other races, it was preparing to destroy the national liberty and freedom of its weaker neighbors outside those boundaries. At that moment, however, Hitler and his associates were profuse in their assurances that they held no such intentions. All that they desired was the consolidation of National Socialism within the Reich, and the fulfillment of Greater Germany by the incorporation in it of Austria. That country was, so they said, already Nazi to the core and would vote overwhelmingly so, if a free plebiscite were held there, unhampered by the Schuschnigg tyranny, which in itself was, they alleged, only maintained in power by Allied support and the fetters of the Versailles Treaty.

From Rominten I went to Schloss Finckenstein, the home of Count zu Dohna, whom I had met on board the *Cap Arcona* in my journey back from South America. It lies in East Prussia near the Vistula and the Corridor, in the heart of the Prussian Junker country, and close to the estate given by a grateful country to Field Marshal Hindenburg after the war. It is a lovely red brick eighteenth-century house with a mansarded roof; and Napoleon, who stopped there on his passage across Germany to his Russian Campaign, is said, on seeing it for the first time, to have exclaimed, *"Enfin un château,"* a remark which, while flattering to Finckenstein, was hardly appreciative of the other residences in Germany which he occupied or which were placed at his disposal. Napoleon made it his headquarters for a considerable period, and it was the scene of his meeting and romance with Countess Walewska. The history of Europe might have been different today if he had listened more generously to the pleading of Walewska and re-created a real Polish kingdom, instead of a mere half-baked duchy, which was an untenable proposition, and which was quickly lost sight of again after Waterloo. The suite which he used as a bedroom and as offices during his stay at Finckenstein is still preserved in its original condition.

My hostess was a good-looking and charming woman, and my host a cultivated but, unfortunately, very sick man. Though he spoke English badly, he took in and read the *Daily Telegraph* and *Daily Mail*, and I was astonished at his extensive knowledge of English politics and politicians. He owned, farmed, and administered himself some 10,000 acres of arable land and 20,000 acres of forest at an apparently very reasonable profit based on fixed prices and close state supervision. One coincidence which befell me there remains imprinted on my memory. A number of English books had been placed in my bedroom; and among them the correspondence of the Duke of Wellington as edited, I think, by a great-niece of his. I opened it quite by chance at a letter addressed by the

Goering

Duke to his fellow plenipotentiary, Lord Castlereagh, after the battle of Waterloo. Prussia, Russia, and Austria were at the time clamoring for the dismemberment of France in order to prevent the danger of any repetition of the Napoleonic episode. The letter ran as follows: "If we ask France to make this great cession, we must consider the operations of war as deferred till France shall find a suitable opportunity of endeavoring to regain what she has lost and, after having wasted our resources in the maintenance of overgrown military establishments in time of peace, we shall find how little useful the cessions we have acquired will be against a national effort to regain them.

"We ought to continue to keep our great object, *the genuine peace and tranquillity* of the world, in our view and shape our arrangements so as to provide for it."

The italics are mine, and it was an appreciation of realities which corresponded so closely to my own view about the Treaty of Versailles that I copied it out on a sheet of Finckenstein paper and have it still in my possession. It is so easy to be wise after the event, and the national hatreds and resentments of 1919 were an impossible atmosphere for the building up of the "genuine peace and tranquillity of the world." Only those who could have done better have the right to criticize, but objective judgment in the light of subsequent developments is not inadmissible. Versailles certainly contained a far fairer adjustment of territory, based on the principle of nationality, than had ever previously existed. But it had not been a negotiated peace, and the legitimate fears of a renewal of German *Machtpolitik* handicapped its authors. It was, in fact, a peace but not peace. In every problem, with its many issues, there is always a crucial point. I do not refer to disarming Germany, to making her pay for defeat, or to depriving her of her colonies; for such as these there was ample justification. The basic fault, in my humble opinion, of the Versailles Treaty was its failure to accord to Germans the same right of self-determination which it granted to Poles, Czechs, Yugoslavs, and Rumanians. At that time the Austrians and Sudeten Germans had clamored for union with Germany, but higher moral principles were waived in favor of political or strategical considerations which could not admit of any accretion of territory for a defeated but always potentially dangerous Germany. I yield to no one in my devotion to the ideals of a League of Nations. It represents, like all ideals, the striving of humanity for better things. However impossible of full attainment, every step forward toward the desired goal is something attempted, something done. Such a League can, however, in my opinion, never be a practical reality unless and until there is something approaching an equality of moral standards among nations, and until moral principles and abstract justice count more for it than so-called higher politics and political combinations.

CHAPTER VII

FURTHER ATTEMPT
TO IMPROVE
ANGLO-GERMAN RELATIONS

UNDETERRED by the ill success of the invitation extended
to Baron von Neurath to visit London in June, and by the
equivocal attitude adopted by the Chancellor in accepting
and then brusquely refusing to permit it, Mr. Chamberlain
made, as I mentioned earlier, a second attempt in the course
of the year to break the ice of bad relations with the Nazi
Government. Arrangements had been made in 1936 by General Goering, as Game Warden of the Reich and an enthusiastic sportsman, to hold a great hunting exhibition at Berlin
in November, 1937. When I arrived at my post in May, I
found that almost every European country was to be represented at this exhibition except Great Britain. Hunting is of
all sports the least calculated to arouse national jealousies
and ill feeling; and it seemed to me, therefore, and particularly in view of Britain's recognized role in the world of
sport, unfortunate that we should not participate. I consequently appealed to the Foreign Office for help in securing
a contribution from His Majesty's Government, even at that
late hour, for this purpose. Thanks to their good offices a
small sum was forthcoming, and the invaluable assistance of
Mr. Frank Wallace enlisted with a view to organizing a
British section. Mr. Wallace had but three or four months

at his disposal; but by means of boundless energy and zeal he succeeded in getting together a highly satisfactory collection of African, North American, and Asiatic trophies, including heads shot by Their Majesties the King and Queen and H.R.H. the Duke of Gloucester. A stuffed giant Panda was, incidentally, among the notable exhibits. It is perhaps not out of place to mention here that in the final adjudication Poland received the first prize for the European section and Britain the first prize for its overseas collection.

As always in Germany the organization was remarkably good and the exhibition a great success. International sportsmen attended it from all over the world. The French Government sent a pack of foxhounds and huntsmen complete with horns and red coats. The German Government for its part did not forget to have a German prewar colonial section with a map. Hitler, possibly with reluctance, as he hates all sport and deplores in principle the taking of animal life, visited the exhibition; and Goering was, I believe, gratified by the British participation in it.

But it chiefly merits mention in this record owing to the fact that it furnished Lord Halifax, at that time Lord President of the Council, with the opportunity for a visit to Berlin. It is true that in accordance with diplomatic tradition, albeit also in order to avoid exciting exaggerated hopes in some quarters and apprehensions in others, the visit was described as entirely private and unofficial; and the Lord President's status as a Master of Foxhounds was accordingly carefully stressed. But the fact remained that it was designed by Mr. Chamberlain to establish that personal contact between a prominent British statesman and the Nazi leaders which

Further Attempt

Hitler was believed to seek and which, it was hoped, might lead to a better understanding. As such and taken by itself, it was entirely successful and, had a better understanding been possible or really wanted by Hitler, the visit would have largely contributed to it. Lord Halifax lunched on arrival with Baron and Baroness von Neurath, who were old acquaintances, and spent his first afternoon visiting the Exhibition, of which, indeed, he was in German eyes one of the principal exhibits. His passage through the dense throngs of people was certainly greeted by the public with evident sympathy and pleasure. He paid it a second visit on the next day; and in the evening he went by train to Berchtesgaden, where he had a long conversation with Hitler. He returned to Berlin on the morning of the 20th and lunched with General Goering at Karinhall. That evening I gave a big dinner party at His Majesty's Embassy, at which he met most of the other leading Nazi Ministers and personalities. After a luncheon party on the following day (Sunday) at which he made the acquaintance of my principal diplomatic colleagues, Dr. Goebbels and his wife came to tea at the Embassy. While my sister Lady Leitrim and Lady Alexandra Metcalfe, who were staying with me at the time, entertained Frau Goebbels, I acted as interpreter between Lord Halifax and Dr. Goebbels. The subject of their conversation was the press of our two countries, and for a while thereafter there was less friction in this respect. Nor can I refrain from observing that the reasonableness and logic which Dr. Goebbels always displayed in private seemed to make, in spite of his reputation, quite a good impression upon Lord Halifax.

The Lord President left that evening for London. His

time during his five days' visit to Germany had been fully occupied, and the general effect was up to a point undoubtedly good. Hitler cannot but have been—and in fact, so I heard, was—impressed by the obvious sincerity, high principles, and straightforward honesty of a man like Lord Halifax. The general German public regarded the visit as a proof of British good will toward Germany and was clearly appreciative. Nevertheless, the official German tendency was to sit back and wait. As Goering said to me after the visit, "Does the Prime Minister really mean business, and will he be able to impose his will upon those circles in England which seek to negative everything which is Nazi, or is not run on the old lines of the League of Nations, French encirclement, collective security, and Russia as the counterpoise to Germany in Europe?" That was the orthodox German view of British policy then; but the fact was that, in spite of all his professions of a desire for an understanding with Britain, Hitler was himself in no hurry. He was astute enough to realize that he had first to cross the Austrian and other brooks. He was not prepared to sacrifice his central European ambitions to that understanding. Good relations with England only meant, for him, the acquiescence of England in his schemes for the redrawing of the Central European map. His professions cost him nothing and were a valuable part of his stock in trade for deluding the German people, which, in the mass, really did want to be friends with the English. It was the patter of the conjurer intended to mislead his audience and distract their attention. And, indeed, up to March 15th, 1939, however prepared one might be for the worst, it was still possible to hope that Hitler might be sincere; that he meant even approximately what he said; that he would, in fact, be satisfied once the unity of Greater Germany was consummated; that the theory of purity of race was genuine; that all he wanted was Germans; and that, once he had got the Austrian and Sudeten sheep into the German fold, he would leave other nations alone and content himself with peaceful occupations and pursuits. Provided one is prepared for the worst, one can and must always hope for the best, until the worst happens. Peace was my goal, and I could not honestly work for it if I acted on the assumption that, whatever occurred or whatever one did, the end would always and inevitably be the worst. My job was not to prophesy the worst, but to do my utmost to prevent its happening.

At the time, therefore, I allowed myself to cherish the dream that the Halifax visit might indeed constitute the beginning of better things. It is but human to clutch at straws, and there was little else on the political horizon which was calculated to promote optimism. The clouds were unmistakably gathering over Austria, and the star of Henlein was already rising in the Sudeten firmament. The Spanish war was still the major preoccupation of the democratic governments, and behind that smoke screen Hitler was steadily and skillfully consolidating his position. Russia had been weakened by her military purges; while, on the other hand, the Rome-Berlin Axis had become a world triangle through the signature by Italy and Japan of the Anti-Comintern Pact. The three countries constituted a new, powerful, and aggressive bloc; and the smaller states were already beginning to wonder whether comparative immunity under the aegis of Germany was not safer than the theoretical collective security offered to them at Geneva.

Generally speaking, 1937 was for Hitler a year of intensive preparation, both diplomatic and military. The economic situation was giving rise to increasing anxiety, but those who foretold early financial disaster failed to reckon with German organized control. When Lord Halifax asked General Goering how the money was found to build all the magnificent new motor roads, the General's answer was "confidence." Much can be done with confidence when any lack of it is strictly *verboten* (forbidden) and very severely punished.

It is probably true to say that the Spanish war afforded Hitler just the breathing space which he required. It preoccupied Europe, and thus enabled him surreptitiously to prepare the ground for the prosecution of his wider ambitions, by fanning the flames of Sudeten discontent, by encouraging the Nazi elements in Austria, by persecuting the opponents of Nazism in Danzig, and by hectoring the Lithuanians over Memel. What was even more useful to him was the fact that the conflicting ideologies of that war split both France and England into mutually hostile factions. It was these animosities which gave him the opportunity not only of strengthening his external political position but of forging quietly but steadily ahead with military and air-force rearmament. In the annual report on Germany which I wrote for the year 1937, one paragraph ran as follows:

The rearmament of Germany, if it has been less spectacular because it is no longer news, has been pushed on with the same energy as in previous years. In the army, consolidation has been the order of the day, but there is clear evidence that a considerable

Further Attempt

increase is being prepared in the number of divisions and of additional tank units outside those divisions. The air force continues to expand at an alarming rate and one can at present see no indication of a halt. We may well soon be faced with a strength of between 4,000 and 5,000 first-line aircraft. The power of the German air force has been still further increased by the intensive development of air defense, which has reached a degree of efficiency probably unknown in any other country. [Goering gave me on one occasion an interesting explanation of why such attention had been paid in Germany to A. R. P. Soldiers, he said, cannot keep their eyes to the front if their families in the rear are exposed to danger.] Even the navy, though well within the 35 per cent proportion is training a personnel considerably above the requirements of that standard. Finally, the mobilization of the civilian population and industry for war, by means of education, propaganda, training and administrative measures, has made further strides. Military efficiency is the god to whom everyone must offer sacrifice. It is not an army but the whole German nation which is being prepared for war.

In the light of that paragraph written in the course of the first week of January, 1938, it seems astonishing that one should have managed to preserve at the time any shred of optimism. It was, however, still possible to conceive that Hitler was acting solely on the principle: *Si vis pacem, para bellum.* I never had a shadow of doubt that his aims were the incorporation of Austria, the Sudeten Lands, Memel, and Danzig. His claims in these respects were based on the principle of self-determination, and a negotiated settlement in regard to them should not therefore have been impossible. Even Hitler's emotion over dead Germans in connection with the *Hindenburg* and *Deutschland* disasters encouraged the illusion that he might recoil from a war in which such misfortunes would be magnified a hundred thousandfold.

Failure of a Mission

Time, which alone could do so, has proved the falsity of these hopes. Hitler and his wild men were not to be satisfied by a mere display of force to achieve their ends. If one makes a toy, the wish to play with it becomes irresistible. And the German Army and Air Force were super-toys, and Hitler was determined to find or, if he could not find, to make an occasion for proving, regardless of the cost to Germany and to the world, what a formidable super-toy maker he was.

As for Hitler's emotion over dead Germans, it was undoubtedly sincere at the moment that he expressed it, and it in fact corresponded with a certain sentimental streak in his character. But it was a typical streak of his two-sided nature, which he could assume or discard at will. It was the same with his indignation over oppressed Germans in other countries (not over those—be it noted—in the concentration camps in his own country). So long as good relations with Poland were necessary to his policy, he evinced no sympathy for the German minority in that country. In order to insure Italy's good will, he proved that he was quite ready to sacrifice the Germans in the South Tyrol, though possibly with the idea of sending them back again there later. Since the war began, he has authorized the infliction of untold hardships on the Baltic Germans, simply in order to oil the wheels of his present Russian policy. On the other hand, when sentimentality served his immediate purpose, as in the case of the pro-Nazis in Austria, the Sudeten, in Czechoslovakia, or the German minority in Poland, he was able equally easily to work himself up into a frenzy on their behalf. As with the oppressed, so it was with dead Germans. He had publicly announced that

Further Attempt

he reckoned on heavy German losses if there was war with Poland. Yet that did not deter him from conceiving and carrying out his Polish campaign, in spite of the fact that he could certainly have attained his ends without loss of life, if he had been willing to be patient. Similarly there can, I think, be little doubt that he will sacrifice without a tremor countless thousands of lives on the Western Front if he believes that by so doing he will succeed in glorifying himself and in maintaining his own position and that of his party in Germany.

I have alluded to my mission to Berlin as a drama. The year 1937 constituted its orchestral overture, of which the Wagnerian leitmotivs were the disciplined tramp of armed men, ever louder and more multitudinous, and the ceaseless clank of heavy machinery forging guns and yet bigger guns, tanks and ever heavier tanks, bombers and still more powerful and destructive bombers. It was a somber introduction to the four-act tragedy which was to follow.

PART II
THE DRAMA

CHAPTER I.   PRELUDE

IT is no exaggeration to say that a domestic incident constituted the prelude to the tragedy itself; and the curtain for that prelude rose on January 12th, 1938, when the German press announced that Field Marshal von Blomberg had been married on the previous day to a certain Fräulein Eva Gruhn, with Adolf Hitler and General Goering as sole witnesses of the ceremony. I had been dining the night before at the Ministry of Propaganda, and our host, Herr Funk, then Undersecretary of that Ministry and today Minister for Economics and President of the Reichsbank, had announced the fact at the end of dinner to some sixty guests, including many Cabinet Ministers, military officers, and Nazi officials, as well as a number of diplomatists. All, without exception, learned the news with amazement, and everyone at once asked who Fräulein Gruhn was without finding anyone to answer. Speculation continued to center round that question until it gradually 'became public property that she was inscribed on Himmler's police records as an attractive lady, but of the lighter virtues. I have never felt quite certain in my own mind that the whole affair was not a calculated plot on the part of that scheming chief of the Gestapo. He must, at least, have known what was going on, even if Hitler and

Goering did not; and it was, furthermore, very much in his personal interests, and those of the extremists, to eliminate Blomberg.

In any case, the shock of this disclosure to Hitler's personal feelings and public prestige was immense. Not only was Blomberg one of his most trusted advisers but also one of his most intimate and possibly most beloved friends. And this best friend had deceived him. On discovering the truth, Hitler's first step was to endeavor to persuade the Marshal to allow the marriage to be dissolved, on the ground that he had been inveigled into it under false pretenses. Blomberg's refusal to agree to this course shook Hitler's faith in the loyalty of his followers both to himself and to Germany. But worse was to follow. Blomberg had probably never, as a political Marshal and as too subservient to the Nazi civilians, been very popular with the Army chiefs. Incidentally he was equally unpopular with the Nazi extremists as not being one of themselves and as being opposed to their excessive interference in military matters. Without waiting for Hitler to find his own way out of the impasse, the Commander in Chief, General von Fritsch, supported by other generals as well as by the sole surviving and highly respected Marshal of the great war, von Mackensen, notified the Führer that Army discipline could not tolerate the retention of Blomberg, married to a lady with such a past, in his post as Minister for War. If there is one thing which a dictator dislikes, it is being dictated to. Partly out of repugnance to having his hand forced and partly out of loyalty to his old friend, he demurred at first to Blomberg's removal. Whereupon General von Fritsch took occasion not only to insist on the point

of military discipline, but also severely to criticize the Führer's foreign policy, more particularly as regards Austria.
This was going further than Hitler would tolerate. As Field
Marshal Goering said to me a month or so later: "What
would Mr. Chamberlain have done if your C.I.G.S. had come
to him and said, 'Quite apart from Army matters, I entirely
disapprove of your foreign policy'? He would have said,
'Thank you, good day,' and dismissed him as Hitler did
General von Fritsch."

That was, in fact, what happened. Fritsch left and Blomberg also. The only question for Hitler then was how to
effect these two main changes with profit, or at least without loss of face to himself. In the end, three weeks later, on
February 4th, and after the first of Hitler's temperamental
fits of uncontrolled rage of the year, these two removals
were announced under a vast camouflage of other changes
and retirements, not only in the Army but also in the Navy,
Air Force, and Diplomatic Service. Except, however, in the
field of diplomacy, little mattered except the removal of
Blomberg and Fritsch, inasmuch as at least 90 per cent of the
changes would have taken place in the normal course of
events a few months later. Hitler himself took over command
of the German armed forces and became supreme War
Lord, with General Keitel, a serving soldier and a gentleman, performing most of Blomberg's executive functions,
but under the direct nominal supervision of the Führer. General von Brauschitsch, a very competent and able officer,
succeeded Fritsch as Commander in Chief. General Goering
became a Field Marshal, thereby becoming the only one on
the active list in Germany. Generally speaking, it may be

said that Hitler succeeded in maneuvering himself out of his difficult position with remarkable adroitness. He had taken a welcome opportunity to effect a purge of the monarchist and conservative elements in the Army. He had put its leaders in their place and kept the party in theirs. The party had hoped for more drastic action against the Army; and the Army, though it had met with a decided if inconclusive defeat, was possibly relieved that worse had not befallen it. But the seeds were sown of the absorption of the Army within the party structure, and they have been germinating ever since. They sprouted considerably after Munich, but it is the war which will decide which of the two shall govern Germany.

It has been necessary to lay great stress on the incident of the Blomberg marriage. Both morally and materially its consequences were of the utmost importance. Not only did it—as mentioned above—cause Hitler his first brainstorm of the year, but there is good reason to believe that it radically altered his entire outlook on life. Thenceforward he became less human; and his fits of rage, real or simulated, more frequent. His faith in the fidelity of his followers was gravely shaken, and his inaccessibility became greatly accentuated.

To whom did Hitler really listen? That is a question I thereafter repeatedly asked; and the reply was always "no one." Moreover, the all-important upshot of the incident was to remove from Hitler's entourage two of his most moderate and respectable advisers, Blomberg himself and Baron von Neurath. The replacement of Neurath by Ribbentrop was a major disaster. The failure of the latter's mission to London had long been apparent, I fancy even to Hitler himself; and he would probably have been removed sooner if any other suitable post had been immediately available to Germany's "Ambassador at Large." The reconstruction gave Hitler the opportunity of giving him the office of Minister for Foreign Affairs, albeit directly, as in General Keitel's case, under his own supervision; and I was inclined to believe that, in making the appointment, the Führer felt that Ribbentrop, who as a yes-man was sympathetic to him, could do less harm in Berlin than in London. I should like to make it quite clear here that I have no personal quarrel with Herr von Ribbentrop, whose original intentions on his appointment to London may have been admirable. But from the beginning I felt that his vanity, his resentments, and his misconceptions of England and English mentality were a serious bar to any prospect of a better understanding between the two countries; and at the end I realized that, as far as lay in his power, no one had done more than he did to precipitate the war. For that there is no hell in Dante's Inferno bad enough for Ribbentrop. It was a consummation which I had long feared and to which I had more than once drawn the attention of his colleagues.

Speaking to Goering and to others before Munich, I had reminded them that if one man had been more responsible than anyone else for the war which began in August, 1914, it was Count Berchtold, the Austrian Minister for Foreign Affairs. I had known him in St. Petersburg when he was Austrian Ambassador there. He was a great Austrian nobleman, but like Ribbentrop he was a combination of vanity, stupidity, and superficiality. And I warned my listeners that if Ribbentrop were not checked, he would one day lead Germany to ruin as Count Berchtold had led Austria. Unfortunately foreign politics were Hitler's main preoccupation; and in his position as Foreign Minister Ribbentrop had more constant access to, and consequently more chance of exercising his influence on, the Führer than any other German Minister. In September, 1938, as well as in August, 1939, Ribbentrop and Himmler were in my opinion his principal lieutenants in the war party of which Hitler himself was the leader.

Finally there is no doubt that the Blomberg incident and the necessity which it imposed on a dictator to obliterate its memory by some striking external success accelerated the tempo of what may be described as Act I of the drama— "Austria."

Between, however, the prelude and the first act, there was an interlude, in the course of which Mr. Chamberlain made his third effort in eight months to initiate with Hitler discussions, the object of which was to lead to those serious negotiations, with a view to the settlement by pacific methods of all outstanding problems, which was the settled policy of Mr. Chamberlain's Government vis-à-vis Germany. That was, too, from beginning to end, the underlying purpose of my mission to Berlin. Admittedly, there may have been certain honest misunderstandings on both sides. Yet, though Hitler was constantly talking of the hand which he had held out to England and complaining that England had rejected it, whenever definite advances were made to him, he always found some way of withdrawing and of refusing to meet us halfway. It is impossible today to believe that this was fortuitous. The Greek tragedy motif was not accidental but calculated. His aims in Europe were not compatible with negotiations

with Britain, and he was determined to secure them first before risking actual negotiations with us and above all before
we became too strong. The naval treaty was "eyewash";
and there can be little doubt that Hitler always contemplated denouncing it, as he did in April, 1939, whenever it
suited his purpose to do so (i.e. after his land and air rearmament was completed). In the meantime, if the Anglo-German Naval Treaty and the guarantee to Belgium could keep
us from interfering with his Central European schemes, so
much the better. That was, I am convinced, the sole motive
of both Treaty and guarantee.

It is so important to realize this that I venture to enumerate
here the various concrete attempts which were made during
the course of my mission to Berlin with a view to initiating
Anglo-German discussions: Firstly, the invitation for Baron
von Neurath to visit London in June, 1937, which failed, as
I have recounted, in consequence of the alleged *Leipzig* incident and Ribbentrop's jealousy; secondly, Lord Halifax's
visit to Berlin, which led to no response from Hitler, but
which was followed, thirdly, by my own equally inconclusive
interview in March, 1938, with the Chancellor, which I am
about to describe; fourthly, Mr. Chamberlain's own visits to
Berchtesgaden and Munich and the Anglo-German declaration which Hitler deliberately tore up when he occupied
Prague on March 15th, 1939; fifthly, the visit to Berlin which
it was arranged for the President of the Board of Trade and
the Secretary of the Overseas Trade Department to make
on March 18th, 1939, and which had naturally to be cancelled after Hitler's action on March 15th; and sixthly, Lord
Halifax's last effort on June 30th, when, in his great and

considered speech at the annual dinner of the Royal Institute of International Affairs, he defined British policy as resting upon twin foundations of purpose. "One," he said, "is our determination to resist force. The other is our recognition of the world's desire to get on with the constructive work of building peace. If we could once be satisfied that the intentions of others were the same as our own and that we *all really wanted peaceful solutions* [the italics are mine]—then, I say here definitely, we could discuss the problems that are today causing the world anxiety. In such a new atmosphere we could examine the colonial problem, the question of raw materials, trade barriers, the issue of *Lebensraum* (living space) and any other issue that affects the lives of all European citizens." There could not have been a fairer offer, but it was ignored.

I have quoted this passage at length, because it truly constitutes the theme associated with the whole of my work during those two strenuous years at Berlin, and unceasingly argued by me in all my talks with Germany's leading statesmen. "If you really want peace, we are honestly ready to talk," was the perpetual burden of my language to all who would listen to it. Some undoubtedly did, but others stopped their ears. The truth was that Hitler did not "really want peaceful solutions." I do not mean that he wanted war with Britain—from that he certainly shrank, but he was anxious to try out his new war machine, and was avid for cheap victories over Czechs, Poles, or others who would stand no chance against the organized and disciplined military might of Germany.

Prelude

Goering had said after Lord Halifax's visit, "Does Mr. Chamberlain really mean business?" To prove that he did so I was recalled to London at the end of January, 1938, and given instructions to seek an interview with Hitler and to discuss the possibilities of a general settlement. If we judged by the German press, as well as Hitler's own statements to casual British visitors, the twin obstacles to a better understanding between our two countries were our constant opposition to Germany in Europe and our refusal to hand back the colonies of which we had "robbed" her. I was consequently told to inform Hitler that His Majesty's Government would be ready, in principle, to discuss all outstanding questions.

I returned to Berlin on February 4th, but in view of the unsettled atmosphere caused by the reorganization following on the Blomberg marriage incident, my actual audience with Hitler was deferred until March 3rd. By that time Mr. Eden had left the Government, and Lord Halifax had succeeded him as Foreign Secretary. Unfortunately—and it seemed fated that it should always be so for my meetings with Hitler—the moment was an ill-chosen one. Dr. Schuschnigg had been summoned to Berchtesgaden on February 12th, and the Austrian kettle was boiling hard and on the point of boiling over. Hitler was consequently in a vile temper and made no effort to conceal it.

I was received in the old Reichschancery, and was asked to sit down on a big sofa against the wall facing the window. On my left on a small stool was Dr. Schmidt taking notes. On his left again, in a semicircle, Hitler himself in an armchair, and next to him and facing me, Herr von Ribbentrop.

Failure of a Mission

I began with a statement of my object in asking to see the Chancellor. It was not, I said, to suggest a bargain (*Kuhhandel*, or cow deal), an accusation which the German press always made against us when we suggested anything but to create a basis for friendship. His Majesty's Government, I said, did not underestimate the difficulties to be overcome but were convinced that they could be overcome if both parties contributed on a basis of reciprocity and on the principle of higher reason as distinct from the use of mere force. His Majesty's Government admitted that changes were possible, but only if effected on the basis of higher reason; they had discussed what appeared to be the main questions between us, such as a limitation of armaments and the restriction of bombing—to which His Majesty's Government would add the abolition of bombing airplanes—as well as a peaceful solution of the Czech and Austrian problems, and the colonial question. What contribution for her part was Germany, I asked, ready to make toward general security and peace in Europe.

It was perhaps the longest continuous statement which I ever made to Hitler, and must have lasted for the best part of ten minutes. During all that time he remained crouching in his armchair with the most ferocious scowl on his face, which my firm, but at the same time conciliatory, remarks scarcely warranted. He listened, nevertheless, till I had finished and then let himself go. Nothing, he said, could be done until the press campaign against him in England ceased. (He never ceased harping on this subject in every conversation which I ever had with him.) Nor was he going to tolerate the interference of third parties in Central Europe. Injustice was

Prelude

being done to millions of Germans, and self-determination and democratic rights must be applied to Germans as well as others. Only 15 per cent of the Austrian population supported the Schuschnigg regime; if Britain opposed a just settlement, Germany would have to fight. If Germans were oppressed there, he must and would intervene; and, if he did intervene, he would act like lightning (*Blitzschnell*). Austria must be allowed to vote, and in Czechoslovakia the Germans must have autonomy in cultural and other matters.

It was clearly not colonies which interested Hitler. After haranguing me for half an hour about the British press, the insupportable meddling of British bishops in German church affairs, the unbearable interference of England generally in matters which, according to him, did not concern her, and about the sad fate of Nazi-loving Germans in Austria and Czechoslovakia, he turned to the question of disarmament and referred to the threat to Germany of the Franco-Soviet pact and of Czechoslovakia's accession thereto. It was, he said, for that reason that Germany had to be so heavily armed, and any limitation of armaments depended, therefore, on the U.S.S.R. The problem was, he continued, rendered particularly difficult "by the fact that one could place as much confidence in the faith in treaties of a barbarous creature like the Soviet Union as in the comprehension of mathematical formulae by a savage. Any agreement with the U.S.S.R. was quite worthless and Russia should never have been allowed into Europe." It was impossible, he added, to have, for instance, any faith in any Soviet undertaking not to use poison gas.

Failure of a Mission

The sentences in quotation marks are Hitler's actual words as recorded in the written and carefully edited notes made and given to me at the time by Dr. Schmidt. In fact the whole of the three last paragraphs are summarized from that written record, as approved by Hitler himself and communicated to me by Herr von Ribbentrop. I have transcribed it at some length, because Hitler's remarks on this occasion constitute interesting evidence, as taken down and to be used against him, of the Hitler technique. When he spoke of a vote in Austria, I asked him if he meant a plebiscite, a suggestion which had long been canvassed in the German press. Hitler's answer was that he demanded "that the just interests of the German Austrians should be secured and an end made to oppression by a process of peaceful evolution." In other words, he begged the question with a vague reply. He did not intend, as he proved later, to tolerate a plebiscite unless it was held under his own direct auspices. His claim for the Sudeten in Czechoslovakia should equally be noted. It was limited to autonomy at that moment. After he had got Austria, autonomy was not enough, though it continued to be the openly declared objective until his army was ready to strike. As soon as it was so, the incorporation of the whole of the Sudeten Lands in the Reich was demanded. When he got them, that again was not enough; and the Czechs, whose independence he had said that he was prepared to guarantee, had to lose that also. Each stage was always the last for him until he had reached it. As soon as that position was gained, he advanced on the next. Nor are his observations in regard to the U.S.S.R., in the light of August, 1939, less illuminating. As for the limitation of armaments and the prohibition or restriction of aerial bombardments, which he had once upon a time expressed such willingness to consider, his attitude toward these problems on this occasion left very little of either of them above the surface. His words were often fair; but, when one attempted to get down to brass tacks, he skillfully eluded the issue. That also was typical of the Hitler technique, and his remark about Russia and poison gas is worth remembering. The U.S.S.R. was still at that time marked out to be the scapegoat, but it was so easy where Hitler was concerned for circumstances to alter cases.

As for colonies he did not seem the least interested in them, and the sum of his reply was that the colonial problem could wait for 4, 6, 8, or even 10 years. He promised, however, to give me a written reply on the subject, and I left Berlin a year and a half later without having ever received it.

We did, however, fitfully discuss such matters, and even studied the globe of the world, which always stands in Hitler's room wherever he is, a practice which I would strongly recommend to all politicians and diplomatists. By that time the scowl on Hitler's face had disappeared, and on one occasion he had even smiled. It was when Ribbentrop intervened with some remark about the British press, which elicited from me the retort that it seemed to me amazing that any man who had lived in Canada and been Ambassador in London should be so profoundly ignorant of British mentality and habits. Hitler seemed to appreciate my onslaught on his Minister for Foreign Affairs, whose ascendancy over him was at that time far from being what it subsequently became. When our long conversation, which must have lasted nearly two hours, was over, I produced from my pocket on leaving an extremely good drawing of the Chancellor which a lady from New Zealand had sent me with the request that I might get it autographed. I asked Hitler to sign it, which he very readily did (in such respects he was always complaisant). Whereupon I observed that, while I, and presumably he, had got no other satisfaction out of our interview, he would at least have given pleasure to one young woman. That also produced quite a genial smile. I cannot remember having ever got another from him.

CHAPTER II

ACT I: AUSTRIA

MR. CHAMBERLAIN'S third attempt to initiate those discussions with Germany which might have been calculated to insure peace in Europe had thus failed, as it was foredoomed that it should, since at that juncture it was only Austria and Central Europe in which Hitler was interested. The episode is, however, important and should be borne in mind. It constitutes evidence of the fact that, except as a means to an end, it was not an understanding with Great Britain but the end itself, namely, dominion in Central and Eastern Europe, that Hitler alone really wanted. But I have somewhat digressed in recounting it, inasmuch as the curtain for Act I of the tragedy had in fact already risen just three weeks earlier, on February 12th, when Herr von Schuschnigg had had his memorable meeting with Hitler at Berchtesgaden.

To have gone to Berchtesgaden at all was the first of Schuschnigg's mistakes; yet the idea was not a new one. Neurath told me afterward that it had been decided in principle as far back as the previous December; and, when I was in London in January, I had warned His Majesty's Government that Hitler was contemplating some immediate action about Austria. The 1936 Agreement between Austria and Germany had never been honestly implemented on either side. Nazi propaganda had never ceased in Austria, and there were consequently between thirty and forty thousand Austrian Nazis still living in Germany to whom, in view of that propaganda, the Austrian Government naturally refused permission to return to their homes. It was these refugees who, embittered by their four years' exile, were mainly responsible on their return to Austria for the persecution and miseries which their former political opponents were eventually destined to suffer. But there is no doubt that the actual summons to Berchtesgaden was part of the camouflage under which Hitler sought to conceal the shock and the deceptions which the Blomberg marriage had caused him. He was consequently in a far from equable or conciliatory frame of mind; and Herr von Schuschnigg, according to his own account, was threatened and browbeaten, and under menaces accepted an arrangement of which he thoroughly disapproved. It required the consent of the Austrian President and Government at Vienna; but this was obtained on February 16th; and Herr von Schuschnigg made the second of his mistakes by remaining in office after an acceptance the effect of which he always intended, as far as possible, to attenuate.

By chance, the news of this acceptance reached Berlin in the course of the banquet which the Reich Chancellor gives annually to the Diplomatic Corps, and gave occasion to the only dispute which I ever had with Baron von Neurath, who, in front of a number of other German Ministers, vehemently accused His Majesty's Government of having actively encouraged the Austrian Government to repudiate the arrangement. To a lesser degree I was attacked by the Chancellor himself later on the same grounds. Equally hotly I denied it.

Austria

It is quite possible that Neurath was genuinely disappointed at the unconcealed British attitude of disapproval, because he feared that, if the ultimate result—of which no German ever doubted—could not be obtained by subterranean propaganda and intrigue, the end would be forcible action with incalculable complications. Hitler himself might also have preferred not to use force, and his *original* plan was gradually to undermine Schuschnigg's position, to procure his overthrow, and to secure his aims comparatively peacefully and less objectionably by means of a pro-Nazi Austrian Government.

It was, however, soon evident that Schuschnigg, who was at heart a loyal servant of the Hapsburgs, had no intention of lending himself to such a maneuver; and the realization of this fact caused Hitler his second fit of uncontrollable rage of the year. He was suffering from this state of violent excitement and resentment when I visited him on March 3rd.

In the event it was Herr von Schuschnigg who, by his third and final mistake, settled any doubts which Hitler may have had as to the best manner of solving the Austrian problem. On the night of March 9th, the Austrian Chancellor suddenly announced to the world by radio that he proposed to hold a plebiscite in Austria on the following Sunday, March 13th, to vote as to whether the country wished to remain independent or to be incorporated in Germany. As no voting lists had been drawn up for several years, only persons over the age of twenty-four would be entitled to vote.

It was the throw of a desperate gambler, and it failed. Schuschnigg's decision was taken without prior consultation, either with his Cabinet as a whole or with Mussolini, who alone was possibly in a position, as he had been in 1934, militarily to support the Austrian Government. The Duce's only reply, when he was eventually informed of it, was to the effect that such a proposal was a bomb which would surely burst in Schuschnigg's own hand.

The news of the proposed plebiscite reached Berlin at midnight on March 9th. It afforded Hitler, that master of opportunism, just the subterfuge which he was seeking. On the following day he summoned his advisers and his generals, and late that afternoon took the decision to cut the Gordian knot with the sword and to occupy Austria by force. He justified his decision on the ground that it was essential to prevent a plebiscite which according to him—and he was undoubtedly correct, for German propaganda would have insured that he should be—would merely lead to bloodshed and the loss of German lives. Nevertheless, I still do not believe, any more than I did at the time, that the rape of Austria in the form which it finally took, or at that date, was definitely premeditated. Hitler would have preferred to incorporate his native Austria into Germany by what he regarded as peaceful means. However clear in his mind Hitler may have been as to his ultimate ends, the decision as to the means for achieving them always depended upon the development of events and was never taken till the last moment.

But there had, of course, been plans in existence since 1934 for armed support of Nazi rebels in the event of revolution in Austria. These were, undoubtedly, rapidly revised; and the concentration of the Army on the border of Austria was completed by dawn on March 12th with very great speed and secrecy. Once it became clear that there would be no opposition, the "invasion" degenerated into spreading troops all over Austria as rapidly as possible, with little regard to war-service conditions. In certain respects it was a slovenly performance, which in itself was proof of inadequate preparation. But it served the Army a useful lesson, as a curtain raiser for possible subsequent forcible action in the case of Czechoslovakia. Moreover, it predisposed the world to believe that what had happened in Austria would be repeated in Czechoslovakia, and thereby helped to promote the subsequent incident of May 21st.

News that troops were on the move against Austria reached me in the early morning of Friday, March 11th. I at once asked the Military Attaché to His Majesty's Embassy to go round to the Ministry of War to ascertain the facts. Colonel Mason-Macfarlane received the answer that there was no information to give and that no troop movements were taking place. He immediately motored to Leipzig and obtained abundant evidence that military operations were afoot, but it was not until 6 P.M. that the War Ministry admitted to the Assistant Military Attaché that Colonel Mason-Macfarlane had been misled in the morning.

Herr von Ribbentrop was at the time in London, whither he had proceeded to present his letters of recall, another fairly evident proof of the unpremeditated moment of the "rape." As Minister for Foreign Affairs he would never have absented himself from Berlin at that moment if he could have foreseen it, and he, in fact, endeavored to return immediately but was told to remain where he was. Indeed, the big question which all Germans asked themselves was, "What will England do?" England, however, left it to words to carry conviction, as Hitler on March 10th had doubtless foreseen. Nor indeed were His Majesty's Government in a position to have saved Austria by their actions. The case against Hitler was not yet a cast-iron one. Austria was German, and many Austrians were wholeheartedly in favor of union with the Reich. The love for peace of the British public was too great for it to approve of a war in respect to which the moral issue was in any possible doubt. The case was the same in the Sudeten German crisis later in the year.

I saw Neurath in the course of the day and made him two strongly worded communications, but verbal protests without the resolute intention to use force if they were disregarded were not going to stop the German troops, which were already on the march. After the reoccupation of the Rhineland in 1936 the policy of hostile words which could not be implemented by hostile action was out of date and ineffective, and merely left behind it feelings of bitter resentment. Germany had become too strong to be impressed by empty gestures, which merely confirmed those like Ribbentrop in their opinion that Britain would put up with anything rather than fight. Lung power was no match for armed power; and Hitler was now prepared to treat all such things as questionnaires, strident rebukes, strong protests, and verbal ultimatums at their word value.

As it happened, Goering had arranged to give a big reception to some thousand guests on the night of March 11th at the "Haus der Flieger," followed by a performance by his State Opera Company. As it afforded me my only opportunity to see the Field Marshal, I reluctantly decided to attend it. The party began at 10 o'clock; and, when I arrived, the air was electric, though the Field Marshal had not yet arrived and was known to be attending a full Cabinet meeting with Hitler. The Schuschnigg and Seyes-Inquart radio messages were being anxiously discussed on all sides, and it was quite obvious that every German present was wondering what was happening. When Mr. Kirkpatrick gate-crashed, with a telegram instructing me to make an immediate communication to Baron von Neurath, one could have heard a pin drop in the great hall while 2,000 eyes watched me reading it. Shortly afterward Goering himself appeared, and, after shaking hands with a few guests, sat down at the central table; and the music began and was followed by a ballet. It was one of the most painful performances at which I have ever been present. Every diplomatist and a great number of the Germans themselves were conscious of the tragedy of music and dance, at a moment when all that which had been left in 1919 of the old Austrian and Hapsburg Empire was crashing to final extinction. I had myself shaken hands with Goering very curtly and coldly. He was obviously nervous and taken aback; and, no sooner had we sat down, than he tore off the blank half of his program, wrote on it in pencil, "As soon as the music is over I should like to talk to you, and will explain everything to you," and handed it to me across the American Ambassador's wife. The last five words were underlined thrice, and in fact, as soon as the performance came to an end, he got up hurriedly and waited for me outside. After a suitable interval I followed him, and for the next three quarters of an hour the Field Marshal's guests were left wondering what was happening.

The Field Marshal's promised explanation consisted in a diatribe against Schuschnigg's lack of good faith, and the impossibility of any other course being followed than that which was being taken. Our conversation, which took place in Goering's private room in the building, was an unpleasant one; but the only point that mattered was that the German troops and airplanes were already crossing the frontier. Nothing in fact could have saved Austria or even have restored her to independent existence except a resort by the Western Powers to a war in which probably the greater part of the Austrian youth would have been found on Germany's side. After fighting Schuschnigg's battle for him to the bitter end, I finally said to Goering that "even supposing the Austrian Chancellor has been unwise, that is no excuse for Germany to be a bully." I also took occasion strongly to urge the Field Marshal to do his utmost to see that the anti-Nazi Austrians were treated with the decency which their loyalty to their country merited. Had Goering been left to his own devices in Austria, I believe that he would have done his best to carry out such a policy. As it was, the embittered Austrian Nazis, backed up by Himmler's secret police and S.S., very soon undid what Goering attempted to do during his brief visit to Vienna after the occupation. My last remark to Goering as we returned to the great hall was that, if he did not wish that Herr Hitler should read what British public opinion would think of his actions, he had better arrange that the English newspapers should not be shown to him for a fortnight. I gave the same advice to Dr. Meissner, the head of the secretariat of the Reichschancery and the man who had served Ebert and Hindenburg in the same capacity as he was serving Hitler. It was not that I wished to spare the latter's feelings, but because I was conscious of his habit of making those who lay in his power, in this case the Austrian anti-Nazis, pay for the resentment provoked by those who were fortunate enough to live outside his jurisdiction.

The die of the fate of Austria had in fact been cast on March 10th. The rest is a matter of simple history. No opposition of any kind was offered to the German troops who entered Austria on the morning of March 12th. After spending the night at Linz and visiting the grave of his mother, Hitler himself reached Vienna on Sunday the 13th; and the curtain for Act I fell amid the cheers of the Austrian mob which welcomed their new Führer and applauded his announcement of the final incorporation of the Ostmark in the German Reich. One of the first acts of the Nazi Government after the occupation was to declare Planetta and the other assassins of Dolfuss to be heroic martyrs for the cause of German unity! Vienna was a landmark in that it constituted Hitler's first step outside the Reich along the path of violence. Moreover, it had been accomplished without actual bloodshed, since, however much they may be regretting it today, there is no doubt that many Austrians, notably the younger ones, were at the time themselves in favor of the *Anschluss*. They little realized at the time that their country would be treated as occupied territory and with complete indifference to its national individuality.

There was for me one last commentary on the proceedings before the act was finally over. March 13th was the German *Heldenstag,* or anniversary for the dead of the Great War. In view of what was happening I declined to attend the ceremony, at which all the heads of missions were wont to be present. Instead, I proceeded to pay a visit to the Austrian

Minister. It was a form of demonstration on my part, and I went there in my motor car with its large British flag flying at the bonnet. I found the Austrian Minister in full uniform, and on the point of going himself to the *Heldenstag* ceremony. I heard afterward that he had given there the Nazi salute and cried "Heil Hitler!" with the others!

THE interval between Act I and the first part of Act II lasted a little over two months. It was by no means a peaceful one. Until the date of Hitler's plebiscites in Germany and Austria, which produced the usual overwhelming majorities in both countries in favor of the Führer, German ears were deafened by daily speeches and nightly broadcasts, to such an extent that the population itself became sick to death of the whole business, and voted "yes" with relief, in order to be done with it. But behind Austria already loomed the specter of the problem of the Sudeten Germans; and Hitler's reference in his Reichstag speech of March 18th to his 10,000,000 unredeemed Germans (of which Austria only accounted for 6,500,000) gave a clear warning to the world as to Germany's next objective. Yet, at the moment of the march into Austria, the German Government had been profuse in its fair promises to the Czechs. Any move on the part of the latter might gravely have compromised the success of the Austrian coup. The Czech Minister was accordingly given positive assurances of Germany's benevolence toward his country. Goering repeated these assurances to me; and I was authorized by him, on behalf of Hitler himself, to convey them to His Majesty's Government. "It would," said Hitler, "be the earnest desire of his Government to improve German-Czech relations"—it was the old refrain and carried ever diminishing conviction.

Nor could there have been any shadow of doubt at all on the subject. In the years between 1933 and 1938 it was a common question to hear, "What does Hitler really want?" It had always been answered—and notably by my predecessor, Sir Eric Phipps, in his valedictory dispatch of 1937—in the same sense: first, Austria, then the Sudeten Lands; and after that, the liquidation of Memel, the Corridor, and Danzig; and finally the lost colonies. From the beginning of my mission I had never found any reason to disagree with the accuracy of a judgment which I entirely indorsed.

Czechoslovakia was the keystone of the French alliance system, and the potential bulwark against German expansion southeastward. But after the *Anschluss* she was left—vis-à-vis Germany—in a completely helpless position both strategically and economically, and it was clear that the integrity of her Versailles frontiers could only be upheld if France and England were prepared either to negotiate or to fight for their maintenance. War or peaceful negotiations were, in fact, the issues at stake. It was equally evident that something had to be done quickly, if Germany were not once more to take matters into her own hands, regardless of the Western Powers. When, therefore, His Majesty's Minister at Prague, in a sober and reasoned telegram, urged His Majesty's Government to intervene, together with France, before it was too late, with a view to persuading the Czech Government to readjust their relations with Germany, I had no hesitation in telegraphing immediately that I concurred wholeheartedly and unreservedly in the sage counsel given by Mr. Newton.

Nor, in doing so, was the only consideration that which one realistic glance at the map of Europe would have sufficed to prove, namely, the indefensibility of Czechoslovakia's strategic and economic position, once Austria had become an integral part of Germany. Though heavily fortified in the north, she had now become highly vulnerable to attack from the south. Quite apart from the national artificiality of this creation of Versailles, which contained in miniature all the diverse racial problems of the old Austro-Hungarian Empire, Czechoslovakia suffered from one fatal defect: her minorities, Polish and Hungarian no less than German, were situated on her very frontiers, and contiguous to the nations which claimed them as their own subjects.

On the broadest moral grounds it was thus difficult to justify offhand the refusal of the right of self-determination to the 2,750,000 Sudetens living in solid blocks just across Germany's border. Its flat denial would have been contrary to a principle on which the British Empire itself was founded, and would, consequently, never have rallied to us the whole-hearted support either of the British people or of that Empire. There were, on the other hand, obvious grounds, strategic and economic as well as historic, for the maintenance of this minority within the Bohemian state; and Dr. Benes, in the months which followed, was quick to take advantage of these points and to make them the foundation of his reluctance to grant an autonomy to the Sudetens which he feared would merely end in their complete secession.

But there was a further consideration which carried much weight. If Germany were not always to be allowed to settle everything in her own way by the display or use of force, then the Western Powers had to display courage, and to effect by diplomatic and peaceful negotiation those revisions of the Versailles Treaty which might alone be calculated to insure permanent solutions. The situation afforded the Western Powers an opportunity to prove that they would not oppose peaceful evolution, any more than they would condone forcible expansion. Genuine autonomy for the Sudetens was a moral issue which we might justifiably press for. Some objective sympathy on the part of Britain for Germany's comprehensible and not even unworthy aspirations for unity might, moreover, have served the useful purpose of showing the Germans that it was not Britain's sole policy to stand in their way everywhere, regardless of whether their aims were legitimate or not. The constant and not always unjustifiable reproach which even the friendliest Germans consistently made to me in Berlin was always on the lines of Goering's remark, "Germany can't pick a flower but England says 'forbidden.'" There might have been more utility in it if, when Germany did try to pick it, we could have effectively prevented her from doing so. There was little when we could not.

Nearly two months elapsed before His Majesty's Government and the French Government agreed to intervene, and in the meantime the position had been clarified to some extent. On the one hand Herr Henlein had rallied under his banner practically the whole of the Sudeten Germans; the Carlsbad program, defining the extent of the autonomy desired by the Sudetens themselves, had been published; and German propaganda on behalf of their "unredeemed" compatriots had become intensified and was crescendo. On the other, the Czech Government had already given indications of that fatal hesitation to appreciate facts which was to cost their country so dear. Most of the Carlsbad program might have been granted at once; and the two or three debatable points in it discussed in a better atmosphere at leisure. Only one solution had any real prospect of success, and that was the conversion of Czechoslovakia from a national state, governed solely by the Czechs, into a state of nationalities, where all, and especially the Sudetens as the biggest minority, had equal and autonomous rights. It had been understood at Versailles that that would be the case. But Dr. Benes undoubtedly felt that such a new creation could not long survive as an entity; and rather than submit to it, he resolved to shelter himself behind the optimistic belief that, in the last resort, France, England, and Russia would save him from the necessity of what he regarded as excessive and dangerous concessions to the German minority.

It was at a meeting in London of the British and French Ministers, in the last days of April, that the two Governments agreed jointly to approach the Czechoslovak Government. At this meeting His Majesty's Government made it quite clear to the French Government that in the event of a German attack on Czechoslovakia they could not commit themselves beyond the statement defining their attitude which had been made by the Prime Minister in the House of Commons on March 24th. After pointing out that Great Britain had no treaty obligations vis-à-vis Czechoslovakia, Mr. Chamberlain had concluded his speech on that occasion with the remark that "where peace and war are concerned, legal obligations are not alone involved, and if war broke out, it would be unlikely to be confined to those who had assumed such obligations, etc." This formula was that used in the various warnings given to the German Government in the course of the next five months.

The Anglo-French joint intervention at Prague began at the end of the first week in May; and on the same day (May 7th), acting in Berlin alone, as had been agreed in London, I notified the German Government of the action which the two Powers were taking at Prague. Actually, at that moment, Herr Hitler was absent in Rome on an official visit, and his Foreign Minister was with him. Immediately on his return, however, a few days later, Herr von Ribbentrop informed me that our démarche had been warmly welcomed (*herzlich begrüsst*) by the Führer, who, so he said, regarded the Sudeten problem as a purely internal question for the Czechs to settle with Henlein. Self-determination in some form or another was, however, he added, essential.

The negotiations at Prague were not my concern, and it is from the German angle alone that I am competent to speak with authority. The fact was that Hitler was in no great hurry: Austria was a considerable mouthful for the German anaconda, his army was being quietly mobilized, and he was quite willing to wait and see if the Sudetens would slip of their own accord peacefully into the German jaws. Even the invasion of Austria, though it had ended in applause and garlands, had not been undertaken without misgiving; whereas a march into Czechoslovakia would be met with those bullets and shells which might so easily lead to European complications. Hitler was, therefore, probably quite sincere when he said that he cordially welcomed the Anglo-French démarche, which he regarded indeed as the first step toward the accomplishment of his own aims. His eventual decision finally to alter his tactics was chiefly due to his own impatience and resentments, but was also—as in the case of Austria—facilitated by the mistakes of his adversaries.

THE second act of the 1938 drama falls naturally into two parts, and the curtain for the first scene rose on May 20th. Benes's justifiable hesitations had fortified the facile suspicions of Germany as to the reality of his intention to grant an adequate measure of autonomy to the Sudeten Lands. The situation in the Sudeten Lands was gradually deteriorating, incidents of a more or less serious nature had become matters of daily occurrence, and a German press campaign based on these incidents and, as usual, greatly exaggerated had reached such a pitch that it was but natural to believe, especially after the recent example of Austria, that another German lightning coup was impending. All the materials for an explosion were thus present when rumors began to spread of a German concentration on the Czech frontier. On receipt of circumstantial reports to that effect from Prague and elsewhere on May 20th, I immediately called on the Secretary of State, Baron von Weizsäcker, and asked him to tell me whether there was any truth in these stories. He denied them; but, taking the incident of March 11th as a precedent, I asked him to telephone to General Keitel on my behalf to remind him of the false information supplied to the Military Attaché of His Majesty's Embassy on that date and to ask the general to acquaint me authoritatively with the facts of the case. An hour later Baron von Weizsäcker assured me, categorically, on the word of General Keitel, that the tales of troop concentrations were absolute nonsense.

Similar assurances were given to the Czech Minister in Berlin as well as to the Czech Government in Prague. But the attitude of the German press and the precedent of Austria lent color to the wildest rumors, and the reports from Prague in regard to German troop movements became more and more detailed. I was actually shown at the Ministry for Foreign Affairs on May 21st a telegram from the German Minister at Prague stating that the Czech War Office had announced that eight to ten German divisions were on the march across Saxony! In fairness to the Czechs it must be realized that much abnormal military activity—judged by normal standards—was continually going on in Germany and that unskilled agents and observers can easily be misled.

On the morning of May 21st, I accordingly sent both the British Military Attachés on an extensive military reconnaisance through Saxony and Silesia (Colonel Mason-Macfarlane actually covered 700 and Major Strong some 500 miles by car between one dawn and the next). They could discover no sign of unusual or significant German military activity, nor indeed could any of the military attachés of other foreign missions in Berlin, who were similarly engaged in scouring the country. But the fat was in the fire; full credence was, not unnaturally, attached abroad to the Czech stories; and I spent most of May 21st at the Ministry for Foreign Affairs registering protests on behalf of His Majesty's Government and officially confirming the warning given in the House of Commons by the Prime Minister on March 24th, as quoted above.

My first interview with Herr von Ribbentrop on May 21st proved the occasion for a certain amount of acrimony on both sides. Owing to a regrettable indiscretion, one of the British newspapers had quoted General Keitel by name as having denied to me the reports of German troop movements. Ribbentrop, who was doubtless offended that I should seek information from anyone except himself, began by complaining of this and said in consequence no military information would ever in the future be communicated to me. I retorted that I could only infer from his attitude that General Keitel's information to me had been incorrect and that I should feel obliged to report to that effect to my Government. He thereupon turned in wrath to the accidental murder of two Germans near Eger, and used as regards the Czechs the most reprehensibly bloodthirsty language. They would, he assured me, be exterminated, women and children and all. When I observed that, while the death of two Germans was greatly to be deplored, it was better that two should die rather than hundreds of thousands in war, his only reply was that every German was ready to die for his country. Incidentally, I believe that the unsuitability of his language on this occasion earned for him a reprimand from his master; and for some time thereafter he remained out of favor. He was to get back again into it when, later in the crisis, his comforting assurances that England would never fight were to give that master the encouragement which he needed for the prosecution of his policy in September.

Prague

In any case, Ribbentrop's attitude on the morning of May 21st did nothing to ease the strain; and on the same afternoon I saw him a second time on instructions from London; and, after notifying him of the action which His Majesty's Government were taking in Prague with a view to inducing the Czech Government to come to a settlement direct with Henlein, I warned His Excellency that France had definite obligations to Czechoslovakia and that, if these had to be fulfilled, His Majesty's Government could not guarantee that they would not be forced by events to become themselves involved. Ribbentrop, who had been highly excitable in the morning, had become sullen in the afternoon. His attitude (doubtless on orders from Hitler, for whom the point continued to be a bitter one till the end) was that all remonstrances should be addressed to Prague and not to Berlin, and he declined to give to Henlein any advice on the lines of that which we were giving to the Czech Government. "If a general war ensued, it would," he said, "be a war of aggression provoked by France, and Germany would fight as she had done in 1914." He repeated this phrase constantly in September. Finally, on the Sunday, I conveyed to him through the State Secretary (Ribbentrop having left Berlin by then to report to the Führer at Berchtesgaden) a personal message from Lord Halifax drawing his attention to the risk of precipitate action's leading to a general conflagration, the only result of which might prove to be the destruction of European civilization.

So far as official action went, this ended the so-called May 21st incident at Berlin. By the Monday morning, all but the most intractable had become convinced that the stories of German troop concentrations were in fact untrue; the municipal elections in Czechoslovakia on the Sunday had passed off without further bloodshed and to the complete satisfaction of the Henlein party, and things might have been expected to resume a normal course.

Before explaining why they did not, it is necessary here to mention a minor feature of this crisis, a feature which, utterly unimportant in itself, was given wide publicity, and which I quote because it actually had a certain bearing on subsequent events. I refer to the story of the special train. As it happens, the Naval Attaché to our Embassy was proceeding on May 21st on normal leave with his whole family. A member of my staff regarded this as a good opportunity to send his own small children away under charge of Mrs. Troubridge. He was informed by the railway company that there was no room on the train but that an extra coach would be added provided it could be filled. Two other members of my staff were accordingly persuaded to enroll their families for the exodus, and thus the coach was filled and ordered. I first learned of this development when I returned from the Ministry for Foreign Affairs about midday, and found the French Ambassador on my doorstep, inquiring whether it was true that I was evacuating the whole of the British colony. The news had by this time even gone as far as London; and I received simultaneously an urgent telephone message from the Foreign Office, requesting me to cancel the arrangements made to this effect. I had hardly put the telephone down when the State Secretary rang me up from the Ministry for Foreign Affairs, telling me that he had received a number of Embassy passports for visas and begging me not to be an alarmist. I told Baron von Weizsäcker that I had only just learned myself of this unfortunate coincidence, that one of the last persons whom I would allow to leave in a crisis would be one of my Service Attachés, that he was going on ordinary leave of absence, and that I did not propose to prevent his doing so, but that I would certainly cancel the extra railway carriage and forbid the departure of any other members of my staff.

As I look back in the light of subsequent events, all this seems rather childish; but I should like to take this opportunity to disclaim any attempt in the May crisis of 1938 to emulate Disraeli's coup at the Berlin Congress. The fact was that everybody's nerves were already worn pretty threadbare even at that early stage. I cannot refrain from quoting another small story in evidence of this. I dined on the night of the 21st with Frau von Dirksen, stepmother of the German Ambassador in London and a friend of Hitler's. The French Ambassador was also there, and in the course of dinner the municipal authorities suddenly began nearby to demolish with dynamite a small hotel, the removal of which was included in Hitler's scheme for the rebuilding of Berlin. I leaned across my hostess and remarked to François-Poncet that the war seemed to have begun. It is doubtful if the remark was a well-chosen one at that moment, and it was possibly a poor example of humor. Several months later Goering said to me, "You were yourself pretty scared during the May crisis." I asked him why he believed this. Whereupon he repeated the above story, which had been seriously retailed to him at the time. I explained that I had only meant it as a joke. Whereupon Goering replied that he himself happened to be in Berlin that night, and had forgotten that the demolition was to take place. "When," he said,

Failure of a Mission

"I heard the first explosion, my immediate reaction was 'those cursed Czechs have begun it.' " If Goering could have jumped to such a conclusion, it is not strange that other people should have had misgivings. The story is at the same time an illuminating one in regard to German mentality. When we were thinking only that Germany was on the point of attacking the Czechs, the Germans were apprehensive lest the latter meant to provoke a European war before they themselves were ready for it.

As I said before, things might have been expected to resume a normal course after the scare of the May week-end. That they did not was no doubt partly due to the attitude of the foreign press. The publicity of the impressive official warning given, as it eventually proved, without due cause at Berlin was unfortunate enough. The defiant gesture of the Czechs in mobilizing some 170,000 troops and then proclaiming to the world that it was their action which had turned Hitler from his purpose was equally regrettable. But what Hitler could not stomach was the exultation of the press. The protagonists of collective security proclaimed the victory of their system. Every newspaper in Europe and America joined in the chorus. "No" had been said, and Hitler had been forced to yield. The democratic powers had brought the totalitarian states to heel, etc.

It was, above all, this jubilation which gave Hitler the excuse for his third and worst brain storm of the year, and pushed him definitely over the border line from peaceful negotiation to the use of force. From May 23rd to May 28th his fit of sulks and fury lasted, and on the latter date he gave orders for a gradual mobilization of the Army, which should be prepared for *all* eventualities in the autumn. He had made up his vindictive mind to avenge himself upon Benes and the Czechs. Once again it was a case of those within his power paying for the humiliation which others had caused him. At the same time, in order to protect himself from any possible reaction on the part of France, he initiated the monumental and costly work known as the West Wall in Germany and abroad as the Siegfried Line. It cost Germany 9,000,000,000 marks (or £750,000,000 at the official rate of exchange of 12 RM to the pound); and the expense of it added to Hitler's resentment. He went so far on May 28th as to fix October 1st as the actual date for the Czech crisis.

Looking back on the past, one realizes how little justified by actual facts was the so-called victory of May 21st. The Germans had never mobilized; nor, though their own newspapers and the recent invasion of Austria were greatly responsible for the illusion, had they actually any intention at that time of a coup for which they were not yet ready and which as they realized required infinitely greater and more careful preparation than had been necessary in the case of Austria. We had cried "wolf, wolf" prematurely, but the fact of the matter was that the world had already lost all confidence in Hitler's good faith, and the liveliness of the general anxiety was the measure of their complete mistrust. Moreover, the upshot of the press campaign was unfortunately twofold: not only did it serve as an excuse for Hitler to come down on the side of his extremists and to approve once again of solutions by force, but it also fatally encouraged the Czechs to believe that their position was secure and Benes in his reluctance to go far enough to satisfy the Sudeten Germans.

Failure of a Mission

In the light of wisdom after the event, it seems most improbable, as it happens, that anything which Benes could have done after May 28th would have sufficed to pacify the offended Dictator. Hitler's prestige had been shaken—his vindictiveness had to find a victim, and an excuse had been found for the use of force. The negotiations dragged on at Prague through May, June, and July, when they reached the inevitable deadlock. My own task during this period was chiefly that of endeavoring, without success, to persuade the German Government that Dr. Benes really meant business and would in the end grant adequate autonomy to the Sudeten.

Diplomatic action having failed, the question then arose as to what the alternative should be. The question of an independent mediator had already been mooted; and in July I had telegraphed to Lord Halifax that, since there was not the slightest prospect of the Sudetens' being willing to accept an agreed settlement on the basis of the maintenance of the purely national character of the Czech state, I had little confidence in the likelihood of the efforts of an independent mediator proving more successful than diplomatic action. I accordingly put forward the suggestion that the Italian Government should be invited to join with His Majesty's Government in proposing to the French and German Governments a four-power conference to settle the problem. At that moment, however, it was feared that it would be difficult to exclude other powers from participating in such a conference; and the decision of His Majesty's Government to invite Lord Runciman, at the request of the Czech Government, to proceed to Prague in a personal capacity as an independent mediator was announced by the Prime Minister in the House of Com-

mons on July 26th. I was instructed on the same day to notify
the German Government and to invite their co-operation in
advocating patience and moderation by Henlein and his adherents. Herr von Ribbentrop's reply was an ill-tempered
comment to the effect that, since the announcement of the
mission had been made before any communication had been
made to the German Government, the latter reserved its attitude and regarded the matter as one of purely British concern.
Hitler had by then other views in mind.

The decision in favor of forcible action had, as I have already mentioned, been taken on May 28th; and the German
Government were thereafter in no mood for conciliation.
The political barometer fell steadily throughout July; and
the reports of quiet but unceasing military preparations in
Germany had reached such a pitch by August 1st that on that
date I asked the Military Attaché to go round himself this
time to the War Office and to inquire on my behalf what was
on foot. Despite Ribbentrop's truculence on May 21st in regard to military information, Colonel Mason-Macfarlane was
there given enough facts to convince him of the seriousness
of the preparations. The only question was how far these
military measures should be regarded as bluff or as a real
menace. My own view at that time was that the Army was
being prepared for *all* eventualities; but that, only if bluff
failed to achieve its German object, would force be resorted
to. It is, however, more probable that Hitler meant to find an
excuse to use force in any case, so far as Czechoslovakia was
concerned.

The Runciman Mission constituted a brief respite during
which I made it abundantly clear to His Majesty's Govern-

ment that, if he failed to achieve the practically impossible before the Nuremberg party rally, we should lose the initiative, which would then and there be seized by Hitler. The Hobson's choice, in fact, which lay before us was whether we were to impose a solution by insistence on the Czech or by force on the German Government.

Lord Runciman had arrived at Prague on August 3rd. Again in the light of wisdom after the event, it may confidently be stated that his mission was doomed to failure before it began. Lord Runciman's negotiations dragged on throughout August with some superficial appearance of unreal good will on both sides, but the sands were running out, and September with its party rally came without any real advance having been made. My repeated appeals for a personal pronouncement by Lord Runciman or at least a report from him to His Majesty's Government recommending the adoption of the principles of self-determination and the Swiss Cantonal system as the only possible basis for negotiation remained without effect. When such a report was eventually published, Munich had come and gone.

So far as Berlin is concerned, it is worth recording two more episodes which occurred before the curtain fell on the first part of Act II. I had sent the British Military Attaché to London early in August to discuss the extent and significance of German military preparations and was subsequently instructed to communicate through Herr Lammers, the Head of the Reichschancery, for direct transmission to the Führer a memorandum from the Prime Minister and Lord Halifax drawing his earnest attention to the apprehensions caused in Europe by these measures. The memorandum led to no apparent result, except to arouse Ribbentrop's strong resentment at its having been sent through the Reichschancery instead of through the Ministry for Foreign Affairs, and it was he and not the Chancellor who ultimately and abruptly replied to the effect that the German Government could not discuss any internal measures which they thought fit to take. But in an indirect sense the communication which I had been instructed to make paved the way for the personal contact between the Prime Minister and Hitler which came later.

The second episode to which I refer was a subsequent visit of my own, under instructions, to London, in the course of which the idea of actual personal contact took concrete shape.

CHAPTER V. *ACT II:* CZECHOSLOVAKIA
SCENE II: MUNICH

THERE was no pause between the two parts of Act II. The curtain merely fell on Prague in order to rise again immediately at Nuremberg, whence the scene shifted rapidly in succession to Berchtesgaden, to Godesberg, to the big scene at Munich, to come down finally at Berlin itself. From the moment that the Nuremberg Congress opened, Prague, as had always been foretold, ceased to be the center of interest.

I am, personally, not likely to forget in a hurry my second visit to Nuremberg in 1938, cooped up for five days in the diplomatic train, without privacy and practically without means of communication. I was already feeling very unwell at the time of a malady which was to put me *hors de combat* for four months in the winter; sleep at night in a wagon-lit compartment was hardly possible, and rest during the day there was none. I had left Berlin on the night of Tuesday, September 6th, meaning to stop a mere thirty-six hours. In the event I stopped five full days. A railway train scarcely lends itself to writing, and I had foolishly omitted to provide myself with any materials for that purpose. Owing to the absence of security, to have taken even a cipher with me was out of the question. When eventually I had to send a letter to London by special airplane, I was obliged to use for the purpose the blank pages torn from some detective stories which I happened to have taken with me.

My vocal activities were, on the other hand, immense. I had two long conversations with Goering, three with Goebbels, one or two with Ribbentrop, two or three with Neurath, half a dozen with Weizsäcker. I conveyed, besides, an endless succession of warnings to a host of other Nazi personalities of scarcely lesser note, the cumulative effect of which, since talking there was almost the equivalent of broadcasting, I hoped would be useful. To all except Hitler, with whom I merely exchanged banalities in the midst of my diplomatic colleagues, the sum of my remarks was the same. "If Germany makes an aggressive attack on Czechoslovakia, France is in honor bound to come to the aid of the Czechs; and, if France is engaged in war, Great Britain will inevitably be drawn in also." I felt that the most immediate matter of importance was so to impress this on the German minds that Hitler, in the big political speech which he was to make at the end of the Congress, would think twice and would not adopt therein an attitude from which afterward, as a dictator, he could not afford to recede.

It was indeed clear from the beginning that Hitler himself was determined to refuse any political contact with the foreigner at Nuremberg. At the diplomatic reception my French colleague, as doyen, or senior member, of the diplomatic body, had tentatively sought his views on the situation by referring to the fall of the political barometer. Hitler had curtly replied to François-Poncet that weather forecasts were always wrong and turned the subject. He was in the midst of his whole Nazi army and after May 21st he was not for a moment going to allow it to be thought that he was subject to any further external dictation. It was my absolute conviction then, and with the enlightenment of time it was even more so, that, firstly, he would have declined on the ground of all his other numerous engagements to receive me if I had asked for a special audience; and that, secondly, if I had given him through Ribbentrop any official warning—which must have become public property—the effect would have been to drive him right off the deep end and would have made an immediate aggression on Czechoslovakia unavoidable.

The idea of a public warning to be given by me to Hitler at Nuremberg, which was seriously considered by His Majesty's Government, was accordingly dropped at my insistence to the above effect. But the most that can be said about Hitler's speech at Nuremberg was that it did not actually slam the door finally on a peaceful solution. It was truculent and aggressive: it claimed self-determination for the Sudetens and promised them Germany's full support, but it set no time limit and demanded no plebiscite. Nevertheless, it set the torch to the inflammable material in the Sudeten Lands, and was the signal for an outburst of demonstrations, rioting, and serious disturbances. The Czechs replied with martial law, and Henlein retorted by abandoning the Carlsbad points as no longer sufficient.

History will be the final judge of the Prime Minister's subsequent actions in flying first to Berchtesgaden and then to Godesberg and Munich. It may be argued in future that since war between the Western Democracies and a dynamic Nazi Germany was inevitable, it would have been wiser to accept the challenge, unprepared though we were, in September,

Munich

1938, rather than to wait till Germany had established her predominance in Central Europe. It would be presumptuous for me to be dogmatic on such points. But what I have today no hesitation in stigmatizing as completely erroneous was the belief held in some quarters at the time, and even persisted in today, that it was possible, with so little material force behind us and on such uncertain moral ground as the refusal of the right of self-determination to the Sudetens, to call by mere words what was alleged to have been, but certainly was not, Hitler's bluff in September, 1938. It is not enough merely to be guided by the facilely popular argument that the only thing in principle to say to a dictator is "No," and to say it as publicly as possible. As I wrote at the time, "If ever we aspire to call Hitler's bluff, let us first be quite prepared to face the consequences." Was France, not to mention England, prepared to face them in September, 1938?

In these circumstances the Prime Minister set into operation his plan for personal contact with Hitler, and shortly after my return to Berlin I received instructions to arrange it accordingly. I did so through Ribbentrop, and Hitler at once agreed. I was given to understand that his first reaction was to save the elder man the fatigue of the journey by going himself to London or at least halfway there. His second was to invite Mrs. Chamberlain to accompany her husband. There was, however, no time to consider counter proposals, and the Prime Minister left London at 8:30 on the morning of the fifteenth and reached the Munich airdrome four hours later.

I had myself left Berlin by train the evening before and had arrived in Munich, where there were certain hurried details as regards ciphering and typing to be arranged with Mr.

Carvell, the Consul General there, in time for breakfast. The British plane did the journey quicker than was anticipated, and I was at the airdrome barely five or ten minutes before it landed. Neither Mr. Chamberlain nor Sir Horace Wilson, who accompanied him, had ever flown before; and I was a little nervous how they might have stood the journey. I need not have been. Mr. Chamberlain stepped out of the machine looking remarkably fresh and quite imperturbable. In reply to some comment of mine he said, "I'm tough and wiry." And he had need to be, inasmuch as by the time he got to bed at 11 P.M. that night he had been traveling by car and rail and airplane for at least ten hours, had had much talk with Ribbentrop and others in between and with a long interview with Hitler and a telegraphic report to his own Cabinet to finish up with. Altogether some sixteen intense hours with scarcely a pause. No mean achievement for anyone, and Mr. Chamberlain was sixty-nine.

From the airdrome at Munich we drove straight to the station for a railway journey of several hours, interspersed with conversations with various notabilities such as General von Epp, the President of the German Colonial League; and lunch in the train with Ribbentrop presiding, etc. On arrival at Berchtesgaden shortly after 4 P.M. we drove first of all to the hotel where accommodation had been hurriedly prepared for us. A bare half-hour's grace was there accorded us before we left again in a fleet of motor cars for the drive of some twenty minutes up the mountain to the Berghof. There Hitler, surrounded by General Keitel and a few other members of his immediate entourage, received the Prime Minister on the top of the small flight of steps which lead up to the entrance of

his unpretentious mountain fastness. The first item on the
program was tea, which was served in a semicircle before the
fireplace situated opposite the great window of the reception
room looking across the mountains to Salzburg. After twenty
minutes of desultory conversation, the Chancellor suggested
to the Prime Minister that they might begin their talk; and
they disappeared, together with the reliable interpreter, Dr.
Schmidt, into Hitler's study. The rest of us remained to sit
and talk together in the reception room for the next three
hours. Hitler's personal staff did their best to feed and entertain us, but it was a wet and misty September evening, and
even the distraction of looking out of the window at the view
was denied us. On the other hand, there was a constant influx
of German press telegrams about incidents in the Sudeten
Lands. One, I remember, reported that forty Germans had
been killed in a clash somewhere with Czech gendarmes. A
British observer (of whom there were already a number in
Czechoslovakia) who was immediately sent to verify the facts
of the case subsequently ascertained that there had, in fact,
been one death. It was a typical example of the method of
exaggeration and actual falsification of news which was followed by the German press at that time and has been ever
since.

It had been my idea that it would be best for the Prime
Minister and Hitler to have their meeting alone and not in
the company of Ribbentrop, as would have been inevitable if
Mr. Chamberlain had been accompanied by Sir Horace Wilson or myself. It was so arranged, but in the event this was
unfortunate, as, thanks to Ribbentrop and contrary to normal
usage, the interpreter's record of the conversation was never

communicated to the Prime Minister, thereby causing him much extra trouble and worry, as well as rendering the procedure of conversations *à deux* subsequently impossible. I have always regretted this, as Ribbentrop's interventions were never helpful and often the reverse. At the later interviews Sir Horace Wilson was always present, and myself sometimes; while Kirkpatrick acted as British interpreter and took records of the meetings.

In the course of this first conversation, which lasted for three hours, Hitler made it clear that the only terms on which he could agree to a peaceful solution by agreement was on the basis of the acceptance of the principle of self-determination. The Prime Minister finally accepted that principle for himself, and undertook to consult his Cabinet and to endeavor to secure its consent to it and likewise that of the French and Czech Governments. Hitler, for his part, declared his readiness to discuss thereafter ways and means, and undertook to meet Mr. Chamberlain again at a date to be agreed upon between them.

The Prime Minister accordingly left by air for London again on the following morning. Lord Runciman was recalled from Prague for consultation, and the French Premier and Monsieur Bonnet were invited to London on September 18th. Mr. Neville Chamberlain loyally executed his side of the bargain and even more, since His Majesty's Government and the French Government agreed to persuade the Czechoslovak Government, in the cause of peace and the maintenance of the vital interests of Czechoslovakia herself, not only to grant self-determination, but to cede without plebiscite to the Reich

Munich

all the limitrophe Sudeten areas in which the population was over 50 per cent German.

In the meantime, however, the internal situation in Czechoslovakia after Berchtesgaden had gone from bad to worse. Thousands of Sudeten refugees had begun to pour over the frontiers, many undoubtedly at Nazi instigation but some also out of real fear of being caught, in the event of war, between two fires. Ultimately there were about 250,000 of these unfortunate people in Germany. The able-bodied were enrolled as "Free Corps" and started to raid back into Czechoslovakia. The casualty lists began to mount up. The Hodza Government resigned and was succeeded by a Government of National Concentration at Prague led by General Syrovy. A press campaign of unprecedented violence was set loose in Germany, and the Poles and Hungarians joined in the hunt. If Germany was going to get the lion's share of the spoils, Poland and Hungary were not going to leave their own claims unsatisfied. The Hungarian Regent and the Polish Foreign Minister hurried to Berchtesgaden. On the other side of the fence Soviet Russia talked vaguely of supporting the Western Powers; while the Czechs themselves were asking for advice as to what to do in the light of the German military concentrations.

In view of the agreement between the Prime Minister and Hitler at Berchtesgaden to meet again, the German press campaign was particularly indefensible. But self-determination, now that the principle had been conceded, was no longer enough for Hitler, though Goering at this juncture gave me his word that Germany would take no action before a second meeting had taken place. Nevertheless, as the Field Marshal

155

pointed out, there was no time to waste; and Germany was not bluffing.

I remember his saying to me on this occasion, "If England means to make war on Germany, no one knows what the ultimate end will be. But one thing is quite certain. Before the war is over there will be very few Czechs left alive and little of London left standing." He then proceeded to give me fairly accurate details of the numbers of modern antiaircraft guns we possessed at the moment as well as of the unpreparedness of England's air defenses generally. He also mentioned, as was doubtless true at the time, that the German Air Force was numerically superior to those of Britain, France, Belgium, and Czechoslovakia combined.

Such was the position when I was instructed to arrange the second meeting between the Prime Minister and Hitler. It took place this time at Godesberg. The visit to Berchtesgaden had been fixed up literally at a few hours' notice, but the Germans had had a week in which to prepare for Godesberg. Nothing this time was left undone to minister to our comfort and to create the best possible impression. A guard of honor was awaiting Mr. Chamberlain's inspection at the Cologne airdrome, and a band greeted him with "God Save the King." He drove from the airdrome to the Petersberg hotel at Godesberg with Ribbentrop. Godesberg itself is one of the beauty spots of the Rhineland, in the country of the Lorelei and the Drachenfels. The Petersberg hotel is famous in Germany. It is situated on a hill, overlooking a wide stretch of country on three sides, with the Rhine on the fourth. The Prime Minister and I were to spend the morning of the morrow pacing the wide balcony, which ran the whole length of the hotel outside the rooms placed at our disposal. It was a lovely autumn morning; and the view was wide and fair to look upon, "Where every prospect pleases, and only man is vile." It is a hackneyed phrase, but it is astonishing how often in this world it recurs to one. Our accommodation in the hotel was spacious and comfortable, and each room had its own bathroom. The proprietor had filled both bed and bathrooms with the special products of Cologne, scent and soap, bath salts and shaving requisites.

On the opposite side of the river to us Hitler had taken up his quarters at one of his favorite haunts, a hotel kept by one Dreesen, who had been a companion of his early struggle for power. It was there that he had taken the decision for the "blood bath" of June, 1934, and it was thence that he flew with Goebbels to Munich for the arrest and execution of Roehm. It was thither that Mr. Chamberlain and his party proceeded for his meeting with Hitler at 5 P.M. on that 22nd of September. To get there it was necessary to cross the river by ferry, which was done under the eyes of thousands of onlookers, who lined the banks in a manner reminiscent of the 'Varsity boat-race day. Hitler met the Prime Minister at the door of the hotel, and led him without delay to a room upstairs, which was normally used for board meetings. They sat down each at one end of the long baize-covered table, and the proceedings began. The German populace by the river had demonstrated its unconcealed and spontaneous pleasure at seeing the British Prime Minister, whom they recognized as the harbinger of peace; but Hitler himself was in an uncompromising mood.

Mr. Chamberlain opened the proceedings by recalling that at Berchtesgaden he had agreed in principle to the right of the Sudeten Germans to self-determination; that he had undertaken to endeavor to obtain the assent of his Cabinet and of the French Government; and that it had been agreed that if he were successful he would return in order to consult with Hitler as to the ways and means of putting the agreement into force. Within a very short lapse of time he had, he continued, been able to obtain the assent of the British Cabinet; the French Ministers had visited London and had likewise agreed; and, furthermore, the acquiescence of the Czechoslovak Government had in addition been secured. He accordingly outlined the steps which in his opinion should now be taken to arrange for the peaceful transfer of the Sudeten territory within the shortest possible time.

When the Prime Minister had finished, Hitler asked whether he was to understand that the British, French, and Czechoslovak Governments had in effect agreed to the transfer of the Sudeten territory from Czechoslovakia to Germany. The Prime Minister replied: "Yes." There was a slight pause, a silence in which Hitler appeared for a moment to be making up his mind. He then said decisively: "*Es tut mir fürchtbar leid, aber das geht nicht mehr.*" (I am exceedingly sorry, but that is no longer of any use.) The Prime Minister expressed his surprise and indignation; he could not be expected, he declared, to return to London with fresh proposals and demands only to be faced once more with the rejoinder that they were no longer adequate.

Hitler thereupon shifted the blame by explaining that it was the Hungarian and Polish claims which had now to be

met. His friendship with these two countries demanded, he
said, that he should give them full support. To which the
Prime Minister retorted that on Hitler's own showing these
claims had not the same urgency as the question of the Sudeten Germans and that the Hungarian-Polish claims could only
be considered after the Sudeten problem had been solved in
an orderly manner. When the discussion thereupon reverted
to Mr. Chamberlain's proposals, Hitler declined flatly to consider them on the ground that they involved too much delay.
Instead, he demanded that the German-speaking areas should
be ceded forthwith and occupied by German troops. This
Mr. Chamberlain in turn declined to accept; and, after three
hours of somewhat exacerbated debate, the meeting adjourned.

The deadlock that night and most of the next day seemed
complete. Hitler, having secured one position, was already
advancing on the next. He was no longer prepared to execute
his part of the bargain at Berchtesgaden and to discuss quietly
the ways and means of a settlement. He was using the claims
of the Poles and the Hungarians and the plight of the Sudeten
refugees, which his own agents had manipulated, as a pretext,
which possibly satisfied his own facile conscience, to break
his word to Mr. Chamberlain. Godesberg was the real turning
point in Anglo-German relations, and I have always felt that
it was there that Hitler made the first of his big political mistakes. He had cheated the British Prime Minister; and, by let-
ting him down, thereby prepared the way for the revulsion
of feeling in England against Hitlerism and its methods which
was to become complete after the occupation of Prague in
March, 1939.

Failure of a Mission

The first interview at Godesberg thus ended without any reference to a subsequent meeting, and until the late afternoon of the following day it looked as if there might be none. Two written communications were exchanged in the course of the day without producing any modifications of the respective positions. The British press even reported that the negotiations had definitely broken down; and in the interval London informed Prague that it could not advise against a Czech mobilization, while pointing out, nevertheless, that mobilization might precipitate a conflict.

The Prime Minister's patience was, however, not yet finally exhausted. He was unwilling to refuse discussion of proposals which he had not actually seen in writing; and at 5 P.M. that afternoon he instructed Sir Horace Wilson and myself to see Ribbentrop and to suggest that Hitler should embody the exact nature of his proposals for the occupation of the Sudeten Lands in an official document. It might have been anticipated that Hitler would reject this request on the ground that he had made his proposals sufficiently clear verbally in the course of the conversation on the preceding day. But the war party in Germany was also not yet finally in the ascendant. Mr. Chamberlain's refusal to renew contact had provoked some consternation among the moderates in the German camp; and Hitler, in view of the high hopes placed by the German people in Mr. Chamberlain's intervention, was reluctant to break off the negotiations and anxious for a further meeting. Ribbentrop was accordingly instructed to inform us that a German memorandum would be prepared in the course of the evening and that we should be informed as soon as it was ready. At 10:30 that night the conversations were resumed.

Munich

Although Hitler was in a much less truculent mood and even made an effort to appear conciliatory, his memorandum showed that he had not moderated his demands, which were presented in a most peremptory form and described by Hitler as his last word. In this document he required the Czechs to begin the evacuation of the predominantly Sudeten areas at 8 A.M. on September 26th and to complete it by September 28th. Thus, the Czechoslovak Government was to be given a bare forty-eight hours to issue the necessary orders, and only four days in which to evacuate the whole of the Sudeten Lands. It is characteristic of Hitler's methods of argument that, when the Prime Minister pointed out that this was a sheer dictate (the word always applied by Hitler to the Treaty of Versailles) imposed on a country voluntarily surrendering a part of its territory without having been defeated in war, the Chancellor replied: "It is not a dictate; look, the document is headed by the word 'memorandum.'"

In the course of the long discussion which followed, Hitler agreed to modify his timetable slightly, and he also made in his own handwriting a number of minor alterations designed to attenuate the asperity of the memorandum. "You are the only man," he said somewhat bitterly to Mr. Chamberlain, "to whom I have ever made a concession." He appeared, however, relieved when the Prime Minister finally said that, while he could not accept or recommend the German proposals, he could nevertheless, as an intermediary, not refuse to submit them to the Czechoslovak Government. Hitler had no desire that the German people should think that the negotiations had broken down as the result of his own intransigency. He was nonetheless bent on the military occupation of Czechoslovakia. He himself was prepared to risk war with Britain; but, on the other hand, his military advisers were not.

On the following morning the Prime Minister left by air again for London. Thanks to the energy and drive of Colonel Mason-Macfarlane the German memorandum and the map with the Godesberg line marked on it were in the hands of the Czech Government the same night. It had meant Mason-Macfarlane's flying back to Berlin, motoring to the Czech frontier, and then walking ten kilometers in the dark through Czech barbed wire and other entanglements, at the constant risk of being shot as a raider by either Germans or Czechs.

The peak of the crisis was reached after Godesberg. The French mobilized half a million men, and the Admiralty, the British fleet. The French Government reaffirmed their intention to support Czechoslovakia if attacked, and His Majesty's Government similarly reasserted their position in accordance with the Prime Minister's statement of March 24th. Staff talks between the British and French Army chiefs were resumed; and the Czech Government, encouraged by these demonstrations of solidarity, refused to accept the Godesberg memorandum. It looked as if war was inevitable over the point as to the date and manner in which the territories which the Czechs had agreed to cede to Germany were to be handed over.

The Prime Minister refused once more to slip over the abyss. On Monday, the 26th, he sent Sir Horace Wilson to Berlin with a personal letter to Hitler in which, after stating that the German proposals, as they stood, had been rejected by the Czech Government, he again urged the Chancellor, since the difference was one of form and not of principle, to agree to negotiate rather than to resort to force and suggested a direct meeting between Germans and Czechs with a British representative as intermediary.

Sir H. Wilson, accompanied by Kirkpatrick and myself, saw the Chancellor at 5 P.M. that afternoon. This interview also was stormy and unsatisfactory. Herr Hitler could only with difficulty be persuaded to listen to the Prime Minister's letter. At one point he shouted: *"Es hat keinen Sinn weiter zu verhandeln"* (It is no use talking any more); and he moved to the door as if to leave the room. Eventually he returned, and the conversation was resumed, but it was impossible to reach any satisfactory conclusion. On the same evening he made a speech in the Sportpalast which was cheered to the echo by his enthusiastic claque of Nazi supporters. It contained a savage attack on Benes personally, and in it he finally burned his boats by declaring that, if the Czech Government themselves had not ceded all the Sudeten Lands by October 1st, Germany would occupy them by that date with himself as the first soldier of the Reich. At the same time he made an appeal for British neutrality by friendly references to Mr. Chamberlain's efforts for peace and to his own desire, as evidenced by the Naval Treaty, for good relations with England. After that speech it seemed impossible for him to go back on his words. The Roosevelt appeal for peace, which was made on the same day, was not even reported in the German papers. It was feared that it might have a depressing effect on the people, who were being feverishly worked up for war.

Sir Horace Wilson spent that night in the Embassy, and in the course of it received instructions to deliver yet another personal message. Therein Mr. Chamberlain, while acknowledging the references to himself in Hitler's speech, guaranteed if Germany refrained from force to see that the Czech undertakings already given would be carried out. Sir H. Wilson accordingly saw Hitler for the second time at 12:15 on the morning of September 27th. He asked the Chancellor if, in the light of the Prime Minister's statement, he could take any message back to London. Hitler replied that the Czechoslovak Government had only two courses: acceptance of the German memorandum; or rejection. In the course of this conversation Hitler shouted savagely on two or three occasions: *"Ich werde die Tschechen zerschlagen,"* which Herr Schmidt, the interpreter, faithfully translated as: "I will smash-sh-sh the Czechs." He showed by his demeanor that he was longing to chastise the Czechs for their insolence; bombs must fall on Prague; the Czech Army must be put to rout; Dr. Benes must be forced to ignominious flight. When it was clear that Hitler's determination to go to war was quite inflexible, Sir H. Wilson said that he was charged by the Prime Minister to give him a message to the following effect: "If, in pursuit of her Treaty obligations, France became actively engaged in hostilities against Germany, the United Kingdom would feel obliged to support her."

Hitler's answer was that he could only take note of this communication. It meant, he said, that if France elected to attack Germany, England felt obliged to attack Germany, also. Sir H. Wilson attempted to refute this interpretation of his statement, but Hitler declined to be convinced. "If France and England strike," he shouted, "let them do so. It is a matter of complete indifference to me. I am prepared for every eventuality. I can only take note of the position. It is Tuesday today, and by next Monday we shall all be at war." On this depressing note the interview ended.

Sir Horace flew back to London early the same afternoon. Nevertheless, his conversations had had their effect; and I was officially informed that night by the State Secretary that Hitler had addressed, through the German Embassy in London, an immediate and important personal letter to the Prime Minister, attempting to justify his attitude and begging Mr. Chamberlain to continue to use his good offices with a view to inducing the Czech Government to see reason. It constituted a perceptible attempt at conciliation and was indicative of a certain nervousness. Therein he gave the Prime Minister the definite assurance, which he was so cynically to disregard six months later, to the effect that, once the Sudeten Germans were incorporated in the Reich, he would cease to be interested in the Czechs and would *do nothing to infringe in any way their independence*. I have included the English translation of this letter, for obvious reasons, as Appendix I at the end of this volume.

A chance episode had, as it happens, produced a salutary revulsion in Hitler's mind. In the afternoon of that Tuesday, a mechanized division had rumbled through the streets of Berlin and up the Wilhelmstrasse past the Chancellor's window and those of the Embassy. For three hours Hitler stood at his window and watched it pass. The Germans love military display, but not a single individual in the streets applauded its passage. The picture which it represented was almost that of a hostile army passing through a conquered city. Hitler was deeply impressed. At that moment he realized for the first time that the cheers of his sycophants in the Sportspalast were far from representing the true spirit and feelings of the German People.

Late in the afternoon of September 27th, I had been advised by the Foreign Office by telephone that instructions were on their way to me for yet another communication to the Chancellor. I accordingly made arrangements to meet the State Secretary at the Ministry for Foreign Affairs at 11 P.M. that night and handed to him a note for immediate translation and submission to Hitler. It contained proposals, agreed to by the French Government and transmitted to Prague, pressing the Czech Government to agree to the immediate transfer of the Sudeten territories on the basis of a timetable guaranteed by His Majesty's Government. The first areas were to be handed over on October 1st, and the creation of an international boundary commission for the settlement of details was also suggested. The proposals went far to meet Hitler's demands, and in the end they constituted the main basis of the final settlement at Munich. Baron von Weizsäcker was noncommittal, though he undertook to arrange that these proposals be conveyed immediately to the Chancellor; and with faint hope I retired to bed on the Tuesday night, realizing that, if nothing new intervened, the announced general mobilization of the German Army would take place the following day at 2 P.M. Since the Army was already concentrated and mobilized, in effect this meant the beginning of the march into Czechoslovakia.

I was aroused at 7 A.M. the next morning (Wednesday) by the French Ambassador, who informed me by telephone that his instructions to make a similar communication to mine had reached him at 4 A.M., that in some respects they went even further than mine, and that he had been requested to see Hitler himself. He said that he had already asked for an audience.

Three hours later, at 10 A.M., he rang me up again to say that he feared the worst, since he had had no answer to his request for an audience and probably would not now receive one. I replied to M. François-Poncet that I would come and see him at 10:30. I then asked to be put into communication with Goering by telephone and was able to get into immediate touch with him. Fortunately the telephone was working well everywhere on that critical day. I told the Field Marshal that the French Ambassador had asked for an audience, that no reply had yet been vouchsafed him, that it was a question of fresh proposals, and that peace or war depended on it. I began to describe the proposals, but Goering cut me short. "You need not," he said, "say a word more. I am going immediately to see the Führer."

I then went round to see the French Ambassador; and, while we were discussing the new proposals, a message came from the Reichschancery that Hitler would see François-Poncet at 11:15. Simultaneously a Secretary brought round to me at the French Embassy a telegram from London, instructing me to give immediately a final personal message from the Prime Minister to Hitler himself. Its gist was that, after reading Hitler's letter of the previous evening, Mr. Chamberlain was still convinced that Germany could obtain her essential requirements without resort to war and that he was ready to come to Berlin at once himself in order to discuss the whole question with Hitler and with representatives of France and Italy. Did Hitler, it concluded, wish to take the responsibility of starting a world war for the sake of a few days' delay in settling the problem?

It is worth recalling the exact sequence of events on that critical day. Goering went to see Hitler between 10:15 and 11:15 and was joined there by Neurath, who had forced his way in uninvited. Both were in favor of a peaceful solution by negotiation. At a meeting of Hitler and his advisers there had been some plain speaking, in which Goering had vehemently accused Ribbentrop of inciting to war. Among other things, it was related that Goering shouted that he knew what war was and he did not want to go through it again. If, however, the Führer said "March," he would go himself in the first and leading airplane. All that he insisted upon was that Ribbentrop should be in the seat next to him. He did say this or something like it, but it was not in the Führer's presence. But I believe that he did call Ribbentrop on that occasion a "criminal fool." Nor, of the various factors which induced Hitler to abandon his idea of a Czech war, was Goering's intervention the least important.

Then came the Poncet interview, in the middle of which, at 11:40 A.M., Hitler left the room to see the Italian Ambassador, who had arrived with a preliminary urgent appeal from Signor Mussolini for the postponement of the so-called general mobilization for twenty-four hours. The Italian intervention proved the final and decisive factor for peace. It enabled Hitler to climb down without losing face. His first remark to me when I saw him at 12:15, immediately after Poncet, was: "At the request of my great friend and ally, Mussolini,

Munich

I have postponed mobilizing my troops for twenty-four hours."

Before actually seeing Hitler himself I had, however, realized that the situation had taken a turn for the better. When I entered the Chancellery, there was an atmosphere of relief in the faces of the less bellicose of the crowd of Nazi soldiers and aides-de-camp who filled the hall. One friend of mine whispered in my ear: *"Das geht besser: halten Sie nur fest."* (It is going better: only stick to it.) I was at once ushered into Hitler's Cabinet room, where I met Goering and Neurath on their way out. I gave Hitler the Prime Minister's message, and his reply was that he must consult again with Signor Mussolini before giving me a definite answer. We discussed fairly amicably the latest proposals of the French and British Governments; and the Chancellor, though a little distrait, was not unreasonable. My interview with him, which lasted over an hour, was also interrupted by a second visit from the Italian Ambassador, this time to say that Mussolini himself was prepared to accept the British proposals for a Four-Power meeting, which had been telegraphed to Rome.

I had been left to argue desultorily with Ribbentrop; and, when Hitler rejoined us, I failed to notice any particular change in his attitude. Yet neither before nor after was he other than comparatively amicable, though he shouted once or twice when he described the orders which he would give to Goering's air fleet, if compelled to do so. I was, however, told afterward that those who listened anxiously within earshot on the other side of the door had feared from the noise that things were going badly. I had, however, become used

169

by this time to Hitler's neurotic outbursts, and had been not unfavorably impressed.

But as a matter of fact, everything was settled before ever I reached the Reichschancery that morning. Peace had been insured when Hitler agreed at Mussolini's request at 11:40 A.M., exactly two hours and twenty minutes before zero hour, to postpone his so-called general mobilization. Had he given the order for it, there could have been no going back; and Czechoslovakia would have suffered the same fate as Poland did a year later. If nothing had happened before 2 P.M. that afternoon, it would have been impossible for Hitler not to have given the order for his troops to march. The Czech Maginot Line was strong, but it would have been turned from the south through Austria; and in any case the campaign would have been settled, as it was in Poland, by the vast superiority of the German Air Force.

Though other factors combined to give Hitler cause for reflection, nothing but the Italian intervention could well have forced open again the door which Hitler had slammed behind him at the Sportpalast on the Monday. The importance attached by Hitler to Mussolini's personal attendance at Munich is a further proof of this. On that supremely critical Wednesday, the Italian Ambassador paid four visits to Hitler in three hours (the fourth was to notify Mussolini's personal attendance at Munich) and was about twenty times in telephonic communication with Rome. The lady telephonist who put through the calls in Rome was given later 2,000 lire by Signor Mussolini in appreciation of the services she had rendered. As Attolico said to me on the way down to Munich, "The communists have lost their chance; if they had cut the telephone wires today between Rome and Berlin there would have been war."

In my final report on the events leading up to the outbreak of war I referred to the untiring efforts for peace of the Italian Ambassador. It was no less true of the 1938 crisis than it was of the 1939 one. His efforts failed this second August, as did those of the rest of us. But I have always in my own mind attributed a notable share of the success in preserving peace in 1938 to Attolico. He was, indeed, absolutely whole-hearted and selfless in the persistence of his exertions to save Europe from the horrors of war; and he devoted all his great tact and energy to that sole purpose. He was, moreover, very ably seconded by his wife, who spoke German fluently, which the Ambassador did not. While the Ambassador was traveling down by train with me to Munich, Madame Attolico, unknown to her husband, was herself flying to her favorite shrine in Italy to pray for that peace which he had worked so hard to insure.

The meeting of the four statesmen at the new Brown House at Munich began at 1:30 P.M. on the afternoon of the following day, September 29th. Mussolini had arrived by train from Rome, and Daladier by air from Paris, shortly before the Prime Minister. All three were enthusiastically acclaimed by the German people, who filled the streets. Their discussions ended thirteen hours later at 2:30 A.M. on the Friday morning. At no stage of the conversations did they become heated. The presence of Mussolini acted as a brake on Hitler, and the fact that the former had tactfully put forward as his own a combination of Hitler's and the Anglo-French proposals, thereby defeating the intention of Ribbentrop, who was anxious to put forward a scheme of his own, made general agreement easier all round. It was largely the necessity for translation into three languages, English, French, and German, which, together with the difficulties of hasty drafting, delayed the conclusion. Mussolini was the only one of the four statesmen who could speak and understand all three languages. The final agreement was reached substantially on the lines of the Godesberg memorandum as modified by the final Anglo-French plan. Four areas of progressive occupation by Germany were established, with dates. Rights of option were guaranteed, plebiscite areas foreshadowed, and an International Commission nominated to deal with the execution of the final agreement. A possible further Four-Power meeting was adumbrated, and the British and French Governments declared their intention to abide by their previous offer of a guarantee of the diminished Czechoslovakia. The German and Italian Governments undertook to participate in this guarantee once the claims of Hungary and Poland had been finally satisfied.

Germany thus incorporated the Sudeten Lands in the Reich without bloodshed and without firing a shot. But she had not got all that Hitler wanted and which she would have got if the arbitrament had been left to war, namely, the strategical frontier which so many Germans desired and which would have included Prague, the seat of the first German university. Czechoslovakia had lost—and a bit more—territories which it would probably have been wiser not to have included at Versailles in the Czech state and which could never, except on the basis of federation, have remained permanently therein. The humiliation of the Czechs was a tragedy, but it was

Munich

solely thanks to Mr. Chamberlain's courage and pertinacity that a futile and senseless war was averted. As I wrote to him when all was over: "Millions of mothers will be blessing your name tonight for having saved their sons from the horrors of war. Oceans of ink will flow hereafter in criticism of your action." Both statements were correct, but the verdict of history will in any case assuredly be that the course which the Prime Minister took was the only right and sane one in the circumstances as they existed. As I wrote at the time, "The day may come when we may be forced to fight Germany again. If we have to do so, I trust that the cause may be one in which the morality of our case is so unimpeachable, the honor and vital interests of Britain so clearly at stake, as to insure us the full support of the united British people, of the Empire and of world public opinion." This would not have been the case in September, 1938.

I left Munich before the Prime Minister had his final meeting alone with Hitler and drew up and signed the Anglo-German Declaration of September 30th. Early that morning the French and Italian Ambassadors, together with the German State Secretary and myself, flew back to Berlin; and the first meeting of the International Commission set up under the Munich Agreement was actually held the same afternoon at 5:30 P.M. Its meetings constituted the final scene of the second act of the drama.

The task delegated to the Ambassadors was ungrateful in principle and most distasteful in detail. I had made up my mind before the first meeting began that, with a view to the future, the best hope for Czechoslovakia lay in direct negotiation, where possible, with Germany, and that plebiscites, which could only lead to trouble, should be avoided at all cost. I did my best to insure both those objectives. I saw Goering, and secured an assurance from him that Germany would not be unconciliatory if the Czech Government frankly sought co-operation with, rather than antagonism to, Germany. I arranged a meeting between the Field Marshal and the Czech delegate on the Commission, M. Mastny, who was also the Czech Minister at Berlin and with whom I had maintained throughout the crisis the friendliest relations. From the moment that Benes resigned, the position became easier, though the Germans, as usual, did little to modify their demands, or to honor Goering's promise to be generous.

There were two major crises in the course of the discussions of the International Commission. The Munich protocols were vaguely worded, and the first arose out of the question as to the extent of the areas to be handed over without plebiscite to Germany, and as to the meaning of the 50-per-cent-majority provision. The German attitude toward the latter was, as it happens, in accordance with the text of the Munich Agreement and the Anglo-French proposal which preceded it; but the Czechs refused to accept it; and Hitler retorted with an ultimatum, demanding occupation up to the language line drawn in the Austrian maps of 1910. There was no map showing the racial areas between that year and 1923, by which time the prewar position had been considerably modified. My French and Italian colleagues on direct instructions from their Governments both accepted the German standpoint; and, when they came to see me at the British Embassy to tell me so, I was left to decide whether to do so also or to say that I could not do so without prior reference to His

Majesty's Government. I decided on the former course
mainly because I hoped thereby, firstly, to avoid plebiscites
and, secondly, to pin the Germans down to a line of their
own choosing, which they would find it difficult afterward
to modify again to their renewed advantage, and thirdly,
because the German contention was actually, in my opinion,
the better founded of the two theses. At the same time, at a
subsequent meeting of the Ambassadors with Ribbentrop, I
made it clear that I deeply resented the method employed by
the German Government, and would, if it were resorted to
again, seek the authority of my Government to resign from
the Commission rather than submit to it. In fact, the Germans
did attempt later to get the Commission to agree to an extensive modification in their favor of the line they had themselves chosen. In an interview which I had with Baron von
Weizsäcker I told him that I would never consent to it and
threatened to resign. The German Government thereupon
abandoned their pretension at the time, but only to secure
their object, or at least part of it, later by direct negotiations
with the Czechs.

The acceptance of the 1910 boundary rendered plebiscites
superfluous, and by October 10th direct co-operation and
negotiation between Czechs and Germans were sufficiently
advanced for the meetings of the political section of the
International Commission to be discontinued *sine die*. Act II
was over.

CHAPTER VI

SECOND ENTR'ACTE:
HITLER'S REACTIONS
AFTER MUNICH

I LEFT Berlin as soon as was practicable after the conclusion
of the work of the International Commission. I had, of course,
the utmost misgivings as to Hitler's good faith and the honesty
of his ultimate intentions toward the Czechs; but a Government had assumed power at Prague which sincerely sought
co-operation with Germany; and, since Hitler had got the
Sudeten Lands, which he had solemnly assured Mr. Chamberlain was his sole object, it was still permissible at least to hope
that he might treat a friendly disposed Czech Government
with some generosity and fairness. Nevertheless, I left for
England about the middle of October thoroughly disheart-
ened, and if I had been a free agent I would never have returned to Berlin. The Hitlerian methods had been too much
in evidence at Godesberg and Munich, as well as at Berlin
during the session of the International Commission, for me
to feel otherwise than disgusted.

Moreover, I was a sick man and had been for some months
past. Within a couple of weeks I was operated upon in a nurs-
ing home, and for four months altogether I remained completely out of everything. It was only thanks to Mr. Stanford
Cade's marvelous skill and care that I was more or less fit,
and even so rather less than more, for duty again about the

middle of the following February. That in itself was a minor disaster. I am not presuming to suggest that anything might have been altered by my presence at Berlin. But four months were too long to be absent from Germany in the dynamic state through which she was passing, and in view of the appetites which had been whetted by the inclusion of 10,000,000 Austrian and Sudeten Germans in the Reich.

Furthermore, events occurred during that interval which had a considerable bearing upon subsequent developments. One of these was the organized persecution of the Jews which took place in November. In revenge for the murder by a young unbalanced Jew of a German diplomatist in Paris, at the instigation of Dr. Goebbels' propaganda press and with the connivance and actual participation of Himmler's secret police and extreme Nazis, squads of German hooligans reverted to the barbarism of the Middle Ages and indulged in an orgy of violent ill treatment of the Jews such as even the Middle Ages could scarcely equal. The motives of this disgusting exhibition, which shocked all decent Germans as much as it did the whole outside world, were twofold. One was utterly ignoble and revolting, namely, the opportunity which the murder afforded to plunder the Jews and expedite their expulsion. The second, within limits, might have been comprehensible. The German authorities were undoubtedly seriously alarmed lest another Jew, emboldened by the success of Grynszpan, should follow his example and murder either Hitler or one of themselves.

The exaggerated and inhuman revenge which the Germans took was, however, from their own point of view an act of incredible stupidity comparable in its effects with the sinking of the *Lusitania* and the shooting of Nurse Cavell in the war.

Thereby they turned the whole of the world's opinion definitely against themselves. The most ingenious propaganda of their enemies could not have achieved a similar success. The revulsion abroad, and particularly in the United States, where Dr. Benes had taken refuge, had, however, one important sequel. It encouraged the anti-German section in Czechoslovakia, or what the Germans were pleased to call the Beneshists, to raise their heads again and to hamper the conciliatory efforts of Dr. Hacha and M. Chvalkovsky for better relations with Germany. It was the hostility of this section which served as an excuse for Hitler to swallow, some months later, the rest of the cherry, of which he had only bitten off the first half at Munich.

The second interesting feature of my four months' enforced absence, was what I can only describe as the reactions of Hitler after Munich.

It must first be clearly realized what were Hitler's objectives in September. Quite apart from his openly expressed desire to complete the unity of Germany by the incorporation of the Sudetens, he was bent on humiliating the Czechs and particularly Benes. After the May crisis the Czechs had announced, *urbi et orbi*, that it was their mobilization which alone had prevented Germany from marching. It was, according to them, they who had put Hitler in his place and had taught him what "No" meant. Such an attitude was enough to infuriate any hypersensitive dictator, and from that date Hitler was determined to get his own back and teach Benes a lesson. After May 21st Hitler deliberately sought an opportunity to crush Czechoslovakia by force. A small war would, he also reckoned, give his new army that confidence and experience which he felt that it required. But anything more than a local war, in which victory was certain, was something quite different, since in a world war it would be his regime and his position as Führer of the German people which would be at stake. In September, however, he had not believed that, when it came to the point, the French nation would be ready to fight for the Czechs or that England would fight if the French did not. He argued as follows: Would the German nation *willingly* go to war for General Franco in Spain, if France intervened on the side of the Republican Government at Valencia? The answer which he gave himself was that it would not; and he was consequently convinced that no democratic French Government would be strong enough to lead the French nation to war for the Czechs. That was the basis of his calculations, and his policy was in accordance therewith. The repeated British warnings, backed by military unpreparedness, had consequently little effect. Nor, in fact, did His Majesty's Government officially ever go further than to say that we would support the French once the latter were involved in hostilities. In his speech at Danzig, after war had broken out, on October 24th last, Herr von Ribbentrop told his listeners that the British Government had promised their assistance to the Czech Government in those days (i.e. September, 1938) and so made a European crisis out of a problem that without British interference would have been solved overnight. Ribbentrop did not say how it could have been solved—though one can imagine the German solution which he may have had in mind—and the actual statement is in itself one of the many falsehoods in that speech. We were, except collectively as members of the League of Nations, under no obligations to the Czechs; we repeatedly said so; and we undertook the ungrateful role of honest broker on that very account, and never gave them at any time any promise of assistance.

The Munich settlement thus deprived Hitler of the great satisfaction—to which he was ardently looking forward—of giving his army a little experience, of appearing himself in the role of a conquering hero, and of wreaking vengeance on Benes and the Czechs. In one sense he may have been not ungrateful to Mr. Chamberlain for having prevented a world war to which his army and people were opposed; in another, any gratitude which he may have felt was far outweighed by resentment at having been compelled to change his mind and at being deprived of his local war. The unanimity with which the French Chamber (unlike the House of Commons in this respect) approved of the Munich Agreement certainly helped to confirm him in this opinion. In yet another sense, too, Hitler felt irritated with himself. A section of his followers were always egging him on to fight England while the latter was still militarily unprepared. They reproached him for having accepted the Munich settlement and thus having missed the most favorable opportunity. An uneasy feeling lest they might have been right contributed to Hitler's ill humor.

Nor was Munich in itself an agreeable experience for him. He found himself there for once in the company of three men who were his equals, instead of being surrounded by sycophants obedient to his slightest gesture. The experience confirmed his dislike for settlement by negotiation. Moreover, the evident popularity of Mr. Chamberlain with the German people not only detracted from his own personal prestige but also gave him food for uneasy reflection. He could dragoon his people, and they would always follow him; but could he count on their willing devotion in all circumstances? It was the first unpleasant rift between him and his people, and it was the peace efforts of Mr. Chamberlain which had started it.

It is certainly a fact that, after Munich, he showed considerable ill will toward those who had argued with him against pushing things to extremes. His Voice had told him that there would be no general war, or that, even if there were, there could be no more propitious moment for it than that October; and for once he had been obliged to disregard that Voice and to listen to counsels of prudence. After Munich, those whom he regarded as the faint hearts in Germany, beginning with Goering and passing through many strata of the party and of the Government officials, fell from grace. On the other hand, this uneasy reflection was the main cause of the rise to favor of the Ribbentrops and Himmlers, and of his subsequent measures for the reinforcement, by means of the S.A., of the party vis-à-vis the Army, which had also been antiwar. But it was his own faint-heartedness which probably infuriated him more than anything else; for the first time he had failed to obey his Voice.

One is obliged to theorize to a certain extent in endeavoring to arrive at an accurate estimate of these underlying forces, since the world problem today starts with individuals. In the final report on events leading up to the declaration of war, which I wrote on my return to England and which I largely reproduce in the final chapter of this book, I remarked that Hitler would prove a fascinating study for historians with psychological leanings in the future. His critics today describe him by many strange names: he may be any or all of them, but I prefer to leave it to the professional psychiatrist to pronounce the verdict. For me he was a sort of Dr. Jekyll and Mr. Hyde. To begin with, he may not have been more than a visionary of genius or a practical dreamer with a sublime faith in himself and in his mission to reinstate Germany in her former position among the nations. *Mein Kampf* shows that he was naturally endowed with a highly developed political sense, but it is unlikely that his original ambitions were as wide as they subsequently became. His initial aspiration may well have been to become Chancellor of Germany, to complete her unity by means of the incorporation of Austria, his own motherland, as a first objective, and to restore to Germany her self-respect and prosperity. The interesting point to elucidate would be when he ceased to be Jekyll and became Hyde. It was probably a matter of gradual evolution. Dictators, having achieved absolutism, lose their sense of proportion. Each success leads to ever expanding aims, while their insatiable desire for their own permanence drives them in the end to put self before their country, and to adventure as the sole means of maintaining their hold. So it was with Napoleon and so it seems to me to have been with Hitler. The Chancellorship, the unity and prosperity of Germany were, in the end, not enough. His flatterers described him as the successor of Frederick the Great and Bismarck; and, as time went on, he felt himself called upon to emulate their military victories as well as their other constructive achievements. During that first visit of mine to Nuremberg I could not, as I have related, forbear asking myself how any human brain could keep its sanity amid all the adulatory worship which his followers accorded to him. When I first met him, his logic and sense of realities had impressed me; but, as time went on, he appeared to me to become more and more unreasonable and more and more convinced of his own infallibility and greatness. In the end Bismarck was no longer an equal. Hitler could and did describe Ribbentrop as a second Iron Chancellor.

He himself had become something far greater, conceivably a sort of Mahomet with a "sword in one hand and *Mein Kampf* in the other." And with such a sword there need be no longer any limit to his ambitions except his own death. His habit of constantly hinting, in public as well as in private, that his life would not be a long one gave rise to rumors about some incurable disease from which he was suffering; but I often wondered whether he did not merely use the idea as an excuse to justify his own restless impatience. He was a skillful mixer of fraud with force, and was always seeking to find for everything excuses which would hoodwink his people into submitting to anything which he might order for them. Even a dictator cannot ignore altogether the feelings and wishes of his people, and Hitler used his internal propaganda with immense skill for this purpose. His constant aim was to persuade them that everything he did was right and justified, that he and Germany were the victims of calculating and hostile foreigners who drove him (Hitler) to act as he did solely in self-defense. In *Mein Kampf* France, then in occupation of the Ruhr, was held up to execration as the chief enemy; during the struggle for power it was the U.S.S.R. and the communists; then England became public enemy No. 1; in the summer of 1938 little Czechoslovakia became the archfiend which threatened the independence of the Reich, and in the summer of 1939 there had to be war "because Poland invaded Germany!" That was part of what Mr. Chamberlain so aptly and feelingly described as the "sickening technique" of Hitlerism. It was always poor little Germany which was being ill-treated.

Yet at the same time, Hitler was always preaching to Germans that they should forget that inferiority complex which is so often attributed to them. I used to ask my Nazi friends how they combined Hitler's doctrine of the superiority of Germans over all other races with this habit of describing Germany as the "poor little downtrodden victim" of unscrupulous neighbors. I told them that it would revolt me to hear my own country so alluded to. One, possibly more perspicacious than the others, remarked to me that Hitler's excessive insistence on the point of the German inferiority complex only meant that he still had it himself. He was probably right.

But I must return to the reactions of Hitler after Munich. It must always be borne in mind that Hitler was no administrative leader, and that his power over his people was mystical rather than executive. He owed his success in the struggle for power to the fact that he was the reflection of their subconscious mind and to his ability to express in words what that subconscious mind felt that it wanted. Once he achieved power, he impressed the people most by his opportunistic or instinctive judgments as to what could or could not be done and as to the right moment to do it. He had acted on several occasions in direct defiance of the advice of his stoutest followers and of his army; yet the event had always proved him to be right. Until Munich. There, for the first time, he had been compelled to listen to contrary opinion, and his own faith in his Voice and his people's confidence in his judgment were for the first time shaken.

Much in his outbursts of spleen after Munich was, in my opinion, due to this psychology. Hitler was always waiting for the right moment and consequently slow to take a final decision; but, once it had been taken, nothing had hitherto turned him from his purpose. Yet he had decided in May to occupy Czechoslovakia by force in October, and in the end he did not. Mr. Chamberlain at least saved Czechoslovakia from that utter ruin and destruction which Goering had foretold, and it seems to me amazing that there should have been people who honestly believed the contrary. I am aware that such people continue to argue that a more categorical attitude on the part of His Majesty's Government would have deterred Hitler from either pressing his claims to the Sudeten or from attacking the Czechs. It is difficult to see how our attitude could have been made more definite than it was—and yet Hitler was not deterred by it. He was convinced that the Czechs could have been crushed in a few days or at most weeks and that this result could have been achieved long before France or England could have brought them any effective assistance. He would never have attacked either France or England and by waiting to be attacked by them he could have rallied behind himself the whole of Germany, as the victim of Western aggression, or preventive war. Once Prague had been occupied, he would then have offered peace, in the belief that the British and French peoples would have been loath to continue a world war for an object which had already been lost and which, even after victory, would have had to be settled more or less in accordance with German desires. I wrote in this sense before Munich; and I did so again a year later before Warsaw, in respect to which the technique was the same. Were his calculations in 1938 in this respect ill-founded? Hitler still believed after Munich that they would not have been, and it was that which rankled.

He had, moreover, a further delusion. He had hoped that the Anglo-German Declaration, which had been signed at Munich, would be accepted in England at its face value, and with relief—if not with enthusiasm. He anticipated that after Munich we should be willing to slow down our rearmament, leaving Germany in the happy possession of what Herr Hitler himself described as the mightiest armaments the world has known. In this position he could have dictated to Europe were he so minded. Instead, Mr. Chamberlain announced in Parliament that England could no longer remain the only unarmed nation in Europe and that consequently the rearmament program must be pushed forward with all speed.

Moreover, once the immediate danger of war had been averted, Mr. Chamberlain was vigorously attacked for the Munich settlement, not only by his political opponents, but even by members of his own party. This circumstance gave Hitler the opportunity of violently abusing the so-called English warmongers during the course of several public speeches in the autumn. In a speech at Weimar, in November, he even made an offensive personal reference to the Prime Minister. At the same time the English press campaign against Munich was answered by a violent anti-English campaign in the German press. The only difference was that, whereas in

England the Opposition papers were concerned, in Germany it was those newspapers which stood closest to the Ministry of Propaganda, such as the *Volkischer Beobachter* and the *Angriff*, which led the anti-English agitation. In this atmosphere there could be no *détente* in Anglo-German relations, but only an aggravation of ill will; nor was the situation improved by the anti-Jewish riots which took place all over Germany in November and which aroused a storm of indignation in England, as well as in all other foreign countries. With each attack on him, Hitler's resentment and irritation grew. The German military machine redoubled its efforts; and, with a view to convincing the German people of the necessity for yet more guns, England was represented to them as preparing for war. Since Mr. Chamberlain was now firmly established in the eyes of that people as a peacemaker, he was described by Hitler in his speeches as likely shortly to be replaced under the British Constitution by a Government which desired war with Germany. "Tomorrow," said Hitler, "Churchill may easily be Prime Minister of England," and he reinforced his arguments about British warmongers by misquoted statements taken from debates in the House of Commons about "the destruction of dictatorships" and "airplanes carrying bombs to Berlin."

"The resentments of a petty mind may ruin an enterprise which would have profited an Empire." Germany was led to the brink of war in September, 1938, in order to satisfy the resentments of a dictator—and over the brink the next September. I do not know what the feelings of the German people are today, but nothing in 1938 shook their confidence in their leader more than the realization of this fact. Every German approved in principle of the incorporation of their Sudeten fellow countrymen in the Reich, but they did not see the point of going to war for something which could so easily be got without war. Was the case very different in 1939 in respect to Danzig and the Corridor?

CHAPTER VII

INTERLUDE: RETURN
TO BERLIN
AFTER FOUR MONTHS

AFTER four months' absence, I returned to Berlin in the
middle of February. Physically I was still unfit, but morally
I was somewhat recovered from the pessimism and the disgust
which I had felt after the conclusion of the work of the
International Commission, which had defined the frontiers
between Germany and Czechoslovakia. My obsession about
the Greek-tragedy motif, too, had somewhat receded into
the background of my mind. This was partly due to reaction
against the rumors which were circulated in December and
January, and to which a considerable measure of credence was
given abroad, in regard to a contemplated German invasion of
both Holland and Switzerland, the seizure of the Rumanian
oil fields, and even a surprise bomb attack on London. I
believed these stories to have been put into circulation largely
by the Nazi extremists themselves in order to distract attention from their real and more immediate objectives; and they
seemed to me, and in fact were, at that moment premature.
But Europe generally and the British public in particular were
justifiably anxious and apprehensive. Yet it was obvious that
Hitler had other fish to fry before embarking on such adven-
tures as those mentioned above. Danzig and Memel, of which
two cities the population was preponderantly German, were

the most obvious of Hitler's next and earliest objectives; and Germany's relations with Czechoslovakia had yet to be definitely settled.

I did not, however, feel that any of these questions should necessarily prove anything like as difficult of solution as that of the 3,500,000 Sudeten Germans. I was personally inclined to think that Hitler, following the line of least resistance, would begin with Memel. Poland had shared in the spoils of Czechoslovakia. She had acquired the whole of the Teschen area after Munich, as well as the coal-mining center of Oderburg, where the population also was largely German. Hitler's followers had protested against this cession at the time, but Hitler had replied that he was not a coal merchant. Polish relations with Germany appeared, therefore, on the surface to be comparatively good. Colonel Beck had visited Hitler at Berchtesgaden in January, negotiations were known to be proceeding between Berlin and Warsaw; and some bilateral modification of the status quo at Danzig seemed perfectly feasible, particularly as the League of Nations had more or less disinterested itself in the affairs of the Free City.

On the eve of Munich Hitler in his written letter to Mr. Chamberlain had, on the other hand, categorically assured him that once the Sudeten Germans were incorporated in the Reich, he had no intention of restricting in any way the independence of the Czechs. At Munich he had undertaken to guarantee the integrity of Czechoslovakia itself, as soon as the claims of Poland and Hungary had been settled and her frontiers delimited. Germany's racial ambitions had now been satisfied. There were no more large bodies of Germans contiguous to the frontier of the Reich, and Hitler himself had publicly said after Munich that he had no further territorial claims in Europe. Memel with its 150,000 and Danzig with its 400,000 Germans seemed small questions compared with Austria and the Sudeten Lands.

Why then should there be war? Was it worth jeopardizing the great gains of Nazism since 1933 for Danzig or Memel or even the Corridor? The settlement of these problems might be difficult and give rise to uneasiness, but there was no reason to anticipate that they would bring Europe again to the brink of war as in 1938. So far as Czechoslovakia was concerned Dr. Hacha had succeeded Dr. Benes as President of that country; and he and his Foreign Minister, M. Chvalkovsky, were known to be in favor of co-operation with instead of hostility to Germany. Discussions were in fact actually proceeding between Berlin and Prague in regard to the text of a German-Czech agreement.

Moreover, there were other grounds for optimism. Before I left London, it had been arranged for the President of the Board of Trade and the Secretary of the Overseas Trade Department to visit Berlin. Their journey, as in the case of Lord Halifax in 1937, was officially stated to be a private one, the ostensible occasion for it being a banquet which was to be given in Berlin to representatives of certain British industries who were discussing trade agreements with their German competitors. But behind the façade of privacy, the real intention of the visit was patent; and, though the primary object was a modest one, it was legitimate to hope that it might lead to more general and concrete trade discussions. From economics to politics was no great step. I had immediately on my return to Berlin spoken of the visit of Mr. Oliver Stanley and

Failure of a Mission

Mr. Hudson both to Field Marshal Goering and Herr von Ribbentrop. Both had expressed appreciation and concurrence, though inclined, with habitual German touchiness, to resent the fact that Mr. Hudson was proceeding from Berlin to Moscow. Both also had used an almost identical phrase in speaking of the position in Germany. At long last, they had said, a dictator, just as much as the government of a democracy, must take into account the wishes of the people. Since it was quite evident that the German people as a whole were as tired as the British and the rest of the world of repeated crises and wanted peace, I took this remark, which sounded so clearly the echo of their master's voice, to mean that Hitler had decided to come down on the side of peace. It was also in concordance with Hitler's own public statement that the Nuremberg party rally of 1939 would be given the title of "peace rally."

I was consequently once again moderately hopeful and not inclined to see the black side of anything. There were enough prophets of evil in the world without my adding to their number. I even felt that there might have been some honest cause for misunderstanding after Munich on account of our rearmament, and I did my best in February to clear up this point in two public speeches which I made at the annual dinner of the German-English Society in Berlin, and at Cologne at the inauguration of a new branch there of that Society. I took as my theme the fact that British rearmament was not only compatible with, but the necessary adjunct of, a passionate love of peace. I referred to the immediate response which had been given by Mr. Chamberlain to a reference by Hitler in January to the necessity for co-operation between

Return to Berlin

Britain and Germany, as well as to the categorical assertions recently made by Lord Halifax that no British statesman, no party in England, nor the British people as a whole would ever contemplate or support an aggressive war. I was able to stress the point by a minor incident which occurred at the end of the banquet in Berlin. I had just finished speaking when the head of the Press Bureau at the Ministry for Foreign Affairs entered the room with a news telegram in his hand, reporting the vote in the House of Commons of a further £150,000,000 for rearmament. He asked me somewhat indignantly how I reconciled my pacific utterances with this evidence of our aggressive intentions. Lord Brocket, as its Vice President, had just got up to speak on behalf of the Anglo-German Fellowship, and I told Herr Aschmann that I would give him my answer when Brocket had finished speaking. I then wrote across the telegram in German the following sentence, and signed it: "Peace can only be insured when Britain is in a position to defend herself." Dr. Aschmann asked me if he could publish my comment. I told him that he certainly could. Needless to say, this was never done; but that phrase was, in fact, the sum of all my arguments and explanations at the time, and it was the true answer to all the specious German casuistry which Goebbels and the war party were spreading at the time to the effect that Britain was hurriedly preparing for war in order to crush her rival, Germany, before the latter grew too strong. Inferiority complex or not, Hitler and his extremists would scarcely have pretended to believe this if they had not themselves contemplated aggression and sought thereby to justify their own military preparations. They might never have decided to risk aggression at all had Britain remained strong after 1920. It was her weakness which had encouraged them to cherish their dreams of European domination. The truth is that peace can never be assured, if one country is allowed to indulge in armaments which are much more powerful than those of her neighbors. Human nature cannot be trusted to that extent, particularly when the standards of civilization in the various countries of Europe are different; and the best check, till the millennium arrives, on excessive appetites and ambitions is such an equality of strength as to make adventure a precarious and risky undertaking for any country. Not the least cause of my optimism in February, 1939, was in fact the belief that the rapidly increasing strength of Britain's armament would serve as a useful deterrent and make Hitler think twice before he threw down the gauntlet.

Another point in favor of peace that February was the fact that the Spanish Civil War was at last drawing to its close, and the risk of further incidents on that score had become no longer a dangerous factor in the situation. Finally, I found that Goering himself, whose presence as head of the Air Force and as a Field Marshal would be indispensable at the outbreak of serious hostilities, had decided to get thin, and by one means or another had actually lost forty-two pounds! Even if one weighs two hundred and sixty or seventy, one cannot lose forty-two pounds with impunity. His heart had been affected by his treatment, and he told me he was going to San Remo at the beginning of March for a long cure. That and his reference to warmongers being fools and dictators being obliged to take the wishes of their people into account were indications of a nature to reassure me. He may have been fooling me, but I doubt it. It is true, on the other hand, that Ribbentrop was now supreme in all matters of foreign affairs and apparently enjoying the unbounded confidence of his master. Even so, realizing that he was merely the echo of the voice of that master, I was not unduly perturbed. Even today and after the event, I still find it hard to accept the view that any particular step was actually contemplated by Hitler for that March. He was never a dealer in exact dates, and I was once told by someone who ought to have known that he only once fixed a date in advance, and that was October 1st, 1938, which he chose on May 28th of that year for the invasion of Czechoslovakia. In the middle of February I do not believe that he had any time limit in his head for the settlement of the Czech question. Everything was still dependent on how the incident which would suit his purpose could be worked up to a head. Certainly his ultimate object was to get Bohemia and Moravia in some form or another back inside the Third German Reich, as they had been in the First Reich; but he was still uncertain exactly how this end was to be achieved. It is true also that he was greatly annoyed at the recrudescence of the anti-German faction in Czechoslovakia and that his agents were encouraging the Slovaks in their quarrels with the Czechs with a view to weakening the latter. But his final plan was still unformed. Everything depended on the development of the situation.

Hitler is an Austrian; and the best-known trait of the Austrians is what is known as their *Schlamperei*, a sort of happy-go-lucky and haphazard way of doing things. I always felt that Hitler had his full share of this characteristic. He had all sorts of general plans in his head, but I greatly doubt if he had preconceived ideas as to how they were to be executed. Unfortunately, as he went on, he became more and more intoxicated with success and confident in his own greatness and infallibility. His plans grew more grandiose, and he combined his *Schlamperei* with an amazing mastery of opportunism. In this he was helped by the thoroughness of the preparations for all, even the most hypothetical, eventualities, which were drawn up by his subordinates. Hitler himself just waited till his opponents made a tactical mistake and then used the plan which seemed best to suit both his own general objective and the opportunity afforded by that mistake.

As it was with Schuschnigg's unfortunate plebiscite in March, 1938, so it was with the Czech Government's equally unwise intervention at Bratislava in March, 1939. However actively in both cases Hitler may have been working to produce an incident, neither was a foreseeable occurrence; and, in spite of the fact that several clever guessers had, a month or so ahead, foreseen March 15th as a day of trouble in Czechoslovakia—and afterward took great credit for their foresight—I do not consider that they owed the success of their lucky guess to anything but chance. If the Czechs had been a little more prudent and if the Stanley-Hudson visit had taken place ten days earlier, i.e. before the Czechs overthrew the Slovak Government of Father Tiso, March might after all have gone out like a lamb and the evil day have been at least postponed. I can only say "might," since, if the pretext of the Czech occupation of Bratislava had not been found, another might just as well have sufficed with the same result. However that may be, when the Ides of March actually came, I could only personally feel that the Greek-tragedy motif which had, I hoped, been exorcised at Munich, was still disastrously at work. Hitler was not going to allow the end to be peace.

At the risk of breaking the thread of the sequence of events, I cannot refrain from mentioning here something which was told me when I returned to Berlin that February. Shortly after my arrival, I happened to meet someone who was in close contact with Hitler and had recently been dining with him. His first remark to me was, "Your reputation has gone up in Germany." I said that that sounded very gratifying but that I should be glad to know why. "As you are aware," my informant said, "there were in Germany last September two currents, a war party and an antiwar party. Your reputation with the latter was always high, but now it is higher still with the former. The war party accuse you of having bluffed Hitler into believing that England would have gone to war if he had attacked the Czechs, and they are furious because they still argue that England would not have fought whatever happened. They say 'That cursed British Ambassador: he bluffed us with his tales at Nuremberg in September, and he bluffed us in May with his special train. What a bluffer.' "

The authority was unimpeachable, and I repeat the story here for two reasons: In the first place it threw some light on Hitler's reactions after Munich; and at the same time it confirmed my belief that he had always wanted his local war, and that he felt that he had been cheated out of it by a combination of Signor Mussolini and Mr. Chamberlain, together possibly with my own language as the mouthpiece of His Majesty's Government. Secondly, the story gave a better answer than I ever could have done to those in England,

and there were such, who believed that my language, particularly at Nuremberg in the preceding September had not been strong enough. What some people are apt to forget or fail to realize is that remonstrance is much more readily listened to and heeded when it comes from a person who attempts to understand another point of view, even when it is not his own. An official representative abroad cannot really serve his own country to the best purpose if he is known to be hostile to the government of the country in which he resides. On the other hand, his language can be much more forcible, without merely arousing a resentment which merely defeats the purpose of that language, if he is known to be trying his best to serve the interests of both his own and the country to which he is accredited. One does not serve one's own country less well thereby, since the two interests are not always incompatible. Far from it. It would, for instance, have certainly been in the interests of both Germany and Britain, as well as of the rest of Europe, to have honestly and reasonably kept the peace.

CHAPTER VIII

THE PARTING
OF THE WAYS

I MUST, however, now turn back to the general situation in
Germany as it appeared to me and as I reported it to the Foreign Office at the time when I went back that February to
Berlin. Nineteen hundred and thirty-eight had been a momentous year for Europe. In the course of a few months and
without bloodshed Hitler had completed the work begun by
Frederick the Great and Bismarck, and by consummating at
long last the unity of Greater Germany through the incorporation in the Reich of Austria (the Ostmark) and the
Sudeten Lands had completely modified the strategic and economic structure of Europe, to the great advantage of Germany and to the detriment of Europe generally but of France
in particular, for which Munich marked the end of her postwar system of alliances. Remarkable though Hitler's achievements sound in the twentieth year after Germany's defeat in
1918, history will, I feel sure, regard them as the inevitable
consequences of that war and of the peace which ended it.
In 1937, when I went for the first time to Nuremberg, General Goering, as he then was, asked me who, taking the long
view, I regarded as the principal beneficiary of the World
War. I replied Italy, which had finally secured her natural
and strategical frontiers, and the Slav States. Goering's reply

was, "No, Germany; since without such a war and without such a defeat, German unity would have been impossible."

Nor did I even then think that he was wrong. Nationalism was one of the features of the age which followed Napoleon, who was its supreme, if unconscious, patron. Italian unity and the Second Reich were the two principal examples of it in the nineteenth century; and Ireland, no less than the re-creation of Poland, Bohemia, the Baltic States, etc., the postwar fruits of it. Even the Jewish question, which is likely to prove one of the chief problems of the twentieth century, is in itself merely a byproduct of nationalism driven to excess. What was indeed almost more remarkable than Hitler's achievements was the fact that the realization of German internal and national unity had been so long delayed. Volumes could be written on this subject; but a brief, yet necessary, glance at the salient features of the background of German history is sufficient to support the truth of this assertion. To begin with, it was the German Emperors of the First Reich (or Holy Roman Empire) who, by pursuing the shadow of universal power, threw away the substance of national German unity. Thus the Hapsburgs of Vienna forfeited their chance, and it fell to the Hohenzollerns of Prussia to be the champions of pan-Germanism. The Austrian Empire was built up at the expense of German unity, and the rivalry between Hapsburgs and Hohenzollerns split Germany in two. It was the heterogeneous elements of the Austrian Empire which mainly prevented Bismarck from completing, in his Second Reich, the full union in the nineteenth century.

The unity of England was completed so early in her history that it is difficult for us to realize that in the middle of

The Parting of the Ways

the seventeenth century, after the Thirty Years' War, which did so much to retard her natural political development, Germany consisted of about three hundred and fifty completely independent states, each with its own separate administration and free to adopt whatever foreign policy might suit its individual inclination. At the outbreak of the Napoleonic Wars at the end of the eighteenth century there were still about one hundred and seventy of these states. Some fifty disappeared as the result of the Napoleonic reforms and of their inclusion in the kingdoms which he set up for his relatives or friends in Germany. The Bismarckian era of the nineteenth century eventually reduced them to the twenty-six states, most of them with their own ruler, government, and legislative assembly, which comprised the Germany of 1914. The chaos and distress of the postwar era enabled Hitler to complete the internal unification of the Third Reich by abolishing the parliaments of the individual states, by transferring to the central government their sovereign rights, and by transforming them into mere provinces of the single state. Had he stopped there the world might have had cause for congratulation. Nor could Hitler have done what he did if it had not been for the defeat of Austria in 1918, which freed the Poles, Czechs, Rumanians, Croats, Slovenes, Italians, etc., from the government of Vienna and left the Ostmark isolated and the Sudeten Germans under the rule of the Czechs, whom they hated and despised. It was always thereafter a mere question of time for these nine or ten million Germans to gravitate by the natural force of attraction into the Germany of the Third Reich. The weakness of Germany alone prevented this occurring immediately after the war, and the unattractiveness of the Nazi system alone delayed it after Germany had become strong again. But the evolution in itself had always seemed to be inescapable, and not even the restoration of the Hapsburg Empire could have done more than postpone its ultimate consummation. Anyway, whether we liked it or not, the unity of Greater Germany had been achieved in 1938; and it remained to be seen what Hitler would do next.

There were, generally speaking, two obvious alternatives for him: either to misuse Germany's great military strength for the purposes of political domination and for the satisfaction of his own restless and ever increasing ambitions or to abandon jungle law in its cruder forms and to return to peaceful collaboration in conjunction with other countries. In a word, after Munich, Germany stood at the crossroads, one finger post pointing toward adventure and the other toward normalcy.

To the ordinary observer every argument of common sense seemed, in Germany's own interests, to indicate that the latter would be not only the happiest for his people, but also the most prudent course for Hitler himself to follow. Leaving the desires of the mass of the German people out of account, even Hitler himself, after his great but exhausting successes during the past six years, should have been yearning for a period of more tranquil existence, during which he would be able not only to consolidate the unity which he had accomplished, but also to give scope to his much advertised and already partially commenced artistic and constructive plans for the beautification of Greater Germany. Moreover, Germany would be all the more powerful later if she were given time to digest the extensive additions of territory which she had just acquired. On every reasonable ground he should have been sincere when he said, as he did about this time, that he was looking forward to a long period of peace. If he had really and solely had Germany's welfare at heart, he must and would have stopped at Munich. It was true that he had not played fair with Mr. Chamberlain at Godesberg. The latter had agreed at Berchtesgaden to accept the principle of self-determination for the Sudetens, but at Godesberg that was no longer enough for Hitler, who had insisted on his pound of flesh by means of a surgical operation instead of by those methods of remedial treatment which negotiation could have ensured. Yet, even so, the plight of the Sudetens themselves at the time, however responsible Hitler's myrmidons may have been for it, was such as to excuse to some extent the immediate application of the knife; and the world would for the sake of peace have accepted the accomplished fact in spite of the unnecessary suffering which had been caused to the victim. If Hitler had pursued a fair and honest and constructive policy thereafter in Central and Eastern Europe, Great Britain was prepared to be disinterested and helpful. Peace was Hitler's for the asking after Munich, and he alone could have ensured it. It is difficult even today to see why he did not.

"Revolutions," as I wrote in my final report of September, 1939, "are like avalanches, which once set in motion cannot stop till they crash to destruction at the appointed end of their career"; and it may be argued that it was not possible even for Hitler himself to check the momentum of the National-Socialist revolution, of which he was the inspired leader. Future historians will argue the point; but I believe that, dis-

Failure of a Mission

agreeable though the task might well have been for him personally, Hitler's position in Germany was such that he could have imposed any course that he willed upon his followers. He was not merely the victim of the movement which he had initiated; he was also the slave of his own growing megalomania. He owed all his successes to his tactical opportunism; and, when once again a chance was afforded him of scoring another such success, as was the case when the Czech Government used force to overthrow the Tiso Government at Bratislava, he lost his last sense of proportion and reason and seized it, regardless of the ultimate consequences to Germany, to the world, and to himself.

Admittedly, if he had wished to follow the road to normalcy, he would have been obliged to break with his extremist minority, with the Ribbentrops and Himmlers, Hesses and Leys, and rabble of his street-fighting days. Possibly also with the youth of the country, which he had spent the last six years in perverting to his own revolutionary uses. The Germans are notorious for their lack not only of balance but also of any understanding of the mentality and reactions of others. The successes of Nazism had been so great that its devotees, and especially the German youth, felt that nothing and nobody could stop them anywhere. After the postwar humiliations, their desire to prove their recuperated strength and importance to the world was a consuming one; nor did they regard anyone in continental Europe as capable of standing up to their bullying. Her postwar experiences had unfortunately taught Nazi Germany that nothing could be achieved except by force or the display of force; and in such a frame of mind any compromise or reversion to static conditions was difficult and would only have been regarded as a sign of weakness.

To all such elements as those just mentioned above, the road to adventure was clearly the most attractive and the most profitable. It is true that they constituted but a small minority; and, as a demagogue, Hitler's natural inclination should have been to please the majority of his people. But minorities, especially in revolutionary times, exercise an influence entirely disproportionate to their actual numbers. It has been estimated, for instance, that at the time of the French Revolution, only 3 per cent of the population of Paris were active and wholehearted revolutionaries. And Hitler himself was an extremist; and his principal advisers, since the disappearance of Blomberg, were the same.

Apart from these active careerists, another dangerous aspect of the situation was Germany's increasing financial and economic difficulties. The strain, both mental and material, under which the German people had been working since 1933 was immense, and required an increasingly violent psychological stimulus to keep it working. It was estimated in 1938 that 60 per cent or more of the sum of her efforts in human beings, labor, and materials was destined for war. No people, even though disciplined and hard working as are the Germans, would put up indefinitely with guns instead of butter or endure an economic policy based solely on *Wehrwirtschaft*, namely, the control of the whole of a nation's economic output in the interests of military preparedness. There was always the question, therefore, whether Hitler would not feel obliged to seek to conquer by force the markets which Germany had lost by over-concentration on armaments, or, in other words, be compelled to follow the road of further adventure, either in order to forestall economic collapse or as the result of it. Economic disaster spelt unpopularity for Hitler and for Nazism; and to many thinking Germans the real problem was whether Hitler could change his economic policy and revert to normalcy without another internal revolution. It had so long been organized on a purely military-autarchic basis, that it would certainly have been difficult to reverse the process and reknit the fabric of free commerce with the outside world without incurring severe dislocation and unemployment. Yet, even in this respect I was always disinclined to accept the oversimplified theory that Hitler would necessarily be obliged to seek further adventure in order to avoid economic collapse. I had too high a respect for the capacity of German organization to regard such a theory as the whole truth. Moreover, a prosperous and peaceful Germany was a British interest; and, as the contemplated visit of Oliver Stanley and Hudson indicated, the outside world, and Britain in particular, was prepared to help her to overcome her financial and economic difficulties.

I am thus convinced that, if Hitler had wished to return to economic, as well as to political and international, normalcy, he could have done so. His extremists might have criticized him or even proved troublesome; but he could have dealt with them no less firmly, though, let us hope, much less sanguinarily, than he did in 1934 with the Roehm faction. There would have been criticism also in some quarters in England at holding out a helping hand to Germany and at not leaving Nazism to stew in the juice of its own making, but the majority of the nation would have approved of a broad-minded British policy in this respect. From the long view, it was clear that Europe could never be stable and peaceful until Germany was once more settled and prosperous. Her prosperity would facilitate her economic rivalry with ourselves but in the end would have benefited both. There was no constructive value in standing aloof and keeping Germany, one of our best customers, permanently lean. The theory that, if Hitler were treated as a pariah, the German nation would itself overturn him and his regime had no foundation in fact and was merely the outcome of wishful thinking. The reverse was actually the case, and the denial of help and the refusal of all sympathetic understanding merely drove the nation to despair and to cling closer to him as the sole defender of German interests.

Be that as it may, I would give much to know what was at the back of Hitler's mind during those fateful six months after Munich when he stood at the parting of the ways.

THOUGH he may never have even considered choosing
the road to normalcy, I do not think that when I returned
to Berlin in the middle of February Hitler had yet decided
what form the path of adventure was to take or when he
would set forth along it. I met him a few days after my
return at a motor exhibition, and he seemed genuinely glad
to see me. Goering, as I have mentioned earlier, was on the
point of leaving for San Remo; and even Ribbentrop, after
he had assured himself that my long absence was due to a
real illness and not to a diplomatic malady and connected with
the withdrawal after the November Jewish pogrom of the
American Ambassador, had been distinctly friendly. My
hopes were thus raised by my first impressions on my return,
but they were quickly undeceived. My first indication of early
trouble was at the annual banquet which Hitler gave to the
diplomatic corps, somewhat later than usual, on March 1st.
After dinner Hitler used to remain standing in the drawing
room, and speak for some five or ten minutes in turn to each
of the heads of missions in the order of their precedence. The
apparent friendliness which he had shown at the motor exhibition was notably absent at this dinner. At the exhibition he
had shaken me by the hand not once but three times. On this

The Occupation of Prague

occasion he carefully avoided looking me in the face when he was speaking to me. He kept his eyes fixed over my right shoulder and confined his remarks to general subjects, while stressing the point that it was not Britain's business to interfere with Germany in Central Europe. I had heard it all before; but, while he said nothing new or startling, his attitude left me with a feeling of vague uneasiness. In the light of wisdom after the event, I have no doubt that he was already weighing the various contingencies in regard to Prague and making his plans for March 15th. He was contemplating his breach of faith with Mr. Chamberlain, and I was reminded of my meeting with him on March 3rd of the year before when he was similarly preoccupied about Vienna.

The brew was in fact, already being stirred by his followers. The Vienna radio was busily inciting Slovaks against Czechs, and a fraternal quarrel between those two Slav kinsfolk was being worked up to serve Hitler with another of those openings which he was so skillful in turning to his own advantage. Within a week the quarrel had become so embittered that on March 10th the Czech President dismissed the Slovak Prime Minister, Father Tiso, occupied Bratislava with Czech troops and gendarmerie, and forcibly installed another Government there with a nominee, Karel Sidor, at its head who enjoyed the confidence of Prague. Once again Hitler's opponents, Slovaks and Czechs alike, had made a false move and played into his hands. The chance was too good a one for Hitler's opportunism to let slide, and arrogantly regardless of the consequences, he proceeded once more to pull the appropriate plan out of its drawer and to act like lightning.

Failure of a Mission

Though the possibility of an armed coup on Czechoslovakia in view of Germany's position and her power to foment trouble in that country could never be discarded, I must confess that almost up to the last moment I found it difficult to believe that Hitler would go quite as far as he did. Was it sheer perfidy and lust for dominion or complete amorality and inability to consider any or anybody's outlook except his own? It was probably a combination of all those four, since the issue was transparently obvious. The ink was hardly dry on the Munich documents; and, if he had really wanted that understanding with Britain which he professed so constantly, so eloquently, and in tones of such injured innocence to seek, he could never have violated as cynically as he did the undertakings which he had given to the British Prime Minister.

Unfortunately the Czechs were incredibly shortsighted and domineering in their treatment of the Slovaks, and the separatists among the latter no less blindly disloyal in their attitude toward the Czechs. It was obvious that the controversy which had arisen between them was exposing both equally to German interference; and during the week which preceded the occupation of Prague I did my utmost to persuade the Czech Minister at Berlin to use all his influence with his Government to induce it to lose no time in settling its dispute with the Slovaks and in withdrawing its troops from Bratislava before it was too late. Like the Polish Ambassador later, M. Mastny had temporarily lost all contact with the Wilhelmstrasse and was completely in the dark as regards Germany's intentions. My warnings to M. Mastny that his Government was playing Hitler's game for him and that its folly would end in disaster either fell on deaf ears or

The Occupation of Prague

he himself failed to impress Prague. The Czech Government persisted in its obstinacy; and on Saturday, March 11th, it was announced that Father Tiso had appealed to the German Government for protection against his Slav kinsfolk.

On the same day the German press, which had up till then devoted little space to the Czechoslovak constitutional dispute, adopted a violently pro-Slovak attitude and made ominous references to Czech interference with German institutions and individuals. It was the customary Nazi method of preparing for one of their more iniquitous actions. Nevertheless, it seemed that the press was still awaiting a definite lead from higher authority, and I was averse to anything being said or published abroad which might incite Hitler to precipitate action (as had happened in the preceding May) and make the position for the Czechs even worse than it already was. It was a reticence which proved futile, but verbal protests would have been equally so.

As in the case of Austria just a year earlier, events moved with startling rapidity; and on Saturday evening and on the Sunday the German press was full of wild tales of Czech atrocities and of Germans flying for refuge. In his ability to make quick decisions and to follow them up with equally quick action, a dictator has a great advantage over a democratic government. Hitler saw a long cherished plan within his grasp. He made up his mind on that Sunday, and he was not going to allow either the Western Powers or his Italian ally to complicate the situation for him again by any unwelcome interference with it. I went to the Ministry for Foreign Affairs on the Monday morning, and saw the State Secretary and adjured him to see that nothing was done to violate the

Failure of a Mission

Munich Agreement or to upset the Stanley-Hudson visit. I found Weizsäcker completely noncommittal, and all that he could assure me was that whatever was done would be done in a "decent" manner. He repeated that phrase more than once.

In the event the only part of the performance which could be regarded as decent was the appointment of Baron von Neurath as Lord Protector of Bohemia and Moravia. It was an invidious task for him; and, apart from the fact that in view of Neurath's reputation as a moderate and as not unsympathetic to the Czechs his nomination was calculated to throw dust in the eyes of Europe, it was surely with his tongue in his cheek that Ribbentrop recommended his former chief for such a job. Nor was it made any easier for Neurath later when a notorious Sudeten bully and gangster, Frank, was appointed to be his State Secretary. Such was Nazi "decency"; yet I cannot blame Weizsäcker. Hitler had taken his decision on the preceding afternoon, and that was the end of the matter. Weizsäcker could not have told me less, but he equally could not tell me more.

The year before, Hitler had finally made up his mind to march into Austria on March 11th, and this year the decision to occupy Czechoslovakia was taken on March 12th. Large numbers of troops were already in Vienna with a view to a review being held there, at which Hitler was to be present, to celebrate the anniversary of the *Anschluss:* others had been concentrated in South Germany with the alleged object of supporting Italian claims, which were at that time being pressed against France. The position on the chessboard was

The Occupation of Prague

propitious, and Hitler resolved to strike once again at the exact moment most favorable to his designs.

I left the Wilhelmstrasse after seeing Weizsäcker that morning filled with the gloomiest forebodings. I tried to comfort myself with the State Secretary's assurance about "decency." Weizsäcker was an honorable man; and I had forcibly impressed upon him the reactions which would be inevitably produced in England if the German Government acted in any respect contrary to the Munich Agreement or did anything of a nature to upset the arrangements for the Stanley visit, which was to take place at the end of the week and for which all the invitations had already been issued. But I was not reassured. When I had spoken in the strongest terms against the use of troops, Weizsäcker had protested that the behavior of the German Army was always "decent." It was not a remark calculated to allay my misgivings. At the same time I felt that official protests on the part of His Majesty's Government would arrive too late, and in any case would merely meet with the same fate as those which had been made at the time of the occupation of Vienna. Nothing but the direct and immediate threat of war would have stopped Hitler at that stage. The Czech Government was alone in a position to save itself by its action. After my conversation with Weizsäcker I accordingly saw the Czech Minister and once again urged him, since he himself was no longer in touch with the German Foreign Office, to propose to his own Foreign Minister, Chvalkovsky, who was known to favor co-operation with Germany, an immediate visit to Berlin. In my view such direct contact could alone save the situation; it might be humiliating but it might prevent the worst from happening. It was not pleasant advice to give, but things might have turned out differently if it had been taken earlier. When not only Chvalkovsky but also President Hacha himself came to Berlin, it was already too late; and the announcement, which was made on the following day, March 14th, that the latter was on his way to appeal to Hitler filled me with consternation. Chvalkovsky was one thing, but Hacha was another. The latter was head of the state and as a gesture it seemed to me unwisely humble and excessive. Hitler had put him where he wanted him and would show neither mercy nor generosity. From that moment I was under no illusion that all was not lost. There was some question of my sitting up on the night of March 14th in order to await the earliest possible news of what was happening at Hacha's meeting with Hitler. But I could do nothing more and preferred to go unhappily to bed. My first glance at the newspapers in the morning was sufficient to confirm my worst apprehensions. It was the final shipwreck of my mission to Berlin. Hitler had crossed the Rubicon.

Up to March 12th the plan had been to send an ultimatum to the Czech Government supported by a display of force. I have some reason to believe that the text of such an ultimatum was actually telegraphed on the Saturday to the German Legation at Prague but cancelled before it could be presented. Its terms would certainly have been harsh but would probably have left the Czechs at least a shadow of independence. But the German controlled press and Himmler's provocative agents, those essential pieces of the machinery of Nazism, were already at work. What had happened after Mr. Chamberlain's visit to Berchtesgaden six months earlier and what was to happen in respect to Poland less than six months later were again being enacted. The tales of Czech atrocities grew, Germans were reported as being ill-treated and massacred, refugees from the German area of Brünn were described as streaming in thousands toward the Austrian frontier, and so on and so forth *ad nauseam*. It was these stories which served as the pretext for Hitler to change his mind, to cancel the ultimatum, and to substitute in its place a full military occupation and the establishment of the Protectorate. He was a genius at finding or creating plausible excuses for all his actions, however iniquitous!

It is difficult to believe that these machinations were not an intrinsic part of Hitler's own schemes; yet it seems but fair to relate that I heard some months later a story which seemed to indicate that they were not. On his arrival at Prague on March 15th, one of the first things which Hitler expressed a wish to do was to visit the hospitals. His entourage, probably soldiers and consequently less well informed than Himmler's blackshirts, asked him for what purpose. "To visit the German wounded victims of Czech ill treatment," was Hitler's answer. As there were none, his followers had some difficulty in persuading him that such a visit would be useless. Possibly they induced him to believe that they existed everywhere except in Prague itself; but, if the story is true—and my source was both a Czech and a good one—it would seem to indicate that some of the party were even more impatient than Hitler himself or even that the Führer was to some extent at least the tool of his extremists. Nevertheless, it was more a question of timing and opportunity than of principle. The Bohemian Protectorate was a long-cherished design, and would have remained an ultimate objective even if his followers had not forced Hitler's hand in March.

Once Hitler's final decision had been taken, everything possible was done to give to the proceeding, at least in German eyes, a spurious air of legality. The Germans are traditionally legal-minded. Father Tiso; the Slovak Catholic priest, had been summoned to Berlin on March 11th and persuaded to place the fate of his small country in Hitler's hands. He was told to proclaim the independence of Slovakia and became its first President, under German protection. Dr. Hacha followed Tiso to Berlin on March 14th, though it is but true to say that he came there of his own volition, in the hope of sparing his country the horrors of invasion and of securing by his abasement at least a measure of generous treatment. Whatever virtues Hitler may possess, generosity is certainly not one of them; personally, I was struck on several occasions, when generosity might have profited him, by the complete absence of that quality in his make-up. Dr. Hacha was an old and weak man, and his daughter traveled with him in order to look after him. He was received with the honors due to the head of a state—or a condemned prisoner before execution—and his daughter was given a bouquet of flowers by Ribbentrop at the station. On their arrival at the Adlon Hotel, she was presented with a box of chocolates from Hitler! But that was the limit to which his generosity went. The Czech Foreign Minister, Chvalkovsky, had accompanied his President; and after an exchange of visits between him and Ribbentrop, Dr. Hacha was granted an interview with Hitler at his Chancellery at one in the morning. A German doctor was thoughtfully ordered to be in attendance there in case Dr.

The Occupation of Prague

Hacha were taken ill in the course of the proceedings; and, if report be true, his services were actually required once, if not twice. Long before Dr. Hacha arrived at the Chancellery, German troops had already entered Czechoslovakia and had occupied the country round Mahrisch Ostrau on the alleged, but possibly not unjustified, pretext of forestalling a Polish occupation of that area. It contained some of the richest mines in Bohemia and was consequently coveted by both Poles and Germans.

Such was the setting for poor Dr. Hacha when he was ushered into the presence of the Führer. The interview between them lasted until 4 o'clock in the morning. Much of the delay was due to the interruption of all telephonic communication between Berlin and Prague. Dr. Hacha expressed fear lest some rash Czech troops might fire on the German invaders. He was told that, if they did so, Prague would at once be bombed by the German Air Force. Field Marshal Goering, who had been recalled from San Remo on March 12th, was present to reinforce this threat; and Dr. Hacha was advised to speak by telephone personally to his Ministers at Prague to convey to them the warning. It was only after much difficulty and delay that he was able to do so. Otherwise it was merely a question of signing on the dotted line; and this he did, thereby handing over the Czech people, "in the interests of pacification," to the German Reich. The proceedings were a complete farce, though it must be admitted that President Hacha might well have adopted a more dignified attitude. He might at least have refused to sign and thereby have deprived Hitler of the satisfaction of being able to pretend to the German people that the occupation of

Failure of a Mission

Bohemia was legitimate and desired by the Czechs themselves. Without signing he could just as easily have recommended, as he did, to the Czech Government that no resistance should be offered to the invaders. He must be excused on the ground of his age and ill-health. He left again next morning for Prague, but by skillful manipulation of the train service Hitler got there before him, and the proclamation announcing the constitution of Bohemia and Moravia into a German Protectorate was announced to the Czech people from the upper windows of the Hradshin Palace on the morning of March 15th. The whole crisis had only lasted five days. Hitler had staged another of his lightning coups; and once more the world was left breathless.

As a coup it was a brilliant success, but in every other respect it constituted an irreparable political blunder. Godesberg was in comparison an unimportant and minor one. By the occupation of Prague, Hitler put himself once for all morally and unquestionably in the wrong and destroyed the entire arguable validity of the German case as regards the Treaty of Versailles. After Prague, Nazism ceased to be national and racial and became purely dynamic and felonious. By his callous destruction of the hard and newly won liberty of a free and independent people, Hitler deliberately violated the Munich Agreement, which he had signed not quite six months before; and his undertaking to Mr. Chamberlain, once the Sudeten had been incorporated in the Reich, to respect the independence and integrity of the Czech people. Thereafter Hitler's word could never more be trusted nor could the most pacifically minded disregard the rape of Prague. It was a repetition of Belgium, 1914, in another form; and it is no exaggeration to say that in 1939, also, the war has been caused by the deliberate tearing up by Germany of a scrap of paper. Up till that March, as I wrote in my final report, the German ship of state had flown the German national flag. On those Ides of March, its captain defiantly hoisted the skull and crossbones of the pirate, and appeared under his true colors as an unprincipled menace to European peace and liberty.

As long as National Socialism remained an article for internal consumption or even confined its aspiration to those solid blocks of Germans who lived on its immediate frontiers, the morality of the German case was a debatable proposition. As far as internal affairs went, the Government of Germany was the concern of the German people, nor would the British nation or the British Empire as a whole have ever willingly consented to go to war in order to refuse the application, where it might be possible and just, of the principle of self-determination. It was not until the theory of German nationalism was extended beyond Germany's own frontiers and the principle of self-determination, having served its purpose, was abandoned in favor of the theory of *Lebensraum* (or unlimited elbowroom for Germany regardless of others) that the Nazi philosophy and its urge for domination exceeded the limits compatible with peace. Prague revitalized France, consolidated England and the Empire, and produced a common front against future German aggression. Its occupation laid the foundation of the present struggle for the ideal of the maximum of freedom and justice as against unprincipled power politics and world dominion.

Nor was the Prague coup only a political blunder of the first magnitude. It was no less a tactical error. Though its superficial success and particularly its execution without bloodshed appealed to the great majority of even moderate Germans and temporarily enhanced Hitler's prestige on that account, there were many Germans who did not hesitate to criticize it for what they described as its faulty timing. In their opinion there were other more immediate questions, such as Memel and Danzig and the Corridor, which it would have been wiser and easier to settle first. Czechoslovakia could so easily have waited, and in due course have been reduced to the necessary state of vassalage by methodical and relentless economic pressure. I still think it strange that Hitler did not follow this course, and that is why I can only imagine that it was a case of his love of displaying his mastery of opportunism proving stronger than his sense of judgment. The Czechoslovak quarrel was just too good a chance to be missed, and so was the opportunity for putting Mr. Chamberlain and M. Daladier in their places for their presumptuous interference at Munich with Germany's freedom of action in Central Europe.

Furthermore, it was easy for Hitler to find for the satisfaction of his own people both military and economic excuses for the gratification of his own personal ambitions and resentments—since even Munich had not assuaged his rage against the Czechs for their attitude in May, 1938. It was, I think, Bismarck who said that: "Who holds Bohemia holds Central Europe." The strategic importance of the two provinces is indeed obvious from a mere glance at the map. It would enormously simplify the task of the German General Staff if Bohemia and Moravia were included in the Reich. The surrender of the Sudeten Lands had compromised the whole

The Occupation of Prague

scheme of Czech defense against German aggression. Disrupted from within as well as from without, Czechoslovakia could not now hold up a German invasion even for a few weeks. The danger, on the other hand, still existed of a coalition between Russia and the Western Powers; and, as Hitler told his generals, England was rapidly preparing for a preventive war. (The fact that Ribbentrop was incessantly preaching that Britain was utterly decadent and would never fight for anybody or anything made no difference to Hitler's arguments to the contrary when it suited him to put them forward.) In such circumstances the approval by his military advisers of the course which he proposed to take was a foregone conclusion; and Hitler gracefully pretended to yield to their insistence. His economic advisers were subjected to similar arguments. Raw materials were Germany's supreme need. The possibility of a British blockade, particularly as the United States had become so hostile as the result of the persecution of the Jews, rendered it indispensable that Czechoslovakia should be incorporated without delay in the German Reich in order to prepare against the eventuality of that blockade. Encirclement on land, the blockade by sea, inflation, and the lack of raw materials were Germany's constant bugbears; and Hitler could always play upon one or another of them to keep his people subservient to his own policy.

Is it, nevertheless, possible that Hitler should have failed to realize the effect which his action would inevitably produce abroad? Whatever specious arguments he may have adduced to satisfy himself and his followers of the rightness of his action, I cannot believe that he would have acted as he did on March 15th if megalomania had not by that time super-

seded all the other characteristics which had raised him from
nothingness to the leadership of a great nation. That did not,
however, prevent him from simulating surprise at the immediate and immense repercussion which the Prague occupation
produced in the world generally. When Goering was informed that the Stanley-Hudson visit would not take place,
he professed the utmost indignation that it should be cancelled
for such a trifle! The Germans are a strange people: they
seem utterly incapable of seeing any side of a question except
their own, or to understand the meaning of civilized decency
and moderation. Many Czechs themselves felt that a Czechoslovakia hostile to Germany, lying as it did between Silesia
and Austria in the very jaws of the German wolf, was an
untenable proposition. The peace of Czechoslovakia's economic existence depended upon the establishment of good
relations with Germany. The text of an agreement to place
her relations with Germany on such a mutually satisfactory
footing actually existed in the Ministry for Foreign Affairs in
the Wilhelmstrasse. In Germany's own interests, a nation of
contented and hard-working Czechs on her frontier and
within her own economic sphere should have been far more
valuable to her than seven or eight millions of resentful and
revengeful vassals. The old Austrian Empire, with its mosaic
of different nationalities and its traditional skill in handling
them, had always found the Czechs the most difficult and
indigestible of all to deal with. They are a race of tough fiber,
and their strength has always lain in their subterranean capacity for opposition. As Jan Masaryk, the Czech Minister
in London, is said to have remarked, "The Czechs will at
any rate give Germany a stomach-ache."

The Occupation of Prague

Germany can hold the Czechs down by brute force today, but in this age of nationality she cannot permanently do so. Whatever be the immediate outcome of the present war, "The Gods remember everlastingly and strike remorselessly. By their long memories the Gods are known." The occupation of Prague on the Ides of March was an immense political blunder. Until then the world, passionately anxious for peace as an end in itself and fully conscious of the horrors of the next war, had watched Hitler proceed from success to success and had appeared to forgive or to be taken in by the hateful methods and technique which he invariably employed. But Prague was the limit. There was no sense of security left anywhere in Europe, nothing but an atmosphere of complete lack of confidence in Hitler's good faith or in his readiness to abide by any undertaking which he might in future give. As I telegraphed on the following day to Lord Halifax, "The annexation of Bohemia and Moravia constitutes a wrong which will be always calling for redress, and though it may have afforded Hitler and Ribbentrop a facile triumph, it would be sad not to believe that in the end it will prove a costly error. . . . His Majesty's Government will doubtless consider what attitude to adopt toward a Government which has shown itself incapable of observing an agreement not six months old." His Majesty's Government took the only course open to them at that moment, by recalling me for an indefinite period to London. My mission to Berlin was already a failure, and from that moment I had no real hopes of peace except in a miracle. Though the ship was sinking, to that precarious hope I clung for another five and a half weary and anxious months.

CHAPTER X. *ACT IV:* POLAND

SCENE 1: THE ANGLO-POLISH
AGREEMENT

THE ostensible motive of my recall to London was to report, but I left Berlin feeling that I might well never return there. It would have been natural and possibly more politic to have withdrawn me altogether. I represented a policy of attempting to seek a *modus vivendi* with the Government of Hitler. That policy had been wrecked by Hitler's act of piracy on the Ides of March, and under ordinary circumstances it would have been more normal to appoint another ambassador in my place. But events were moving rapidly, and His Majesty's Government presumably preferred not to swop horses in the middle of the stream.

My stay in London was a period of suspense and anxiety during which events of great moment were taking place. The world, and, above all, public opinion in England, had been profoundly shocked by the occupation of Prague and the violation of the whole spirit of the Munich Agreement. After Munich, the British people were united, as they had never been since 1920, in support of a single policy. Hitler felt that, in these circumstances, it would not add much to the universal execration of his aggression against the Czechs and of his ill faith toward Mr. Chamberlain, if he quickly settled at the same time the problems of Memel and Danzig. Orders were accordingly given to Ribbentrop to browbeat the Lithuanians and the Poles into accepting the German conditions for a solution of both these questions. With the Lithuanians he was successful, and Memel was surrendered to Germany on fairly reasonable terms. But the Poles were made of sterner stuff. They had, moreover, been double-crossed by Hitler in respect to Slovakia, which they had regarded as within their sphere of interest; and resentment had been added to mistrust. When, therefore, Ribbentrop peremptorily dictated to the Polish Ambassador in Berlin the conditions which Hitler would be graciously pleased to impose on the Polish Government, M. Lipski was instructed to break off the negotiations which had been proceeding for some months in respect to Danzig and the Corridor, while offering to reopen them on the basis of free and equal discussion.

The air was electrical, and full of rumors. The German Army was already on a semiwar footing, and for some time past had been accumulating stores and war material on the Polish frontier. Hitler was infuriated by the Polish reply, and for a moment it looked as if hostilities might begin at any moment. Alarmed by the threatening attitude adopted by the German Government, the Polish Government mobilized part of its own forces; and on March 31st Mr. Chamberlain, with the unanimous approval of the House of Commons and of British public opinion, announced that His Majesty's Government had undertaken an obligation of mutual assistance to Poland in the event of any aggression which might endanger the independence of that country. It was a momentous decision, but after Prague no nation in Europe could feel itself secure from some new adaptation of Nazi racial superiority and jungle law. In twelve months Germany had swallowed up Austria, the Sudeten Lands, and Czechoslovakia. Verbal protests were so much waste paper; and a firm stand had to be taken somewhere and force opposed by force; otherwise, in the intoxication of success Hitler, in the course of another twelve months, would continue the process with Poland, Hungary, and Rumania. Berlin was already talking of reconstituting prewar Austria-Hungary and governing the whole of Central Europe from Berlin. The principles of nationalism and self-determination, which had served Hitler to create Greater Germany, were now completely out of date. They had been cynically thrown overboard at Prague, and world dominion had supplanted them. If peace were to be preserved, it was essential that it should be made crystal clear beyond what limit Germany could not go without provoking England to war. In 1914 His Majesty's Government had been accused of not making this plain enough. There may have been some justification for this reproach, and Mr. Chamberlain's Government were determined that the risk should not be incurred again.

The danger signal, which all who ran might read, was accordingly hoisted, in respect to Poland. Nor did His Majesty's Government stop there. Poland's was a reciprocal agreement; but, since Germany's designs appeared to be limitless, unilateral undertakings were similarly given a few weeks later in respect to Rumania and Greece.

Britain thus made her position unmistakably plain. Yet the upshot only shows how difficult it is to please Germans. In 1914 we were accused of having caused the war because we had not said beforehand what we intended to do. In 1939, because we did make our position crystal clear, we are equally being accused of having provoked the war by intimidating Germany. So Germany always pleads her own cause and never sees any side to a question but her own. The truth is that so long as German action had been confined to predominantly German areas, the British nation, in spite of its profound disgust at the methods employed by Hitlerism, had not been inclined actively to intervene. A preventive war for the sole object of hindering the unity of Greater Germany on a national basis would never have been tolerated either by the nation or by the Empire. No British statesmen could ever have failed to take this consideration into account. But even the profound love of peace of the British nation would not permit it to tolerate the absorption by Germany of one independent country after another. The world had been taken by surprise on March 15th, but there must be no more surprises. War would be the inevitable outcome of the next aggression by Germany. If Hitler wanted peace he knew how to insure it; if he wanted war, he knew equally well what would bring it about. The choice lay with him, and in the end the entire responsibility for war was his.

From the outset, however, it was quite obvious that, in spite of the Anglo-Polish Agreement and whatever might be the ultimate outcome of war, neither Britain nor France was in a position to render any effective immediate aid to Poland if she were attacked by Germany's overwhelmingly powerful Air Force and highly mechanized Army. No physical courage would avail against the superiority afforded by these technical and material advantages. It could only be a question of at most a few months before Poland would be overwhelmed, i.e. long before any blockade or pressure on the Siegfried Line from the west would be available to help her in her one-sided struggle. Immediate support if she were to have any, must come from the east, and Russia alone was capable of giving it.

Once again, as in the case of Czechoslovakia—and one cannot stress the point too often—it was a proposition of political geography. Situated as she is, the fate of Poland depended, and will always depend, on Germany and Russia, between which she lies, and which are both infinitely bigger and stronger than she is. Germany was the menace to her in April, 1939; and Russia's good will and material assistance were consequently indispensable to Poland's immediate safety. With this consideration in mind, and with a view to the necessary inclusion of Russia in the peace front against further German aggression, the British and French Governments began the negotiations with the U.S.S.R. which were to drag on throughout those precious four months, only to end in Russia's abrupt *volte-face* toward the end of August.

Our negotiations with them gave, meanwhile, a magnificent opportunity to Goebbels' propaganda to represent Germany once more as being encircled by the Western Powers. Britain, as the chief architect of this alleged encirclement, was once again proclaimed to be Germany's public enemy No. 1. She never really ceased to be so during the whole of my time in Berlin, except when Hitler's designs against Czechs and Poles induced him temporarily to promote the latter to that proud position. Every opportunity was utilized to criticize and sneer at Britain, to stress her external difficulties and her internal troubles, and to assert her decadence and the decline of her prestige. Clearly the Russian negotiations were a form of encirclement, but in no offensive sense and solely as a means to resist aggression. But as vicious propaganda to whip the flagging German spirits to prepare for the war which Hitler was now definitely contemplating at an early date, it was highly successful; and during those four months it certainly served his purpose. Throughout them he was mobilizing men and more men; and the cry of encirclement, which must always appeal to a country which, like Germany, has eleven foreign frontiers and is consequently prone to claustrophobia, stifled the complaints of those whose sons were called up or whose families were being subjected to increasingly stringent food regulations.

It ceased, of course, to have the same effect when Germany woke up one morning to find that Soviet Russia had overnight become Germany's friend and ally instead of her potential enemy. That was, however, yet to come; and in the interval the extremists and Goebbels made hay while the sun shone.

Not the least cynical part of the encirclement propaganda stunt was that, throughout it, Hitler was himself making every effort at Moscow to turn the defensive encirclement, of the Western Powers against Germany, of which he complained so bitterly, into an offensive Russo-German encirclement against Poland. Persistent rumors of these counter negotiations, also as to the persons who were conducting them, reached us in Berlin; and, indeed, the effort thus to break the peace front was only to be expected. Nevertheless, after the actual dispatch in August of the French and our own military missions to Moscow, I no longer thought that they would be successful. I could not imagine that Russian perfidy was as great as all that. I must add that I had, and with better justification as the event proved, equally little confidence that our own negotiations would be more so, particularly after the inexplicable dismissal of Litvinov in the early stages of our negotiations.

After five weeks' absence from my post I was eventually instructed by His Majesty's Government to return to Berlin. I got back there on April 24th. In view of the new and heavy obligations which we had undertaken in Eastern Europe and in order to give weight to the seriousness of our intention to fulfill them, it had been decided to introduce the military training bill, which imposed, for the first time in modern British history, a measure of conscription in England in peacetime. The immediate motive for my return to Berlin was in order to notify the German Government of the fact (it was not the least of Hitler's triumphs) and to explain the circumstances to them before the actual statement on the subject was made in the House of Commons. Before leaving England I was, however, told that I should make no notification until I received from London the exact terms of the announcement, which had first to be communicated by the Government to the Opposition parties in the House of Commons. It had been originally proposed in principle to make this announcement on the following Tuesday, April 25th; but, in the event, my instructions did not reach me till the Tuesday night and were to the effect that the announcement would only be made in the House on the Wednesday afternoon. By this time the intention of His Majesty's Government was an open secret, and I decided for this and other reasons that it would be preferable to make the notification to the State

Secretary rather than to Ribbentrop himself. I accordingly telephoned, myself, to the State Secretary in the early hours of the Wednesday morning, and told him that I had a communication which I wished to make to the German Government before the afternoon. Baron von Weizsäcker, after remarking that he was aware of the object of my visit, said that he could receive me at midday; and it was to him that the official notification of the intentions of His Majesty's Government was ultimately made.

It would not have been worth while recounting this episode, if the press had not seen in it an opportunity to start a story that I had been rudely rebuffed by Ribbentrop. A former British Cabinet Minister, who might have known better, even went so far as to give a lurid description in some newspaper of His Majesty's Ambassador waiting, cap in hand, on Ribbentrop's doorstep. Even if it had been true, I should not have thought that it was greatly in England's interests or in accordance with her dignity to blazon a fact abroad which could give no satisfaction to anyone except Ribbentrop himself. But in point of fact, it was not even true. The prior notification to the German Government of the Prime Minister's statement about conscription, a purely British concern, was indeed not a communication which needed necessarily to be made to the Foreign Minister in person. Moreover, I fully realized that my withdrawal from Berlin after Prague had deeply offended the Nazi Government, which would be only too anxious to show that they resented it; and, if I had asked Ribbentrop to see me, it is more than probable that he would have found pleasure in finding some excuse to delay doing so. It was an obvious pitfall which I had wished to avoid.

Failure of a Mission

Two days later, on April 28th, Hitler made his speech in the Reichstag in which he announced the offer which he had made to Poland on the basis of the return of Danzig to the Reich, of economic guarantees for Poland at the port of Danzig, of an extraterritorial German corridor through the Corridor and, as a sop, of Polish participation in the guarantee to Slovakia. At the same time Hitler declared that, in view of Poland's rejection of this—as he called it—generous offer, it would not be repeated; and he thereupon denounced the ten-year German-Polish Agreement for the settlement of all questions without resort to war, which he had signed with Marshal Pilsudski in 1934 and which had thus still five years to run. He simultaneously and unilaterally denounced the Anglo-German Naval Treaty of 1935. He took at the same time the opportunity to pour ridicule on President Roosevelt's proposal for a ten years' truce, and on the latter's list of thirty countries which should be guaranteed against aggression. Exactly a week later Colonel Beck replied, stating the Polish case, which was, briefly, to the effect that Poland was perfectly ready to reach a settlement of these questions but only on the basis of a treaty freely negotiated on a footing of equality and safeguarding the vital interests of Poland.

The deadlock was thus complete; and the position in respect to German-Polish relations at the beginning of May, 1939, was strikingly similar to that which had prevailed as regards Germany and Czechoslovakia in May, 1938. The subsequent course of events was equally so. But there were also big differences. It was apparent from the start that the Poles would never yield to force, as the Czechs had done. Nor had Britain had any treaty obligations to the Czechs, as she had

The Anglo-Polish Agreement

after March 31st to the Poles. Mr. Chamberlain could not again go to Munich. Nor was it a case of solid blocks of Germans living in territory contiguous to the Reich. There would have been, it is true, a considerable measure of right in Germany's case, if it had only been a question of a passage across the Corridor or of Danzig itself with its 400,000 German population. Yet, even so, that case had been thoroughly vitiated by her actions subsequent to Munich. After Prague it was clear to Poland, as to the rest of the world, that all Hitler's promises were mere tactical expedients. Was Danzig, like the Sudeten, merely to be the first bite of the cherry, with the whole Corridor, Posen, and Silesia as the second, and ultimately Polish independence itself as the third? Something more than mere verbal guarantees, such as had been offered at Munich but never implemented, would be required if the justifiable apprehensions of the Poles were to be allayed. The Poles were brave and perhaps too fond of talking of their bravery; but the "Hotspurs of Europe," as H.A.L. Fisher describes them in his fascinating history of Europe, had every cause for anxiety, and, in the event, every need for their bravery.

In those still early days in May, with four uneasy months yet to elapse before the curtain fell for the last time on war, my estimate of the general situation was as follows: Provided no unforeseen incident or new combination of circumstances intervened, Hitler, whose tactics were always the same, would wait and in the meantime prepare for all eventualities, exactly as he had done in the preceding summer. If he could then succeed in getting Danzig without war, that would satisfy him for the moment: if he could not get it without war, he would fight in the end, but only at the moment which seemed a propitious one to him. The initiative would always be his; and, even if he held his hand temporarily as regards Danzig and the Corridor, it would not mean that he had renounced his claims and ambitions, but merely that the favorable opportunity which he was seeking had not presented itself. Finally, I was convinced that no solution which fell far short of his offer or ultimatum to Poland on April 28th would ever be a lasting one. For, as I pointed out at the time to His Majesty's Government, the Polish question was not one of Hitler's making. As an Austrian he was possibly better disposed toward Poland than any Prussian could be. The Corridor and Danzig were a real German national grievance, and some equitable settlement had to be found in respect to these questions if ever there was to be genuine peace in the future between Germany and Poland. This was, in reality, fully appreciated by His Majesty's Government; and in every subsequent speech made by the Prime Minister or Lord Halifax, and in every conversation which I had later with Hitler or any of the Nazi leaders, our desire to achieve an equitable settlement was emphasized no less frankly than our resolution to resist force by force.

CHAPTER XI. *THIRD ENTR'ACTE*

AS in 1938, so once again in 1939, the summer months were spent in fruitless negotiation. Moscow had now become the center of the stage; and His Majesty's Government and the French Government sought sincerely but in vain to persuade the Russian Government definitely to assume the same obligations toward Poland as we ourselves had undertaken. As soon as one alleged obstacle to Russian co-operation was overcome, Stalin produced another with unfailing regularity and with the same persistence as we displayed in overcoming each difficulty in turn. Nor did we cease during the same period constantly using our good offices at Warsaw, with a view to the avoidance of the kind of incident which Hitler was so skillful in turning to his own purposes. For my part in Berlin I was preaching patience and giving solemn warnings to all and sundry. My main and indeed almost sole object was to convince the Germans that any further act of aggression by them would mean war with Britain. It was at the end of May, for instance, that I had my conversation with Goering which I reported at the time and which constituted one of the documents included in the Blue Book issued by His Majesty's Government on the outbreak of war. I made it quite clear to the Field Marshal that, while nobody desired more than we did an amicable arrangement between Germany and Poland in respect to Danzig and the Corridor, we were determined to oppose in the future force by force. Though Ribbentrop was at that time making great play with his own special brand of propaganda, to the effect that Britain would never fight over Danzig, the Field Marshal himself did not, on that occasion, appear to doubt that such was our fixed resolve. He rather seemed or pretended to believe that Britain contemplated a preventive war in any case against Germany. He probably took his cue from Hitler, who with his phenomenal capacity both for self-delusion and misrepresentation is still arguing that his justification for war was that belief. Goering was accordingly at pains to explain to me at length why no power or combination of powers could prevail against Germany in Europe. He expatiated on the inability of France to stand a long war, on the military unpreparedness of the Poles and of their lack of real unity, on the unwillingness of the U.S.S.R. to give Poland any effective assistance, on the harm which a war would cause to the British Empire, and on Germany's invincible might.

It was at this time and throughout the summer quite useless to argue about the equal rights of the Poles to *Lebensraum* and economic existence; and in the end I gave up trying to do so and concentrated on the inevitable consequences of aggressive action. The invariable retort of every German was that Britain had given a blank check to the Poles or had placed her sword in their hands. It was once again a case of the fable of the wolf and the lamb, just as it had been in regard to the Czechs the year before. Everything that the Poles did or said was wrong and, moreover, entirely due to British encouragement. Even Weizsäcker was impervious to reason or logic in that respect. The Germans could only think in terms of their own *Lebensraum* and had made up their minds that the Poles would never agree to any modification of the status quo so long as they had the backing of England. All Hitler's plans were made on that assumption.

My conversation with Goering led consequently nowhere in particular, as was, I fear, the fate of all my conversations, however stimulating, with him. But, whatever may have been in Hitler's mind, war did not appear at that time to be either the desire or an immediate preoccupation of Goering. It was on that occasion he showed me with pride the colored sketches of the tapestries which he proposed to hang in his new dining room at Karinhall. I described them in my official dispatch as drawings of "naked ladies," but I am glad to have this opportunity of saying that I did so in no disrespectful or suggestive spirit. Had I anticipated that my dispatch would ever be published, I should certainly have written "nude figures" in place of the cruder expression which I actually used. These drawings were in fact very artistic; and I should not have referred to them at all if it had not been to point the argument of patience, which had been the gist of all my talk with Goering that morning. That was why, when he read out the names of Mercy and Purity, etc., I took the opportunity to observe that I failed to see Patience among them. Goering, who never missed a point, roared with laughter at the innuendo.

Incidentally, I learned, after the publication of the Blue Book, the origin of these drawings. Miss Alice Head, who is Mr. William Randolph Hearst's legal agent in England, wrote to me from St. Donat's Castle to say that the tapestries in question, which were Flemish of the middle sixteenth century and known as the "Four Seasons," were the property of Mr. Hearst and were to have been purchased by Goering from him. They were actually at the Castle, and the price to have been paid for them was £5,000 in English money. She added that Goering's representative was to have come to the Castle on August 16th to complete the deal, but that shortly before that date she was informed that his departure "had been delayed." Miss Head concluded her letter to me by observing, not without insight, that "As events developed, I knew of course that the deal was off."

During the next four months the chief impression which I had of Hitler was that of a master chess player studying the board and waiting for his opponents to make some false move which could be turned to his own immediate advantage—so long as Russia's final attitude remained unpredictable, he himself would not move. His army, of whom a considerable section, communism or no communism, were always preaching the superior value of a Russian alliance, would never have allowed him to risk a world war in which Russia might be actively on the side of Poland. Germany's military nightmare is the war on two fronts; and, if Poland did not seriously count in that respect, the inexhaustible military reserves and numerically powerful Air Force of Russia did, in spite of the drastic Army purges to which she had been subjected in the preceding year. At the same time, though Hitler might sit and wait, it could be taken for granted that he would never be contented with less than or even as much as he had offered to Poland on April 28th. His extremists and many other Germans did not even approve of the settlement which he had adumbrated on that occasion; and, without greatly stretching one's imagination, one can be fairly certain that Hitler himself never meant that offer to be a final solution. It was for him merely a matter of moving a pawn one square forward. He was always moving pawns; and what did it matter to him, as long as he won the game, whether he cheated or not, and moved his knight on occasion like a bishop or his castle like a knight. He could always hope that nobody was looking or, if somebody was, find some excuse for protesting that it was not he but his adversary who had first broken the rules. It was the so-called *Wahnsystem,* or capacity for self-delusion, which was a regular part of his technique. It helped him both to work up his own passions and to make his people believe anything that he might think would be good for them.

When he comes up before the bar of the Last Judgment, he will certainly argue with apparently complete self-conviction that he would have spared Europe the horrors of war if the Poles had accepted his reasonable and generous conditions. It will, I submit, be false. He knew full well that what he really wanted was something more, namely Posen and Silesia and their freedom itself, which the Poles would never surrender without war. He knew that to achieve his full ambition war in the end was inevitable, and his vast armaments were created in readiness for that final consummation. Moreover, as I have said before, he regarded himself as the reincarnation of Frederick the Great and Bismarck, whose portraits and busts adorned his offices in Berlin, Munich, and Berchtesgaden. Mars was the god whom they had served, and Hitler's fame would be incomplete without his own sacrifices to that deity, which at long last had to be greater than theirs. Nor can one leave out of account his inferiority complex. He felt that neither he nor the German nation would ever really succeed in getting rid of that until the memory of the defeat of 1918 had been obliterated by victory in another world war—after which Germany would rule the earth.

So he waited more or less patiently, since his army would not be finally ready for all eventualities until the end of August. That, in spite of all the secrecy of its preparations, was fairly evident. And, when it was announced that the twenty-fifth anniversary of the Tannenberg victory was to be held there on August 27th and that it would coincide with the visit of a German warship to Danzig, it did not need much prescience for me to abandon my rooted aversion to the popular habit of fixing dates for crises and to write to Lord Halifax, as I did early in July, and foretell that the last week of August was likely to be zero hour.

We had reached the last act of the drama, and the curtain for it had gone up on that momentous March 31st when Mr. Chamberlain had announced in the House of Commons our agreement with Poland. Both parties were now sparring for position. We sought at Moscow and Ankara to build up a peace front against aggression; while the Germans were working at Moscow, in the Baltic States, and in the Balkans to make gaps in that front. Both were to win successes and to suffer defeats.

But in the meantime there was a lull which, unless some unforeseen incident occurred, was likely to last for several months; and I reported to that effect at the beginning of May. While there was great activity in military affairs, nothing was being done at the moment which might not reasonably be attributed to normal exercises during an abnormal period. More and more reservists were being gradually called to the colors (I lost one German footman in May and another in July); but the tempo had not yet become accelerated. Hitler was once more as in 1938 waiting on events and preparing for all eventualities, but he had as yet taken no decision, and would take none till circumstances should turn, as he hoped, in his favor. Until the second half of August, when his army would reach its maximum preparedness and the crops be gathered in, the initiative might still be ours, if we could before then build up a solid peace front and behind it persuade Poles and Germans to negotiate. If the opportunity of those summer months were lost, then it was always to be anticipated that Hitler himself, relying on the strength of his army, would recover or seize the initiative. He could scarcely afford to hold the party rally at Nuremberg in September without being able to announce some development of the situation. On the other hand, if the party rally took place, with the vast effort of organization which its celebrations required, it was probable that there would be no war in 1939, since the habitual rainy weather in Poland in October would be likely to make it impossible for the highly mechanized German Army to win the rapid victory which was regarded by the German Army commanders as essential to success. Apart, in fact, from the danger of a serious incident's occurring in the interval or of Hitler and ourselves being placed in a position from which neither of us could withdraw, there was every reason to feel fairly confident of the temporary security of the lull. The whole problem, to my mind, was how to reach the Nuremberg party rally without disaster.

Thus the summer began. Early in May Ribbentrop met Count Ciano in the north of Italy, and an agreement was reached for converting the Rome-Berlin Axis into a definite military alliance, which was eventually signed with much pomp and circumstance in Berlin on May 22nd. The formal announcement of this military alliance which, so far as she herself was concerned, Italy had been partly induced to sign in view of her suspicions lest the British negotiations with the U.S.S.R. and Turkey might be directed against herself, constituted no particularly new situation. The Axis had always been regarded as sufficiently strong without the emphasis of a military alliance signed, sealed, and delivered. Undoubtedly the most interesting clause in it was its first article, which made the alliance conditional on Italy's being kept fully informed in advance of any German intentions which might provoke an international conflict. It was a hint on Italy's part that Rome was not merely tied to Berlin's apron strings and that friendship might be overtaxed if it had to stand the strain of another unannounced coup, as at Prague. The alliance thus seemed to afford a slight guarantee to the rest of the world against the repetition of any such lightning stroke. But, above all, it provided Italy with an opportunity to circumscribe the area of hostilities if Hitler were to take action without first informing Mussolini and securing his consent.

In May, also, Esthonia and Latvia, which were feeling justifiably distrustful of Russia's ulterior intentions and were apprehensive of the extent of our negotiations at Moscow, combined together to reinsure their position by means of nonaggression treaties with Germany. At the time this seemed a further diplomatic victory for Ribbentrop; but it was an ephemeral success, which availed neither Germany nor the Baltic States when Stalin entered the war as the ally of Germany.

May was quickly over, and we were no nearer the formation of the peace front than before. M. Litvinov had been dismissed, and the British and French Ambassadors at Moscow were beginning again with M. Molotov. In the last days of May, I urgently represented to the Polish Ambassador the desirability of resuming conversations at the Ministry for Foreign Affairs, but his answer was that he could do nothing till the German Government had given some evidence of its good will and readiness to talk. The latter for its part took the line that Colonel Beck's speech on May 5th had closed the door and, until he himself reopened it, there was nothing to be done.

June followed, and was the last month when I myself had even any comparative peace of mind. So far as Berlin was concerned it began with the state visit of the Prince Regent of Yugoslavia, who was accompanied by his wife, Princess Olga, the sister of H.R.H. the Duchess of Kent. It was the first royal state visit to Berlin; and Hitler laid himself out, not unsuccessfully, to charm his guests. Nor was any effort spared by the German Government—by means of a review of troops which lasted for nearly four hours—to impress Prince Paul with the military might of Germany. Hundreds of airplanes flew in formation overhead, barely missing the tops of the houses, while an endless succession of tanks and guns and other mechanized forms of warfare constituted an imposing spectacle. The crowd, nevertheless, showed some discrimination by reserving its chief applause for the two or three regiments of cavalry, with their drum majors on horseback, which, albeit in field gray uniforms, were all that was left of the colorful glory of the pre-1914 military displays. It was a monotonous performance which filled one with sadness and horror at the destructive folly of modern civilization.

I had hoped that, in view of their connection with the British Royal family, Prince Paul and Princess Olga would have done me the honor of having luncheon or dinner at His Majesty's Embassy. But the German arrangements were too thorough and complete to permit of this; and, if it had not been for Field Marshal Goering, I should have had no opportunity of seeing them except at a gala performance at the Opera, which was the sole function during the visit to which the diplomatic corps was invited. Even this civility was, I always felt, partly due to the attitude which I had adopted when Signor Mussolini visited Berlin in September, 1937. Neurath was Minister for Foreign Affairs at the time; and, when I learned that the diplomatists were not to be asked to any of the parties given in the Duce's honor, I told the Baron that in such circumstances I was certainly not going to stop in Berlin and be one of the hired applauders of the Axis. And, in fact, I left Berlin. But thereafter, whenever there was a state visit, the heads of the foreign missions were regularly invited to the Opera, which always formed part of the arrangements for the entertainment of state guests. Their Royal Highnesses spent, however, the last two nights of their visit at Karinhall, and Goering was good enough to ask me down there to spend an afternoon with them. It was a tactful thought inspired by the knowledge that the Prince and Princess were old friends of mine from the days when I was Minister at Belgrade.

By far the most heartening feature of the month of June was the marvelous success which attended the tour of the King and Queen in Canada and the United States. It reconsecrated one's faith in the solidity and permanency of Anglo-Saxon idealism, as exemplified in the British Commonwealth of Nations, and reconvinced one of the futile transiency of Nazi ideology and of the theory of dominion imposed by force. Encouraged by such reflections, we celebrated the King's birthday once more on June 9th; and some three or four hundred British subjects attended the reception which I gave at His Majesty's Embassy on that date. It was the last entertainment of any size which was held there before the war. I also gave a big dinner party on the following day, June 10th, which happens to be my own birthday. Three years before, I had completely forgotten the date until the day itself was over, and I had decided this time to arrange a party in advance so as to insure that I did not forget it again. My particular friends in the diplomatic corps were the Italian and Belgian Ambassadors and their wives. No party was complete in Berlin, at any rate for me, without the Attolicos and the Davignons. Madame Attolico was unfortunately absent in Rome; but her husband was present and proposed my health, very unnecessarily but very charmingly. The South African Minister and his wife were, of course there, as was Kirk, the United States Chargé d'Affaires. Among the Germans were Baron von Weizsäcker and his wife, both of whom I greatly respected; Herr Laurenz and Baron von Steengracht with their very attractive wives; and Oberstjäger-meister Menthe, my companion on several shooting expeditions, and his wife. Yvonne Rodd, who was studying singing in Berlin, also came; and the rest of the party was composed mostly of members of the Embassy staff. I recollect that it was a very pleasant and happy evening, but it also was the last formal dinner party which I gave in Berlin.

On June 25th I motored to Hamburg to attend the local Derby and to visit some old friends of mine from Belgrade, Mr. and Mrs. Abbott. He had been Secretary of the American Legation in Yugoslavia when I was Minister there, and was afterward appointed American Consul at Hamburg. As it happened, a Polish horse was expected by many to be going to win the race, but he finished down the course to the keen satisfaction of all loyal Germans. The atmosphere was already strained; and I remember feeling rather sorry for my Polish colleague, who was also present. Yet everybody was friendly and courteous and appeared honestly glad to see one.

Looking back on it all, one can only be impressed by the tragedy and futility of the present war. There was no hostility to England among the mass of the people in Germany. Goebbels' frenzied propaganda may, since the beginning of the war, have been successful in working Germans up to hate; German youth is being, and has for some years past been, educated up to hate us; and Nazi extremists, full of the mystical faith which seeks to impose German leadership on a world of German vassals, will always hate the chief barrier to the fulfillment of their overweening ambitions. Resentment against the English, who nicknamed him "Brickanddrop," may inspire Ribbentrop's hatred; and the "fury of the woman scorned" may fan the passions of Hitler himself. But the German people had no natural hatred of the British, and it is the saddest thing in the world that the two should fight. The spontaneous applause with which Mr. Chamberlain was greeted at Godesberg and at Munich was characteristic of the real feelings of the German people.

Personally, up to the last, I never felt anywhere that I was other than welcome. I attended two large parties at the end of that month; one was given by Funk, who after having succeeded Schacht as Minister for Economics had later replaced him as President of the Reichsbank; and the other by Lutze, who was the Chief of the S.A., or brownshirts. Funk was the most hospitable of men and happiest when he was having a glass of wine or beer with as many friends as he could get together. Lutze had been an officer in the war of 1914, and I much liked both him and his wife. Everyone who was anyone in Nazi circles with the notable exception of the Ribbentrops, Himmlers, *et hoc genus omne* were present at these parties. For me, they were not so much social entertainments as opportunities to exchange views with all who were ready to listen and to talk. I did my utmost in these numerous conversations to enlist the support of those most closely in touch with Hitler, with a view to inducing him to make some gesture which would open the door, if it were only an inch or so, for a response on Mr. Chamberlain's part. But the negotiations with Russia, as long as they continued, were represented to me as an insuperable obstacle to any conciliatory initiative on Hitler's part. Alas, it was all talk; for it was not che Lutzes and the Funks, or even the Brauschitsches and Lammers who decided policy. The last thing which Hitler himself wanted was to start serious discussions with England, and one could not but have the uncomfortable impression that, while I and others were spending our time in talking, Hitler was secretly making his plans for action. Excessive publicity, on the other hand, was ruining even the faint prospect of any satisfactory upshot of the Moscow negotiations, and in the meantime the two parties who should have been talking at Berlin and Warsaw were silent.

Thus, almost before one knew it, June was gone, and we were in July. The month began with an agreement between Italy and Germany for the compulsory transfer to the Reich of the Tyrolese population of the Upper Adige. However great the hardship and distress imposed thereby on the historic inhabitants of those lovely valleys, it was a measure calculated to remove all possible cause of friction between Italy and Germany. It was a sop on Germany's part to the Axis partner, and was not discouraging as such. But otherwise it was becoming more and more apparent that, if the Russian negotiations were not brought to an early conclusion and if discussions were not reopened between Berlin and Warsaw, a Polish crisis before September would be unavoidable. The stories of persecution of the German minority in Poland were still being relegated to the back pages of the official German press, but it was only because Russia's attitude was not defined and Hitler's own military arrangements were not yet completed. Goebbels had already, a fortnight before, made a provocative speech at Danzig on the subject of the ill treatment of German nationals, and the tales of such persecutions were being industriously bruited abroad. Incidentally, I had the impression that Goebbels' speech on that occasion caused considerable anxiety at Rome; and it may well have been one of the reasons for the visit of Count Ciano to Ribbentrop at Salzburg in August, to which I shall refer later. The number of German refugees into the Reich was growing, and passions were beginning to be inflamed. In such an atmosphere incidents were bound to, and did, occur. The zeal of minor officials often goes beyond the instructions of the central authorities. When representations were made to the one party on the subject, the invariable retort was to refer to the faults on the other side. To a great extent such unfortunate situations are always a pot and kettle affair. The Germans laid claim to a German minority of over a million in Poland, and the Poles to a somewhat similar number of Poles in Germany. Both were probably exaggerated, but the point was of little importance, since the minorities were undoubtedly there. In some districts, such as the Silesian mining areas, where those with Polish names were mostly Germans and vice versa, they were in inextricable confusion. On balance, however, I have no doubt in my own mind that the complaints of the Germans in Poland probably had the greater foundation in fact. The Poles in Germany were nearly all of the laboring class, and as such less liable to ill treatment by the German Government, which required all the labor which it could muster. The Germans in Poland were largely either landowners or belonged to the middle class of liberal professions. They were objects of envy rather than of service to the Polish state. Above all, they were being used by the German Government, not as forerunners of German culture but as advance guards for German interference and dominion.

Failure of a Mission

I went to London for a few days in connection with private business at the beginning of July and warned His Majesty's Government that the clouds were gathering. But Russia remained the stumbling block. The Labor and Liberal parties, as well as a section of the Conservatives, were vociferously clamoring for an agreement with the U.S.S.R. at any price and, by their public insistence to that effect, merely encouraging Stalin and Molotov to keep putting that price up. We always seemed to be on the eve of an agreement with the U.S.S.R., only to find the next day that some new difficulty had been raised and had to be overcome. By July the Russian negotiations had ceased to have for me even the superficial appearance of any reality, and I still believe that from the outset Moscow never meant them to terminate in agreement with us. Moscow had become the seat of an oriental despotism, and the ideological basis of the Soviet regime was now nothing but a sham and a delusion. Stalin's sole objective was to embroil Germany with the Western Powers and to make one or the other pull the chestnuts out of the fire for himself.

The moment at which Hitler began his own negotiations with Stalin must remain for the time being a matter for conjecture. But it can scarcely have been coincidence that in Hitler's speech of April 28th his usual hostile references to the U.S.S.R. were conspicuous by their absence; that on May 3rd Litvinov, the Russian protagonist of the League of Nations, was relieved of his post as Commissar for Foreign Affairs; and that a few weeks later a new Soviet Ambassador to Germany was received with marks of quite unusual courtesy. Why should it have been otherwise, since the British agreement with Poland had relieved Russia of all fear of German aggression against herself and, instead of being obliged any longer to consider her own safety, she could now afford to think only of her personal advantage? Peradventure, if England had been willing to traffic in the honor of neutral Baltic States, the end of our negotiations might have been different. Hitler was less scrupulous or maybe he was in turn duped by Stalin. It was important for Russia that the population of the Polish Ukraine, which was more Orthodox Russian than Catholic Polish, should be in Soviet hands rather than constitute a lure to German expansion via Poland. A fourth partition was always a possible eventuality; and, if Moscow could restore her influence in the Baltic States and raise a barrier in the Ukraine to the German *Drang nach Osten*, the Reich would be driven back toward the west again; and that was and must always be the supreme aim of Russian policy. These and other similar considerations cannot fail to have been constantly present in the mind of the ruler of the Kremlin. At the same time he personally admired Hitler, or at least his successes, and was quite ready to take a leaf out of his book and follow the example of his opportunism.

The cards were, in fact, stacked against us; and the peace-front negotiations dragged on interminably between London and Moscow. Stalin, too, was studying the chessboard. On the other hand, instead of there being any relaxation of the tension at Danzig, the position there was growing more and more strained. The remilitarization of the Free City, alleged by the Germans to be purely defensive and in anticipation of a possible Polish attack, was proceeding apace. The so-called safety measures which were being taken in this connection were, however, equally adaptable for offensive purposes and were naturally causing alarm to the Poles, who had other reasons, in addition, for apprehending the intention of the German Government to effect a sudden coup there. Arms were being openly smuggled in large quantities into the city, and the Poles had been obliged on that account to reinforce their customs inspectors by a considerable number of additional frontier guards. By way of reprisal they had also taken some economic measures of a nature to prejudice the trade of the Free City.

The ingredients for a formidable explosion were thus being gathered, and only lacked a spark to blow peace sky-high. In the full realization of this I decided, at the end of July, to seek for myself the opportunity of a personal meeting with Hitler. He was at Bayreuth at the time, attending the Wagner festival. Though absolutely unmusical, I like Wagner. As a young man I studied German in Dresden, which then was the proud possessor of the best opera in Germany. Thanks to Gerald Tyrrwhitt, now Lord Berners, who was in the same *pension* as I was, I had learned there all the leit-motivs (or musical terms) of the *Ring* by heart and had never forgotten them. I had twice attended the whole of the *Ring* in Berlin, and I used this as an excuse to pay a visit to Bayreuth on the twenty-ninth of July. So far as my real objective was concerned it was a complete failure. I had car trouble on the way down; and, when I arrived there, I found that Hitler was away inspecting the Siegfried Line, accompanied by Ribbentrop—an ominous combination. He got back on the last afternoon of my visit, but I only saw him at a distance in the Opera House. The sole satisfaction that I got out of Bayreuth was to hear a marvelous performance of the *Valkyrie*, to see a few personal friends, and to make the acquaintance of the English wife of Siegfried Wagner.

Even so, if he had wanted to speak to me, Hitler could have done so; for he must have been informed that I was there. But contact with the British Ambassador was not part of the game for him. He was as yet, I believe, still undecided as to what to choose as the suitable pretext for his next step. He was still poring over the chessboard, testing nerves, and waiting for his adversary to make a false move or scheming how he could induce him to do so. There was yet a month to go before his army would be absolutely ready to strike, and the British and French military missions were preparing to leave for Moscow. What the position was at that moment in respect to his own negotiations with the U.S.S.R. it is, of course, impossible for me to say. But he may well still have been uneasy lest Stalin might double-cross him, as he subsequently double-crossed us; and, anyway, the German Army was not yet completely mobilized. So he bided his time, and waited for the conjunction of circumstances which would facilitate his final decision.

The technique was exactly the same as in 1938. The German Army was being secretly mobilized within easy reach of the chief strategic points. Every eventuality was being taken into account, and plans had been drawn up to meet each of them. If the favorable circumstances for which Hitler was waiting failed to materialize, he could always hold the September rally and protest the innocence of his intentions. If they did materialize, it would be only too easy for him to fabricate the spark, whenever it was needed, to set Europe ablaze. To produce the crisis he had but to give the word to the Danzig Senate to declare the reattachment of the Free City to Germany. He could always have done this at any moment throughout the summer, and the fact that he did not was proof either of his hesitation or his unpreparedness.

There were three parties in Germany at this time. One, far removed from Hitler's entourage and representing the mass of the people, was all for peace and still hopeful that Hitler's wizardry would enable him to achieve his aims without war. A second was equally all for war at any price. It was confident in the might of Germany's Army and Air Force and in her invulnerability to attack from the west. It was the party in closest touch with Hitler, and was constantly pressing him to go ahead regardless of the consequences, and arguing that in any case Britain either would not or could not fight. There was also a third party, which appeared really to believe that Britain's military preparations were being deliberately undertaken with a view to a preventive war and which consequently argued that war in 1939 was better for Germany than war in 1940 or later. I was repeatedly told by those in closest touch with him that Hitler himself professed to share this view. Those who have base motives themselves tend to attribute similar motives to others. It was not conviction in his case but empiricism which induced Hitler to represent to his army leaders that England was preparing for a preventive war. No other argument was more calculated to make them wholehearted partisans of the immediate war upon which, as the event proved, he was now, and had probably always been, bent.

Third Entr'acte

German propaganda throughout the summer illustrated the contradictory opinions of these two latter parties. Apart from the official press slogan of encirclement, which was calculated to rally the support of all Germans, however peacefully intentioned, persistent reports were being spread abroad on the one hand that Britain would never fight for Danzig and on the other that she was preparing to make war on Germany at the first opportunity favorable to herself, with a view to crushing her before she became too formidable as a political and economic rival. Both reports were skillfully designed to serve Hitler's purpose. It was hoped by the former to derive immediate profit, by undermining the confidence of the Poles and by shaking the belief of the United States and of the smaller powers in the determination of Britain to resist any further aggression. The second was not only intended to overcome any lingering hesitation on the part of the military leaders about the risks of war but destined for use, as it is now being used, when war did come to convince the German people that Hitler was not responsible, but that it had been forced upon him by a jealous Britain. Nothing was more typical of Hitler's elasticity than these maneuvers. If something did not serve one purpose, it could always be made to serve another; and every eventuality had its solution ready and prepared.

The war atmosphere was spreading apace. France, too, was now mobilizing; and the country was united behind M. Daladier. England was also girding up her loins; and in the middle of July extra fleet exercises had been announced, extra ships were placed in commission, and some naval reservists were called up. The underlying idea was to convince Hitler of our

readiness for war. It apparently failed to convince Ribbentrop, who to the last continued to assert that England would
never fight. I say "apparently" with intention, since I am still
unable to credit even Ribbentrop with being so obstinately
foolish as seriously to believe that England would fail to honor
her obligations. There is no shadow of doubt that he was all
the time saying so to Hitler and to everyone. But that he believed himself what he said seems to me incredible.

By 1939 Hitler had become so great in his own esteem
that he could afford to describe his Foreign Minister as the
second Bismarck. He often said so to others, and no one was
surer that it was so than Ribbentrop himself. But the world
had yet to be persuaded that it was so, and for this a war
was necessary. To insure war any means were legitimate. If
he could persuade Hitler, who possibly needed little persuading, to go to extremes by representing England as afraid of
war, all the better. Bismarck had provoked the 1870 war by
falsifying the Ems telegram, and Ribbentrop's idea of emulat-
ing Bismarck was to give his Führer and his countrymen a
false estimate of Britain's intentions. Was not his refusal to
give me, at the eleventh hour, as will be recounted later, the
text of the German proposals for a solution of the Danzig and
Corridor problem a similar maneuver on what he regarded as
Bismarckian lines? Was he not afraid lest war might be
averted if these proposals were seriously discussed? I cannot
say for certain, for the evidence is only circumstantial. But
it may well have been so; and the only other alternative was
a complete disregard of any other opinion except his own.
Goering once said to me, "What you don't like in Ribbentrop

Third Entr'acte

is his tenacity (*zähe*)." I told the Field Marshal that tenacity and stupidity were sometimes confused.

As for Hitler, the British naval measures were but grist to his mill. He was by now too intoxicated by success and by belief in his own greatness and infallibility to care what England did; and our military preparations merely reinforced his theory of the preventive war. On the other hand, our difficulties with Japan at Tientsin and the I.R.A. bomb outrages in England undoubtedly did serve greatly to fortify the arguments of those who were telling Hitler that Britain would be unable to go to war.

If you have a long armistice and nothing to show at the end of it, you will be in danger of war. Disraeli said something to that effect at the time of the Russo-Turkish conflict in 1878, and it was very applicable to the situation at the end of July. A state of half-war, amounting to a kind of armistice had existed in Europe since March; and by July we were drifting rapidly toward war. On August 4th the British Parliament was adjourned; and July, too, was over.

CHAPTER XII. *ACT IV: SCENE II:* WAR

ON the surface the situation had altered little during the month that was past, and the barometer still appeared to stand at "no change." But there were ominous signs of its dropping. There was, on the one hand, still no contact between Berlin and Warsaw, and the Polish and German Ambassadors at Berlin and Warsaw were sitting like Achilles in their tents. Mutual recrimination over the persecution of minorities was growing in volume, and Danzig was seething with rumors and excitement. On the other hand, the successful conclusion of the negotiations between London-Paris and Moscow seemed as far away as ever. It was true that the British and French military missions were now packing their trunks for their trip to Moscow; and, when they actually arrived there on August 11th, it should have been but natural to conclude that this meant that Stalin, while still seeking to drive the hardest bargain which he could in Russian interests, had finally made up his mind to co-operate in some form or other with the Western Powers in resistance to further German aggression. But against that had to be set the disturbing development that Moscow was now unblushingly showing the cloven hoof and was asking for a free hand in the Baltic States. Russia's real objective was thus becoming apparent;

and, with Germany secretly in the market, the scales were being heavily weighted against the Western Powers. They could not barter away the honor and freedom of small but independent countries, but Germany could.

It is to be hoped that someday light will be thrown on the question as to whether Stalin from the beginning was in collusion with Hitler with a view to spinning out his negotiations with us until Germany was ready to strike or whether both Germany and ourselves were merely his catspaws. I incline to the latter view myself, but it is mere guesswork, and I am prejudiced. From the outset I regarded the Russian negotiations as something which had to be attempted, but which lacked all sense of realities. I never believed in any effective or altruistic assistance being afforded by the Russians to the Poles. The most that I hoped was that, if the U.S.S.R., however half-heartedly, joined the peace front, Hitler would regard discretion as the better part of valor and come down on the side of peaceful discussion. But I always believed that Moscow's chief aim was to embroil Germany and the Western Powers in a common ruin and to emerge as the *tertius gaudens* of the conflict between them. This was, up to August, similarly the professed view of all Germans from Hitler downward who commented on our Russian negotiations.

I raised this point with Hitler himself when I saw him at Berchtesgaden on August 23rd. Ribbentrop was at Moscow on that day engaged in signing the Russo-German Treaty, and Hitler expatiated to me triumphantly on the value and great advantages of the new alliance, which he said was definite and permanent. I reminded him of his previous attitude toward the Soviets; expressed the opinion that he might find

Russia's friendship even more dangerous than her enmity; and added, speaking quite personally and on purely moral grounds, that, if an agreement had to be made with Moscow, for whom communism was now merely the cloak for intense nationalism and whose ulterior motives seemed to me highly suspicious, I had rather Germany made it than ourselves. Hitler was for a moment confused and taken aback. He retorted, however, that it was all our fault: it was we who had driven him into Russia's arms. But it was the answer of a man who was seeking to excuse himself.

The silence between Berlin and Warsaw and the lack of progress in our talks at Moscow were, however, not the only indications that the barometer might suddenly and rapidly fall. Apart from the deterioration of the situation at Danzig, the German Army was rapidly nearing the completion of its premobilization preparations. Three or four days at most would now suffice to put it on a full war footing. The arrangements for the Tannenberg celebrations on August 27th were proceeding systematically; and men and material were being steadily drafted eastward via Königsberg into East Prussia. Hitler would shortly be able to choose his own moment for precipitating the crisis, and I was more than ever certain that the last week of August would prove to be zero hour. Colonel Beck was at this time inquiring what instructions the British and French Governments proposed to give to their Ambassadors regarding the Nuremberg rally in September. The Polish Ambassador, whose position in Berlin had become entirely equivocal, would conform, he said, with whatever was decided as regards his British and French colleagues. When I was asked by the Foreign Office what my views were on this point, my answer was that it was still quite uncertain whether the 1939 Nuremberg party day would ever take place at all but that, if we did safely reach September, I should have no hesitation in gladly attending some at least of the celebrations there. But should we get to September in safety? That was the only consideration which was exercising my mind at that time.

As it was generally understood that Hitler would himself be present and would speak at the Tannenberg anniversary and as I feared that he would make that occasion the starting point of the crisis, I did my best to find out something about his intentions with regard to that speech. I could discover nothing; and, in fact, I was probably mistaken. Hitler's action was not to be dependent on a speech. The Tannenberg anniversary was merely cover for his military preparations against Poland, just as the military review for the Vienna anniversary in March had been for his Prague coup. His methods never varied in their essentials. Behind the façade of a plausible excuse Hitler was merely preparing once more for all eventualities and waiting for the favorable moment to take the initiative. Everything comes to him who waits and who schemes while waiting. It was the method best suited to his own temperament and his characteristic Austrian *Schlamperei* —particularly as plans for any and every eventuality were all ready at the German War Office and Air Ministry for executing at any moment and at lightning speed, whatever move Hitler might finally decide upon. The button was merely waiting for Hitler to press it.

The clouds were, in fact, gathering fast; and the first mutterings of the storm were heard on August 4th. On the same date that the British Parliament was adjourned the Polish customs inspectors at four posts on the Danzig-East Prussian frontier were notified that they would not be permitted thenceforward to carry out their duties. Alarmed at the gradual sapping of Polish rights and interests in the Free City, the Polish Commissioner General was at once instructed to deliver a note to the Danzig Senate warning the latter that the Polish Government would react in the strongest manner if the work of the inspectors were interfered with. The Senate subsequently denied that it had issued any official instructions to the effect alleged; but the German Government took the opportunity of what it described as the Polish ultimatum to address to Warsaw a peremptory verbal note, which was handed by the State Secretary to the Polish Chargé d'Affaires at Berlin on August 9th. The Polish Government was therein warned that any further note addressed to the Free City in the nature of an ultimatum or containing threats of reprisals would at once lead to an aggravation of Polish-German relations, the responsibility for which would fall on the Polish Government. The latter retorted on the following day by a similar verbal note denying the judicial right of Germany to intervene in the affairs between Poland and the Free City and warning in its turn the German Government that "any future intervention by the latter to the detriment of Polish rights and interests at Danzig would be considered as an act of aggression."

There is no doubt that the latter phrase was just the sort of pretext which Hitler required to justify his future actions in his own eyes and in those of his people. It enabled him once again to display his skill in turning events to suit his own

War

purpose. The Polish note of August 4th to the Danzig Senate had led to the provocative German verbal note to the Polish Government of August 9th; and the terms of the Polish reply of August 10th, and particularly the just-quoted sentence in it, provided Hitler with a motive for the indispensable brainstorm. Up to that week of verbal notes, public enemy No. 1 was still Great Britain and her alleged policy of encirclement. From that date the stories of Polish atrocities and references to German honor began to take the leading place in the German newspapers.

The 1938 stories of Czech atrocities against the German minority were rehashed up almost verbatim in regard to the Poles. Some foundation there must necessarily have been for a proportion of these allegations in view of the state of excitable tension which existed between the two peoples. Excess of zeal on the part of individuals and minor officials there undoubtedly was—but the tales of ill treatment and expropriation, castration and murder were multiplied a hundredfold. How far Hitler himself believed in the truth of these stories must be a matter for conjecture. Germans are prone in any case to convince themselves very readily of anything which they wish to believe. Certainly he behaved as if he did believe; and, even if one gives him the benefit of the doubt, these reports but served to inflame his resentment to the pitch which he or his extremists desired.

It is impossible to exaggerate the malign influence of Ribbentrop, Goebbels, Himmler, and company. It was consistently sinister, not so much because of its suggestiveness (since Hitler alone decided policy) nor because it merely applauded and encouraged, but because, if Hitler did appear to hesitate the extremists of the party at once proceeded to fabricate situations calculated to make Hitler embark upon courses which even he at times seems to have shrunk from risking. The simplest method of doing this was through the medium of a controlled press. Thus what happened in September of the year of Munich was repeated in the following March before the occupation of Prague, and again in August, before the attack on Poland. Dr. Goebbels' propaganda machine was the ready tool of these extremists, who were afraid lest Hitler should move too slowly in the prosecution of his own ultimate designs. By August 17th the anti-Polish campaign in the press was in full swing.

Before that date, however, two attempts were made, in different quarters, to pour oil upon the troubled waters. Firstly, in the middle of, and alarmed at the heated exchange of, notes between Germans and Poles, Dr. Burckhardt, the High Commissioner for the League of Nations for Danzig, flew to Berchtesgaden in a last effort to place the position in the Free City on a more satisfactory footing. He saw Hitler on August 11th. The latter was intransigent but vague. He was not yet in possession of the text of the Polish reply of August 10th, which had only been communicated to the Ministry for Foreign Affairs in Berlin on that date, or he would have been still more uncompromising. He was vague because he was awaiting news of a meeting which was taking place thirty miles away between his own Foreign Minister and that of his ally, Signor Mussolini, at the same time as he was seeing Dr. Burckhardt.

As I have mentioned earlier, the minatory language of Goebbels' political speech at Danzig at the end of June had already caused the Italian Government some uneasiness. Signor Mussolini had largely contributed to the preservation of peace at Munich in 1938, and he endeavored to play the same part again in 1939. His was the second of these attempts to pour oil on the troubled waters during that August; and he was to make yet a last one when September came. He unquestionably realized that Europe was drifting to war and that, unless something were done at once, there was a grave risk lest Italy might be dragged into the vortex. He accordingly made arrangements for his Foreign Minister, Count Ciano, to visit Ribbentrop at the castle which the latter had recently acquired near Salzburg.

It seems probable that Ciano there proposed, as he did in September, some form of international conference. Ten days earlier it might have been difficult for Hitler to refuse to take such a suggestion into serious consideration. But, once again, the fatality of the Greek-tragedy theme and Hitler's responsibility therefor was in striking evidence. The acid exchange of notes in Danzig and between Berlin and Warsaw had taken place on the very eve of Ciano's visit.

After seeing Ribbentrop on the 11th, Ciano had an interview with Hitler himself on August 12th. The latter had by that time received the text of the Polish verbal note of August 10th and was able to stage a scene whereby, by posing as the offended party, he could justify his refusal to accept any proposal for an international conference. Ciano's attempt at mediation having thus failed, he returned to Italy; and the Italian Ambassador at Berlin was hurriedly summoned to Rome. Signor Mussolini had been unable to divert Hitler from his plan to crush Poland, but he had at least provided against the automatic entry of Italy into war on Germany's side.

Hitler's carefully calculated patience was, in fact, by now exhausted; and on August 18th I telegraphed to Lord Halifax that I had come to the definite conclusion that, if peace were to be preserved, the present situation could not be allowed to continue and that the only alternative to war must be some immediate and mediatory action. In this connection I repeated a suggestion which I had made some time previously, namely, that a personal letter should be addressed by the Prime Minister to Hitler and be delivered by some emissary from London. Two days later I again telegraphed to the same effect and stated my conviction that Hitler had now finally decided upon some form of immediate action which would force the issue. I alluded to the increased German military strength which had been assembled in East Prussia under cover of the Tannenberg anniversary and again expressed my apprehension lest that celebration might prove the starting point for the action which Hitler contemplated. I have little doubt that such was Hitler's original and premeditated intention. A few days later, definite information, in fact, reached me that the long-expected but carefully concealed German military concentrations were already in progress and that instructions had been given to complete them by August 24th. One report actually mentioned August 25th as the date fixed for the German advance into Poland. I believe that the orders to that effect were actually signed by Hitler.

The truth undoubtedly was that by this time not only were Germany's military preparations sufficiently advanced for Hitler to take the initiative but also he could now definitely count upon Russia's complicity in his infamous designs against Poland. The exact date on which he was able to do the latter will be, for obvious reasons, one of the most interesting points which history will have to reveal to us. That and the price, moral and material, which Hitler paid for U.S.S.R. complicity. In any case, so far as the rest of the world was concerned, it was late in the evening of August 21st that the bombshell was exploded announcing that negotiations had been concluded for the signature of a Russo-German nonaggression pact and that Ribbentrop would fly to Moscow on August 23rd to sign it. The secret, which on the German side had been known to not more than a few persons, had been well kept. The first impression in Berlin was one of immense relief, partly at the removal of the dreaded Russian air menace, but more particularly because, in the minds of a public which had been led to believe by Goebbels' propaganda that the British negotiations with the U.S.S.R. were really encirclement with a view to a preventive war, the conclusion of a Russo-German nonaggression pact meant that peace was assured, since Britain would not, it was told, fight for Danzig or Poland without Russian aid. Once again the faith of the German people in the ability of their Führer to obtain his objective without war was reaffirmed. Its satisfaction was, however, short-lived and the disillusion considerable when it was realized that Britain's word to Poland did not depend on Russian support. Those who had fought the war of Nazism against communism were furthermore puzzled by this complete *volte-face*. The Nazi theory of racial purity had been discarded in March, and in August the second of its basic principles, namely anti-communism, was thus equally relegated to the scrap heap. To most Germans the old hereditary enemy is Russia, nor was their confidence greatly fortified by this exhibition of Russian ill faith towards the Western Democracies. Nevertheless, as a diplomatic coup, the Russo-German Pact was a strikingly successful and surprising one. It is devoutly to be hoped that it may prove, in respect of both parties to it, as Pyrrhic as are most diplomatic victories.

At the moment when Herr von Ribbentrop was preparing to fly to Moscow, I received shortly before 9 P.M. on August 22nd instructions to convey without delay a personal letter from the Prime Minister to Herr Hitler. The State Secretary was away at some airdrome seeing Ribbentrop off to Moscow; but I managed to establish contact with Herr Hewel, the liaison officer at headquarters between the Ministry for Foreign Affairs and the Chancellor. He was sympathetic and helpful, and later in the evening I got into touch with Weizsäcker himself. In the course of that night, after several telephonic communications, an interview was arranged for me with Hitler for the following day at Berchtesgaden; and I left Berlin at 9:30 A.M. on August 23rd accompanied by both Weizsäcker and Hewel in an airplane provided for me by the Ministry for Foreign Affairs. Once again on the way down, which took just over two hours, I was deeply conscious of the motif of the Greek tragedy. A week earlier my message might have made some impression, but now the whole position had been compromised by the Russian Treaty.

I reached Salzburg about midday and I had my first audience with Hitler at Berchtesgaden at 1 P.M. in the presence of Baron von Weizsäcker and Herr Hewel. For the purpose of reference I include the text of the Prime Minister's letter

War

and of Hitler's reply as Appendixes II and III at the end of this volume.

The three main points of the Prime Minister's letter were (1) insistence on the determination of His Majesty's Government to fulfill their obligations to Poland; (2) their readiness, if a peace atmosphere could be created, to discuss all the problems at issue between our two countries; and (3) their anxiety, during a period of truce, to see immediate direct discussion initiated between Germany and Poland in regard to the reciprocal treatment of minorities. Hitler's reply, which was no less uncompromising than I had anticipated, was to the effect that Great Britain's determination to support Poland could not modify his policy as expressed in the German verbal note to the Polish Government of August 9th; that he was prepared to accept even a long war rather than sacrifice German national interests and honor; and that, if Great Britain persisted in her own measures of mobilization, he would at once order the mobilization of the whole of the German forces.

At my first interview with him on that day Hitler was in a mood of extreme excitability. His language as regards the Poles and British responsibility for the Polish attitude was violent, recriminatory, and exaggerated. He referred, for instance, to 100,000 German refugees from Poland, a figure which was at least five times greater than the reality. Again I cannot say whether he was persuaded or persuaded himself of the reality of these figures. At my second interview, when he handed me his reply, he had recovered his calm but was not less obdurate. Everything was England's fault. She had encouraged the Czechs last year, and she was now giving a blank check to Poland. No longer, he told me, did he trust Mr. Chamberlain. He preferred war, he said, when he was fifty to when he was fifty-five or sixty. He had himself always sought and believed in the possibility of friendship with England. He now realized, he said, that those who had argued to the contrary had been right and nothing short of a complete change in British policy toward Germany could ever convince him• of any sincere British desire for good relations. My last remark to him was that I could only deduce from his language that my mission to Germany had failed and that I bitterly regretted it.

I flew back from Berchtesgaden to Berlin the same evening. I had, in fact, little hope that either the Prime Minister's letter or my own language to Hitler, however direct and straight-forward, would give him pause. The Russian Pact had, I felt, created in his opinion a situation which was favorable to his designs; and I believed his mind to be definitely made up. Though he spoke in a Neronic vein of his artistic tastes and of his longing to satisfy ,them, I derived the impression that the corporal of the last war was even more anxious to prove what he could do as a conquering generalissimo in the next. What the world or Germany might suffer was of no conse-quence so long as his lust to show what he as leader of Ger-many could do was satisfied. More than once he repeated to me that, if he had been Chancellor of Germany in 1914, she would never have lost that war in 1918.

Nevertheless, the visit to Berchtesgaden may after all have postponed the disaster for a week. Ribbentrop flew back to Germany with the signed Russo-German Agreement; and Hitler returned to Berlin the night of August 24th. I have, as I have mentioned earlier, some reason to believe—though I cannot confirm it—that the order for the German Army to advance into Poland was actually issued for the night of August 25th-26th. It is difficult otherwise to find justification for the various orders and arrangements which came into force on August 26th and 27th. In the afternoon of August 27th itself all telephone communication between Berlin and London and Paris was unexpectedly cut off for several hours. The celebrations at Tannenberg were cancelled on the 26th and the party rally at Nuremberg on August 27th; all naval, military, and air attachés at Berlin were refused permission to leave the city without prior authority's being obtained from the Ministry of War. All German airports were closed from August 26th, and the whole of Germany became a prohibited zone for all aircraft except the regular civil lines. All internal German air services were also suspended. Moreover, as from the 27th a system for the rationing of foodstuffs and other commodities throughout Germany came into force. That this latter and—for the public—depressing measure should have been adopted prior to the outbreak of war can scarcely be explained except on the assumption that war should actually have broken out on August 26th.

The fact may well be, as I imagine it was, that Hitler had had in consequence of the Prime Minister's letter one last hesitation and countermanded the orders to his army; whereas the other arrangements were allowed to proceed unchecked. But it was not the horrors of war or the thought of dead Germans which deterred him. He had unlimited confidence in the magnificent army and air force which he had re-created, and he was certainly not averse to putting them to the test so far as

Poland was concerned. In two months, he told me, the war in the east would be ended; and he would then, he said, hurl 160 divisions against the Western Front, if England were so unwise as to oppose his plans. His hesitation was due rather to one final effort to detach Britain from Poland. Be that as it may, at about 12:45 on August 25th I received a message to the effect that Hitler wished to receive me at the Chancellery at 1:30 P.M. At that meeting he made to me the verbal communication which forms Appendix IV of this volume.

Briefly put, Hitler's proposals therein dealt with two groups of questions: (a) the immediate necessity of a settlement of the dispute between Germany and Poland, and (b) an eventual offer of friendship or alliance between Germany and Great Britain. My interview with Hitler, at which Herr von Ribbentrop and Dr. Schmidt were also present, lasted on this occasion over an hour. The Chancellor spoke with calm and apparent sincerity. He described his proposals as a last effort, for conscience' sake, to secure good relations with Great Britain; and he suggested that I should fly to London myself with them. I told His Excellency that, while I was fully prepared to consider this course, I felt it my duty to tell him quite clearly that my country could not possibly go back on its word to Poland and that, however anxious we were for a better understanding with Germany, we could never reach one except on the basis of a negotiated settlement with Poland.

Whatever may have been the underlying motive of this final gesture on the part of the Chancellor, it was one which could not be ignored; and with Lord Halifax's consent, I flew to London early the following morning (August 26th), on a German plane which was courteously put at my disposal.

War

Two days were spent by His Majesty's Government in giving the fullest and most careful consideration to Hitler's message, and on the afternoon of August 28th I flew back to Berlin with their reply. (See Appendix V.) Therein, while the obligations of His Majesty's Government to Poland were reaffirmed, it was stated that the Polish Government were ready to enter into negotiations with the German Government for a reasonable solution of the matter in dispute on the basis of the safeguarding of Poland's essential interests and of an international guarantee for the settlement eventually arrived at. His Majesty's Government accordingly proposed that the next step should be the initiation of direct discussions between the Polish and German Governments on that basis and the adoption of immediate steps to relieve the tension in the matter of the treatment of minorities. Furthermore, His Majesty's Government undertook to use all their influence with a view to contributing toward a solution which might be satisfactory to both parties and which would, they hoped, prepare the way for the negotiation of that wider and more complete understanding between Great Britain and Germany which both countries desired. Finally, after a reference to a limitation of armaments, His Majesty's Government pointed out that, whereas a just settlement of the Polish question might open the way to world peace, failure to do so would finally ruin the hopes of a better understanding between our countries and might well plunge the whole world into war.

Could any reply have been more precise or straightforward? It made it easy for Hitler to avoid the calamity of war, if he had really wished to do so. It offered him the clear choice between, on the one hand, negotiations in which we guaranteed our good offices with a view to reaching a compromise satisfactory to both parties; and on the other, war in which we should fight on Poland's side, if Germany attacked her. It was the last chance but, with Russia's connivance, nothing was now going to satisfy Hitler except a fourth partition of Poland. In these circumstances I am still at a loss to understand why he postponed his aggression from August 26th to September 1st. What, indeed, was the underlying motive of the proposals which he handed to me on August 25th? He received the fairest possible reply from His Majesty's Government; yet it made no difference whatsoever to his plans. Why then did he make those proposals? Did he genuinely have a last hesitation at the thought of war? Or was it merely with the idea of hoodwinking his German people to believe that he had tried to the last to avoid war?

Before, however, continuing the record of events after my return to Berlin on the evening of August 28th, it is necessary to give a brief account of what had happened during my absence in London. At 5 P.M. on August 25th Hitler had received the French Ambassador and given him a letter for communication to M. Daladier. Its general tenor was a suggestion to France, with which Germany was stated to have no quarrel, to abstain from further support of Poland. It was a last attempt to detach France from both Poland and Great Britain. It received a dignified answer from the French Government, which was published two days later. Appeals for peace had also been made at this time both to the German and Polish Governments as well as to other powers by the Pope and the President of the United States of America. Though they received a favorable response from the Polish

Government, they received scant consideration from Germany. On the evening of August 25th the Anglo-Polish Pact had been signed in London. Though it had been under negotiation for several months, its signature gave great offense to Hitler, who was at first inclined to regard it as the reply of His Majesty's Government to his message to them. His immediate retort was the announcement on the morning of August 26th that Herr Forster had been appointed Reichs-oberhaupt, or Head of the State of Danzig. At the same time the German concentrations against Poland began to reach their final stage.

Thereafter there was a lull for two days pending my return to Germany with the reply of His Majesty's Government. I left London at 5 P.M. on August 28th, and at 10:30 P.M. that evening I was received by Herr Hitler at the Reichschancery and handed to him the British reply, together with a German translation. Hitler was once again friendly and reasonable and appeared to be not dissatisfied with the answer which I had brought to him. He observed, however, that he must study it carefully and would give me a written reply the next day. Our conversation lasted for well over an hour, and it was nearly midnight before I arrived back at the Embassy. It was, I think, the only one of my interviews with Hitler at which it was I who did most of the talking. Possibly for this reason there is no account of it in the German White Paper which was published after the outbreak of war. I used every argument which I could think of to induce him to see reason and to come down on the side of peace. The choice, I pointed out, lay with him. Peaceful negotiation would mean the friendship of Britain, which he was always telling me that he desired: on the other hand an aggression against Poland meant war. I even appealed to his sentiment by quoting a passage from a book, which I happened to know that he had read, about the days in which England had fought side by side with Germany against Napoleon and about the ideas which the Germans had then held about honor and the given word. Blücher, when hurrying to the support of Wellington at Waterloo, had urged his tired troops on in the following words, "Forward, my children, forward; I have given my word to my brother Wellington, and you cannot wish me to break it." Thereafter the old Field Marshal was always known in England as he was in Germany, as "Marshal Forward." I reminded Hitler of this story. He may have been momentarily impressed, but it availed nothing.

I might mention, incidentally, that both on that evening and the next, when I visited Hitler again and was handed his reply, nothing was left undone to enhance or to impress me with the solemnity of the occasion. From the Embassy to the Reichschancery is a mere three or four hundred yards; but, as Berlin was undergoing a week of trial black-outs, the Wilhelmstrasse was in complete darkness. A considerable but quite expressionless crowd had collected in the square, opposite the entrance to the courtyard into which my car had to drive. Though the people were silent, they gave me no sensation of hostility. Up to the bitter end that remained the attitude of the Berliners. A guard of honor was drawn up in the courtyard to the right of the main door, and I was received with a roll of drums. Dr. Meissner and Brückner, Hitler's faithful A.D.C. and bodyguard, were awaiting me on the doorstep. The former remarked to me that he was glad to see that I was wearing a buttonhole. I had always worn a dark red carnation in Berlin except during the three critical days of the week which preceded Munich. When I was seeing Horace Wilson off at the Tempelhof on his return to London during that week, I had been asked by some German newspaper correspondents why I had forgotten my buttonhole. I told them that I had not forgotten, but that I considered it to be inappropriate at a moment of such grave crisis. The story had got around, and I regarded Meissner's remark as significant. Was Hitler then preoccupied as to what the answer of His Majesty's Government would be? But it was probably merely Meissner's own wishful thinking or preoccupation. I wore my carnation again the next day; but, that time, as I was leaving after my interview, I told Meissner that I feared that I should never wear one again in Germany.

That first evening, however, the reply which I was bearing from His Majesty's Government made it so easy for Hitler to avoid the calamity of war that I could still afford to hope for the best. Though he had been noncommittal, he had been calm and even conciliatory.

Such information, indeed, as reached me during the course of the following day tended to represent the atmosphere as well disposed and to foreshadow readiness on Hitler's part to open direct negotiations with the Poles. I was consequently all the less prepared for the reception which I got on being summoned to the Reichschancery again at 7:15 on the evening of August 29th. Perhaps I should have been, as the German midday press had reported the alleged murder of six German nationals in Poland; and this story, which was probably fabricated by the extremists in fear lest Hitler was weakening, together with the news of the Polish general mobilization, was just the kind of thing which was most calculated to upset him. I immediately sensed in any case a distinctly more uncompromising attitude than the previous evening on Hitler's part when he handed me the answer (see Appendix VI) which he had promised me.

Therein Germany's demands were declared to be the revision of the Versailles Treaty by means of the return of Danzig and the Corridor to Germany and the security for the lives of German national minorities in the rest of Poland. In reply to the British proposals for direct German-Polish negotiations and for an international guarantee of any settlement, it was stated, firstly, that the German Government, in spite of skepticism as to the prospect of their success, accepted direct negotiations with Poland, solely out of a desire to insure lasting friendship with Britain; but, secondly, that, in the event of any modifications of territory, the German Government could neither undertake nor participate in any guarantee without first consulting the U.S.S.R. I read the note through carefully, while Hitler and Ribbentrop watched me; and, in spite of the ominous reference to Moscow, I made no comment till I reached the phrase at the end of it in which it was stated that "the German Government counted upon the arrival in Berlin of a Polish Emissary with full powers on the following day, Wednesday, the 30th August." I pointed out to His Excellency that this phrase sounded very much like an ultimatum (*"hatte den Klang eines Ultimatums"*). This was strenuously and heatedly denied by Hitler himself, supported by Ribbentrop. It was a case of the "dictate" and "memorandum" of Godesberg over again. According to Hitler this sentence merely emphasized the urgency of the moment, not only on account of the risk of incidents when two mobilized armies were standing opposite one another but also when Germans were being massacred in Poland. In this latter connection His Excellency asserted that "I did not care how many Germans were being slaughtered in Poland." This gratuitous impugnment of the humanity of His Majesty's Government and of myself provoked a heated retort on my part; and the remainder of the interview was of a somewhat stormy character. It was closed, however, by a brief and, in my opinion, quite honest—since it represented his feelings at the moment—harangue on Hitler's part in regard to the genuineness of his constant endeavor to win Britain's friendship, of his respect for the British Empire, and of his liking for Englishmen generally.

Nor was Hitler's constant repetition of his desire for good relations with Great Britain conscious hypocrisy. He combined, as I fancy many Germans do, admiration for the British race with envy of their achievements and hatred of their opposition to Germany's excessive aspirations. It is no exaggeration to say that he assiduously courted Great Britain, both as representing the aristocracy and most successful of the Nordic races and as constituting the only seriously dangerous obstacle to his own far-reaching plan of German domination in Europe. This is evident in *Mein Kampf;* and, in spite of what he regarded as the constant rebuffs which he received from the British side, he persisted in his endeavors up to the last moment. Geniuses are strange creatures; and Herr Hitler, among other paradoxes, was a mixture of long-headed calculation and violent and arrogant impulse provoked by resentment. The former drove him to seek Britain's friendship and the latter finally into war with her. Moreover, he believed his resentment to be entirely justified. He failed to realize why his military-cum-police tyranny should be repugnant to British ideals of individual and national freedom and liberty or why he should not be allowed a free hand in Central and Eastern Europe to subjugate smaller and, as he regards them, inferior peoples to superior German rule and culture. He believed he could buy British acquiescence in his own extensive schemes by offers of alliance with, and guarantees for, the British Empire. Such preliminary acquiescence was indispensable to the success of his ambitions, and he worked unceasingly to secure it. His great mistake was his complete failure to understand the inherent British sense of morality, humanity, and freedom.

I left the Reichschancery that evening filled with the gloomiest forebodings. Hitler, while reiterating his desire for British friendship, had asserted that he did not intend to sacrifice therefor what he called vital German interests. When I had protested against the time limit for the arrival of a Polish plenipotentiary, he had clearly indicated that his general staff were pressing for a decision. "My soldiers," he said, "are asking me 'Yes' or 'No.' " His army and his air force were ready to strike and had been since August 25th. They were telling him that one week had already been lost, and that they could not afford to lose another, lest the rainy season in Poland be added to their enemies. (When I passed through the anteroom on my way back to my car, it was full of Army officers, Keitel and Brauschitsch among them. Meeting them there did not tend to dispel my apprehensions.) I had asked Hitler what he

War

meant by "vital German interests." He had referred me to his reply, which stated that the German Government would immediately draw up proposals acceptable to themselves for a solution of the Polish question and would place these at the disposal of the British Government before the arrival of the Polish negotiator.

Everything seemed, therefore, to depend on two things: the nature of those proposals and the immediate consent of the Polish Government to the dispatch of a negotiator, or plenipotentiary, to Berlin. The first did not depend on me, but I endeavored to insure the latter by asking the Polish Ambassador that evening to call on me while I was drafting my telegrams to London, by giving him an account of the German reply and of my conversation with Hitler, and by impressing upon him the need for immediate action. I had never been under any illusion as to Poland's capacity to resist for more than a brief period Germany's highly mechanized Army and overwhelmingly superior Air Force. I never concealed this opinion from my Polish colleague; and I implored him, in Poland's own interests, to urge his Government to nominate without any delay someone to represent them in the proposed negotiations at Berlin. But I was equally under no illusions as to what this meant, and I telegraphed at the same time to Lord Halifax to the effect that Hitler had made up his mind to achieve his ends, by a parade of strength, if that sufficed, but by the use of force, if it did not. "The only result," I added, "can only be either war, or once again victory for him by a display of force and consequent encouragement to pursue the same course again next year or the year after."

Failure of a Mission

His Majesty's Government lost no time in replying to the German note of August 29th; and by the early hours of the morning of August 30th (4 A.M.) I had already conveyed to the Ministry for Foreign Affairs an interim answer to the effect that the note would be carefully considered, but observing that it would be unreasonable to expect that His Majesty's Government could produce a Polish representative at Berlin within twenty-four hours and that the German Government must not count on this.

Later in the course of the day, I received three further messages for communication to the German Government. The first was a personal one from the Prime Minister to the Chancellor notifying the latter of the representations made to Warsaw in regard to the avoidance of frontier incidents and begging the German Government to take similar precautions. (I transmitted this in the afternoon to its destination in a personal letter to the Minister for Foreign Affairs.) The second similarly notified the German Government of our counsels of restraint to Poland and asked for reciprocation on Germany's part. The third pointed out that the demand that a Polish representative with full powers must come to Berlin to receive the German proposals was unreasonable and suggested that the German Government should follow the normal procedure of inviting the Polish Ambassador to call and of handing him the German proposals for transmission to Warsaw with a view to arrangements being made for the conduct of negotiations. This last communication also reminded the German Government that it had promised to communicate its detailed proposals to His Majesty's Government, who undertook, if these offered a reasonable basis, to do their best in Warsaw to facilitate negotiations. The good intentions of His Majesty's Government were, in fact, patently clear; and, had Herr Hitler honestly desired or preferred a pacific settlement, all the arrangements to that end seemed to be in full swing.

I had arranged to see the Minister for Foreign Affairs at 11:30 P.M. to make these communications to him. Shortly before the appointed time I received in code the considered reply of His Majesty's Government to the German note of August 29th. I was accordingly obliged to ask that my meeting with Ribbentrop should be postponed for half an hour in order to give me the time to have this last message deciphered. In the concluding passages of that reply His Majesty's Government, while fully recognizing the need for speed in the initiation of discussions, urged that during the negotiations no aggressive military operations should take place on either side. They further expressed their confidence that they could secure such an undertaking from the Polish Government, if the German Government would give similar assurances. They also suggested a temporary *modus vivendi* at Danzig, such as would obviate the risk of incidents which might render German-Polish relations still more difficult.

I saw Ribbentrop at exactly midnight, before which hour the German Government had ostensibly counted on the arrival of a Polish emissary at Berlin. I say "ostensibly" since it seems hardly possible that it cannot have occurred either to Hitler or his Minister for Foreign Affairs that it was utterly unreasonable to expect a Polish plenipotentiary to present himself at Berlin without even knowing in advance the basis of the proposals about which he was expected to negotiate.

Failure of a Mission

The Army leaders had been representing to their Führer that even twenty-four hours' delay involved the risk of bad weather's holding up the rapidity of the German advance into Poland; but, even so, in view of what now occurred, it is difficult not to draw the conclusion that the proposals in themselves were but dust to be thrown in the eyes of the world with a view to its deception and were never intended to be taken seriously by the German Government itself.

Be that as it may, it is probable that Hitler's mood in the hour when he had to decide between peace or war was not an amiable one. It was reflected in Ribbentrop, whose reception of me that evening was from the outset one of intense hostility, which increased in violence as I made each communication in turn. He kept jumping to his feet in a state of great excitement, folding his arms across his chest and asking if I had anything more to say. I kept replying that I had; and, if my own attitude was no less unfriendly than his own, I cannot but say in all sincerity that I had every justification for it. When I told him that I would not fail to report his comments and remarks to my Government, he calmed down a little and said that they were his own and that it was for Herr Hitler to decide. As for inviting the Polish Ambassador to come to see him, such a course would, he indignantly said, be utterly unthinkable and intolerable.

After I had finished making my various communications to him, he produced a lengthy document which he read out to me in German or rather gabbled through to me as fast as he could, in a tone of the utmost scorn and annoyance. Of the sixteen articles in it I was able to gather the gist of six or seven, but it would have been quite impossible to guarantee even the comparative accuracy of these without a careful study of the text itself. When he had finished, I accordingly asked him to let me read it for myself. Herr von Ribbentrop, who always mistook rudeness for strength, refused categorically; threw the document with a contemptuous gesture on the table; and said that it was now out of date ("*überholt*"), since no Polish emissary had arrived at Berlin by midnight. I observed that in that case the sentence in the German note of August 29th to which I had drawn his and his Führer's attention on the preceding evening had, in fact, constituted an ultimatum in spite of their categorical denials. Ribbentrop's answer to that was that the idea of an ultimatum was a figment of my own imagination and creation.

I do not desire to stress the unpleasant nature of this interview. The hour was a critical one, and Ribbentrop's excitability at such a moment was understandable. It seemed to me, however, that he was willfully throwing away the last chance of a peaceful solution; and it was difficult to remain indifferent when faced with such a calamity. I still believe, as I did at the time, that Ribbentrop's exhibition of irascibility and bad manners that evening was partly due to the fact that he suspected that I had purposely postponed calling on him till midnight, i.e. until the hour by which the ultimatum, which he and Hitler had assured me was no ultimatum, for the arrival of a Polish plenipotentiary had expired.

Yet in the German note of August 29th it had been stated that their proposals would, if possible, be placed at the disposal of the British Government before the arrival of that plenipotentiary. Why then should Ribbentrop have himself waited till after midnight before making the pretense of reading them to me. But, above all, why did he refuse even then to hand them to me? Not even Hitler could honestly have expected the Polish Government to appoint a plenipotentiary to discuss proposals in regard to which it was completely in the dark. Did Ribbentrop and his master not wish them to be communicated to the Polish Government lest the latter might in fact agree to negotiate? It is the only conclusion which one can draw from this episode, since it might have made all the difference to the instructions given to M. Lipski on the following day if the Polish Government had been cognizant of the official text of the German proposals. In themselves and taken at their face value, they were not unreasonable and might well have served as a basis for negotiation. That is why one can only assume that Ribbentrop did not wish them to be discussed, and his attitude that night was not only one of ill manners, but also of ill faith. He endeavored to conceal this later by a deliberate distortion of the truth. In the note which was handed to me by Weizsäcker the next evening and which contained at last the text of those proposals (see Appendix VII) it was stated that Herr von Ribbentrop had given the British Ambassador on the occasion of the presentation of the last British note precise information as to the text of the German proposals which would be regarded as a basis of negotiation, etc. The German White Paper on the origins of the war repeats this complete perversion of the actual facts. None of the points at issue in the memorandum were discussed at all. Let those who wish to form their own opinion as to what Ribbentrop euphemistically describes as "precise information," read for themselves the English translation of the text of those proposals. Let them imagine that text being read to them in German, so fast as literally to be unintelligible in any language. Did Ribbentrop have such a high opinion of my memorizing faculty as to think that, after listening to his jabber of words, I could be in a position to give either His Majesty's Government or the Polish Government an authoritative account of the exact sense of a long and complicated text? Yet that apparently was what Ribbentrop was pleased to call "precise information" about a document of vital importance, upon which peace or war depended and which consequently needed to be not only read but studied with the utmost care and circumspection.

I returned to His Majesty's Embassy that night convinced that the last hope for peace had vanished. I nevertheless saw the Polish Ambassador at 2 A.M., gave him an objective and studiously moderate account of my conversation with Ribbentrop, mentioned the cession of Danzig and the plebiscite in the Corridor as the two main points in the German proposals, stated that, so far as I could gather, they were not on the whole too unreasonable, and suggested to him that he might recommend to his Government that they should propose at once a meeting between Field Marshals Smigly-Rydz and Goering. I felt obliged to add that I could not conceive of the success of any negotiations if they were conducted with Ribbentrop.

Though M. Lipski undertook to make this suggestion to his Government, it would by then probably have been in any case too late. There was, in fact, for Herr Hitler only one conceivable alternative to brute force, and that was that a Polish plenipotentiary should humbly come to him, after the manner of Dr. Schuschnigg or President Hacha, and sign on the dotted line to the greater glory of Adolf Hitler. And even that must happen at once, since his army was impatiently asking "Yes" or "No."

Early the next morning I obtained from another source in touch with Goering more definite, if unauthorized, details of the German proposals; and these I at once communicated through the Counselor of His Majesty's Embassy to the Polish Ambassador, who spent that morning on the telephone to Warsaw. It was M. Lipski's last chance to telephone; for, when evening came, the German Government saw to it that that and all other methods of communication with the Polish Government were denied to him. His Majesty's Government, too, were using all their influence at Warsaw; and about the middle of the day I transmitted to the Ministry for Foreign Affairs a further message from His Majesty's Government to the German Government notifying them that the Polish Government were taking steps to establish contact with them through the Polish Ambassador at Berlin and asking them to agree to an immediate provisional *modus vivendi* at Danzig, for which purpose M. Burckhardt was suggested as intermediary. To this communication I never received any reply. There was, however, a further delay of some twelve hours. The Polish Government had, it was announced, authorized their Ambassador to establish contact with Ribbentrop; and Hitler waited to learn what message M. Lipski would bring. The question, in fact, was whether his qualifications would be those of a plenipotentiary empowered by the Polish Government, in spite of its ignorance of the exact terms of the German proposals, to conduct and conclude negotiations or not. On no other terms was Hitler prepared to postpone action. His army was ready, and Poland must be taught a lesson. She must crawl or get her whipping.

During the day there had been much activity on the part of Field Marshal Goering. I think that Goering himself would have preferred a peaceful solution, but in matters such as these it was Hitler's decision which alone counted; and, whatever Goering might feel, he was merely the loyal and submissive servant of his master. Moreover, as I have already described, he had come down definitely on the side of peace a year before; and it might have been difficult for him to adopt this course a second time. He invited me, however, to come to see him that afternoon; and I did so at 5 P.M. in the company of Sir G. Ogilvie-Forbes. Inasmuch as I had heard that the text of the proposals which Ribbentrop had refused to give me was to be broadcast on the radio that evening, my first remark was to point out to the Field Marshal that this procedure would probably and finally wreck the last prospect of peace and to beg him to do his utmost to prevent their publication. Goering's reply was that he could not intervene and that the German Government felt obliged to broadcast their proposals to the world in order to prove their "good faith."

Instead he talked for the best part of two hours of the iniquities of the Poles and of Hitler's and his own desire for friendship with England and of the benefit to the world in general and the advantage to England in particular of such a friendship. It was a conversation which led nowhere; and I could not help feeling that his remarks, which from his point of view were perfectly genuine but which I had heard often before, were chiefly intended for the edification of his listeners. I augured the worst from the fact that he was in a position at such a moment to give me so much of his time. He had a few days before been made president of the new German Defense Council for the Reich (or War Cabinet); and he could scarcely have afforded at such a moment to spare time in conversation, if it did not mean that everything, down to the last detail, was now ready for action.

Incidentally the composition of that council was evidence of Hitler's acumen. He had selected for it all the most respectable of the Nazi leaders, such as Herr Frick, Dr. Lammers, Dr. Funk, who might be counted upon, with Field Marshal Goering, himself the most popular of them all with the general public, to inspire the confidence of the German people. The worst extremists and the most unpopular with the people were omitted from it. To them was to be confided the less enviable task of dealing with the neutrals, of organizing the interior, and of ruthlessly repressing any internal discontent. My general impression of this last talk with Goering was, in fact, that it constituted a final but forlorn effort on his part to detach Britain from the Poles. Nevertheless, the Field Marshal seemed sincere when, having been called to the telephone, he returned to tell us that M. Lipski was on his way to see Ribbentrop. He seemed relieved and to hope that, provided contact was only established, war might after all prove unnecessary. The meeting between the Polish Ambassador proved, however, quite futile. M. Lipski stated that he was acting solely in his capacity as an ambassador without plenary powers to discuss or to negotiate and handed to the Minister for Foreign Affairs a brief communication to the effect that the Polish Government were weighing favorably the proposal of His Majesty's Government for direct discussion and that a formal answer in this matter would be communicated to the German Government in the immediate future. He did not ask for the German proposals, and Ribbentrop did not offer to give them to him. Their meeting lasted but a few minutes. When, after his interview, the Polish Ambassador attempted once more to telephone to his Government, he found that it was no longer possible for him to do so. Hitler had, in fact, chosen his moment to precipitate the conflict. He did not want direct negotiations with the Poles. It was zero hour.

Earlier in the course of that day I had rung up the State Secretary and, after reminding him that the German Government had promised to communicate their proposals to His Majesty's Government, and how helpless I was without the authorized text of them, had asked him to suggest to Ribbentrop once more that they should be sent to me. I heard no more from Weizsäcker until late in the evening, when on returning from my call on Goering, I received a message asking me to call upon him at 9:15 P.M. Similar messages had been sent to the French Ambassador and to the United States Chargé d'Affaires, giving them appointments for 9:30 and 9:45 respectively. I accordingly called on Weizsäcker at the hour named and received from him the text of the proposals, together with the explanatory statement to which I have already referred. As both these documents were being broadcast at 9 P.M., I asked the State Secretary what was the point now of making these communications to me. Weizsäcker observed that he was merely carrying out his instructions and that he could make no further statement to me. I could only infer from this reply that Hitler had taken his final decision. I therefore drafted that night a telegram to London to the effect that it would be quite useless for me to make any further suggestions since they would now only be outstripped by events and that the only course remaining to us was to show our inflexible determination to resist force by force.

In point of fact the advance into Poland had been ordered immediately after Lipski's meeting with Ribbentrop, and in the early hours of September 1st without any declaration of war the German Army crossed the frontier, and the German Air Force proceeded to bomb the Polish airdromes and lines of communications.

In accordance with Hitler's usual technique everything was then done by the German authorities to prove to the German public that it was the Poles who had been the aggressors instead of the opposite. Cynical notices were communicated at 6 A.M. to His Majesty's Embassy notifying me that the Bay of Danzig was closed both to navigation and to flying in view of the possibility of military operations "against hostile attacks by Polish naval forces or by Polish aircraft." Goering also sent me a message to say that the Poles had begun the war by blowing up the bridge across the Vistula at Dirchau; while Hitler himself issued a proclamation to the German Army declaring that the Polish state had refused the settlement which he offered and had appealed to arms, that the Germans in Poland were being persecuted by a bloody terror, and that the Poles were no longer willing to respect the frontier of the German Reich. Every German newspaper repeated the lie that it was the Poles who had begun the fighting. Finally at 10:30 A.M. Hitler met the Reichstag, which had been summoned for that hour, and similarly announced

to the assembled members that he had been "forced to take
up arms in defense of the Reich." It was a deliberate travesty
of the facts, and never can there have been or ever be a case
of more premeditated and carefully planned aggression.

Late that same evening I was instructed by Lord Halifax
to notify the German Government that the latter by their
action had created conditions which called for the imple-
mentation by the Governments of the United Kingdom and
France of their undertaking to come to Poland's assistance
and that, unless His Majesty's Government received satisfactory assurances that the German Government had suspended
all aggressive action and would be prepared to withdraw its
forces from Polish territory, His Majesty's Government
would, without hesitation, fulfill their obligations to Poland.
I was instructed at the same time to request an immediate
reply, and was authorized, if asked, to explain that this communication was in the nature of a warning, and was not to be
considered as an ultimatum.

I handed this communication in writing to the Minister for
Foreign Affairs at 9:30 P.M. that evening. Ribbentrop received
it without other comment than that the sole blame rested on
the Poles, that it was they who had first mobilized and who
had first invaded Germany with troops of the Regular Army.
He made no inquiry as to the exact nature of the communication but merely said that he must submit it to the Führer.
I told him that I realized that this would be necessary and
that I should be available at whatever hour he might be in a
position to give me the Reichschancellor's reply. The French
Ambassador, who had been instructed to make a similar com-

munication, did so immediately after me and received a reply on the same lines.

Earlier in the afternoon of that day, I had, in accordance with Lord Halifax's instructions, officially requested the United States Chargé d'Affaires to be good enough to take charge of British interests in the event of war. All ciphers and confidential documents were burned, and the whole of the staff left their normal residences and were concentrated in the Adlon Hotel next door or in the Embassy itself. These and many other arrangements were carried out with a maximum of efficiency and a minimum of confusion, which did the utmost credit to the organization and competency of the very excellent staff of His Majesty's Embassy. The chief responsibility for this rested upon Mr. Holman, as head of the Chancery.

September 2nd was a day of suspense. The Poles were, it was reported, putting up a brave resistance in the face of surprise and overwhelming numbers, in spite of the vast superiority of the German Air Force and mechanized forces. No reply was received from the German Government throughout the day to the British and French warnings.

In the meantime the Italian Government was making one last effort to save the situation. The Italian Ambassador had come to see me at midday on his way to the Ministry for Foreign Affairs. Signor Attolico told me that he must know one thing immediately: Was the communication which I had made the previous evening to Herr von Ribbentrop an ultimatum or not? I told His Excellency that I had been authorized to tell the Minister for Foreign Affairs if he had asked me—which he had not done—that it was not an ultimatum but a warning. I mentioned to Signor Attolico that I understood that the Italian Government were putting forward a suggestion for the cessation of hostilities and the immediate summoning of a conference of the interested powers. In this connection I said that I felt bound to express the opinion that such a proposal would never be entertained unless at the same time all the German troops were withdrawn from Polish territory. I urged him to press for this. The Ambassador retorted that I could not speak for my Government. I admitted that fact, but said that I could not imagine the possibility of ourselves, and much less of the Poles, agreeing to any lesser course.

There had never been, in fact, for Hitler but the two solutions: the use of force or the achievement of his aims by the display of force. "If you wish to obtain your objectives by force, you must be strong; if you wish to obtain them by negotiation, you must be stronger still." That was a remark which he made to a foreign statesman who visited him that year, and it expresses in the most concise possible form the Hitler technique. It was exactly what he had displayed in September, 1938. He was no more bluffing then than he was bluffing in August, 1939. The fear of a war on two fronts, with Russia hostile or at least unfriendly, might possibly have deterred him and his military advisers from action against Poland. There was no Eastern Front to give him cause for hesitation in 1938, and he could have counted then on Hungarian as well as Polish support in his nefarious plans for the dismemberment of Czechoslovakia. But for Munich he would without a shadow of doubt have invaded that country on September 29th that year, just as surely as he invaded Poland on September 1st the next, and war for us would have come eleven months earlier. In both cases the methods employed were identical: the gradual mobilization of the German Army over a period of months and its secret concentration at the appointed positions, whence the advance could begin at almost any moment and within a very few hours.

Possibly if Hitler had secured his objectives by this display of force, he might have been content for the moment, with all the additional prestige which another bloodless success would have procured for him with his own people. But it would only have been to start again once the world had recovered from the shock, and even his own people were beginning to be tired of these repeated crises. Millions of Germans had begun to long for a more peaceful existence. Guns instead of butter were becoming more and more unpopular except with the younger generation, and Hitler may well have wondered what might happen to his Nazi revolution if its momentum were allowed to stop. Moreover, the financial and economic position of Germany was such that things could scarcely continue as they were without some form of explosion, internal or external. Of the two alternatives the most attractive from the point of view of his growing personal ambitions and those of the clique which was nearest to him was war. So he chose war.

It is scarcely credible that he or Ribbentrop would have acted as they did if bloody war, rather than a bloodless victory, had not seemed the fairer prospect for them. As with Benes, so it was now with Beck. Hitler had always meant to teach the latter a lesson for what he regarded as the base ingratitude of the Poles in refusing the "generous" demands which he had made to them in March. His only maneuvers since that date were with the object of creating circumstances favorable to his plans or of inducing Britain and France to abandon their Polish ally and to leave him a free hand in Central and Eastern Europe. To this end, encouraged by Ribbentrop, he worked unceasingly. One of Hitler's greatest drawbacks was that, except for two official visits to Italy, he had never traveled abroad. For his knowledge of British mentality he consequently relied on Ribbentrop as a former Ambassador to Britain, who spoke both French and English and who had spent some years in Canada and whom he regarded as a man of the world. But Ribbentrop's counsels in regard to England were consistently false.

Even the most absolute dictator is susceptible to the influence of his surroundings. Nevertheless, Hitler's decisions, his calculations, and his opportunisms were his own. As Goering once said to me, "When a decision has to be taken, none of us count more than the stones on which we are standing. It is the Führer alone who decides." If anything did count, it was the opinion of his military advisers. It was they, I fancy, who told Hitler that further delay would be fatal lest the seasonal bad weather in Poland might upset their calculations for her swift overthrow. The Army grudged him even the week between August 25th and September 1st which his last attempt to secure British neutrality had cost it.

Yet, even·so, the advice of his soldiers was probably merely cover for the prosecution of Hitler's own plans. His impatience and precipitate action on the last day of August can scarcely have been other than premeditated. All through the summer he had been waiting on events to turn in his favor and had been making his preparations to seize the opportunity when it was offered to him. The Russian Pact appeared to give him the advantage which he was seeking; and thereafter there was no time to lose if mud was not to be added to Poland's allies. When, therefore, the Polish Government delayed forty-eight hours in sending its plenipotentiary to beg for terms at Berlin, and even then sent only an ambassador without plenary powers, in spite of the expressed readiness of Poland to enter into direct negotiations, Hitler finally made up his mind not to keep his army waiting any longer.

Late in the afternoon of September 2nd I communicated to the State Secretary for the information of the German Government the verbatim report of the Prime Minister's speech in the House of Commons on that date. Therein Mr. Chamberlain stated that, while His Majesty's Government could not agree to the proposal of the Italian Government for a conference while Poland was being subjected to invasion, they would be willing, if the German forces were withdrawn from Polish territory, to regard the position as being the same as before the forces had crossed the frontier. It was the last chance of avoiding the great catastrophe of war at the last minute, but the German Government remained silent.

In the early hours (4 A.M.) of September 3rd I was accordingly instructed by His Majesty's Government to arrange for a meeting with the Minister for Foreign Affairs at 9 A.M. There was some difficulty in establishing contact with the Ministry at that hour, but I was finally informed that Dr. Schmidt was authorized by the Minister to accept on His Excellency's behalf any communication which I might make to him. I accordingly handed to Dr. Schmidt precisely at

War

9 A.M. the final ultimatum from His Majesty's Government, pointing out that over twenty-four hours had elapsed since I had requested an immediate answer to our warning communication of September 1st. that since then the attacks on Poland had been intensified, and that, unless satisfactory assurances were received by His Majesty's Government before 11 A.M., British summer time, of the suspension of all aggressive action against Poland and of the withdrawal of the German forces from that country, a state of war would exist between our two countries as from that hour. Dr. Schmidt received this communication and undertook to deliver it immediately to his chief. As no reply from the German Government was vouchsafed by 11 A.M., the German Representative in London was informed in due course at that hour that a state of war existed between Britain and Germany. By ten minutes past 11 A.M. every British consular officer in Germany had been advised by the staff of His Majesty's Embassy at Berlin that this was the case.

Shortly after 11 A.M. I received a final message from Ribbentrop asking me to call upon him at once. I did so at 11:30; and he lost no time in giving me on this occasion a lengthy document to read beginning with a refusal on the part of the German people to accept any demands in the nature of an ultimatum made by the British Government and stating that any aggressive action by England would be answered with the same weapons and the same form. The rest of the document was pure propaganda, destined presumably for home and neutral consumption, with a view to attempting to prove to the German people and the world generally that it was Britain alone who was to blame for everything which had happened.

My only comment on reading this completely false representation of events was: "It would be left to history to judge where the blame really lay." Ribbentrop's answer was to the effect that history had already proved the facts and that nobody had striven harder for peace and good relations with England than Herr Hitler had done. His last remark to me was that he wished me well personally, to which I could only reply that I deeply regretted the failure of all my efforts for peace but that I bore no grudge against the German people. Thereafter I saw no further German official except the member of the Protocol who accompanied our special train as far as Rotterdam. My last official communication to the German Government was a note which I presented on the instructions of His Majesty's Government inquiring whether the German Government would observe the provisions of the Geneva Protocol of 1925 prohibiting the use in war of asphyxiating, poisonous, or other gases and of bacteriological methods of warfare—the German Government later replied to this through the Swiss Minister in London giving the required assurance on the understanding that His Majesty's Government would similarly observe the provisions of the Protocol.

The French Ambassador had presented at noon a similar ultimatum to the German Government to expire at 5 P.M. For a few hours after 11 A.M. the telephonic lines of His Majesty's Embassy at Berlin continued to function, but about 4 P.M. all telephonic lines were cut off; and both the staff at the Adlon Hotel and the Embassy itself were isolated from all external contact. Members of my staff, however, had visited the Protocol at 11 A.M. with a view to arranging for our departure. They were treated with every civility and consideration and were informed that a special train would be placed at our disposal the following morning. Our only contact thereafter with the outside world was through the American Embassy. Its aid and help were invaluable. No trouble was too great for the Chargé d'Affaires, Mr. Alexander Kirk, and the members of his staff. They did everything that was possible to smooth over the difficulties of those last twenty-four hours; and our only pleasant recollection of that time is our appreciation of the great sympathy and willing assistance which we received from the American Embassy.

CHAPTER XIII

DEPARTURE FROM BERLIN

THE drama had reached its inevitable climax; and on the declaration of war at 11 A.M. that Sunday morning, September 3rd, the curtain fell for the last time. After returning from my interview with Ribbentrop at midday, I did not leave the Embassy again until Mr. Kirk rendered me one last service by driving me in his own car to the station the next morning. Up to those last twenty-four hours I had gone about freely in the streets of Berlin, either on foot or in my motor with its British flag; and I am glad to take this opportunity to bear witness to the fact that throughout those anxious weeks and up to the very end, when we crossed the German frontier, neither I nor any member of my staff were subjected at any time to any discourtesy or even a single gesture of hostility. It was a very different eve of war to that of August, 1914. Then a howling mob had surged in front of the Embassy, had broken its windows, and hurled abuse at its inmates and at Great Britain.

My impression was that the mass of the German people, that other Germany, were horror-struck at the whole idea of the war which was being thus thrust upon them. It is true that I could only judge of Berlin itself and that I was not in a position to witness the reaction of German youth or of the soldiers in the troop trains which were leaving for the Polish front. It is true also that the trial black-outs, the bread cards, and the strict system of rationing, which were already in force, were not exactly cheerful beginnings to a war. But what I can say is that the whole general atmosphere in Berlin itself was one of utter gloom and depression. Every country has the government which it deserves, and the German people must share the responsibility for the present war with those to whose authority they so meekly and readily submitted. But they have a share also of the immense pity which I feel for all those who have got to suffer because the Nazi war party, which had been foiled in September, 1938, won the day in Germany in August, 1939, and because one man was ready to sacrifice their united happiness to the satisfaction of his individual lust for military glory, which must be greater even than that of Frederick the Great.

In order to see for myself the mood of the people after the attack on Poland, I went that last Saturday afternoon for a walk down Unter den Linden, the main street of Berlin. Few people were about, and everyone seemed completely apathetic. I happened to want a drug called Codein and went into a shop to buy it. The chemist glumly told me that he could not give it to me without a doctor's prescription. I mentioned that I was the British Ambassador. He repeated that he was sorry, but the regulations on the subject were quite definite. So I said again, "I don't think you understand; I am the British Ambassador. If you poison me with your drug, you will get a high decoration from your Dr. Goebbels." The chemist's lugubrious face lit up with pleasure at this feeble joke, and he at once gave me all the Codein that I wanted. But there was something very pathetic about it.

I had the same sensation when I left the Embassy for the last time with Kirk. About a hundred yards from the door there was always a policeman on traffic duty where the Wilhelmstrasse crosses Unter den Linden. At that particular corner the policemen, who were not members of Himmler's Gestapo but mostly old soldiers of the municipal police force, used generally to salute me when I passed. That morning, when the policeman saw me coming, he carefully turned his head the other way and pretended to be preoccupied with the traffic coming in the other direction. He naturally could not salute me, and at the same time he did not wish to ignore me. He bore no ill will to a man who, as he and all Berlin knew, had striven to the last for peace.

When we left on the Monday morning in a body from the Embassy, where the whole remaining staff, thirty men, seven women, and two dogs, had been concentrated, a small crowd gathered outside and watched our luggage being put onto military lorries. It was an absolutely silent crowd; and, if there was hatred or hostility in their hearts, they gave no single sign of it. There were doubtless a number of Gestapo agents among them in plain clothes, and yet the people were speechless, when a little vocal abuse of the "encirclers" and "warmongers" would probably have been gratifying to their masters. But the older people in Berlin had not been misled by Goebbels' propaganda; they knew full well that the Embassy had done its utmost to preserve the peace.

Once again there was hardly a soul to be seen in the streets all the way from the Wilhelmstrasse to the Charlottenburg

station, where the special train was awaiting us. The whole
effect was one of apathy and unhappiness or bewilderment.
As Colonel Denis Daly, who had succeeded Mason-Macfarlane
as Military Attaché but three months before, said to me,
"This is a funny war." It was true; from the attitude of the
German people, no one would have guessed that we had
declared war on them or could feel that they wanted to fight
us. The impression persisted right through Germany. In 1914
the blinds of the trains provided for the British and French
Missions had had to be kept drawn throughout the journey.
This time they were drawn on one or two occasions, when
we stopped for a while at the larger stations such as Hannover;
but, as the conductor apologetically said, it was merely to
save me from being inconvenienced by the curiosity of idle
spectators. The older man in the street in Germany was
stunned with horror at the idea of war. But, as one of them
had said to me, "The others are too strong. What can we do?
We are too small. We can do nothing." German youth may
have been enthusiastic, but age certainly was not.

The French Embassy, headed by Coulondre, had left Berlin at 9 A.M. on the Monday morning, about two and a half
hours before we did, and by the same route via Holland.
Up to within a few miles of the Dutch frontier, the arrangements made for our departure went without a hitch. But,
when we reached the small station of Rheine, on the Monday
evening, we were suddenly informed that we were to be
held up there pending further orders. Some difficulty had
apparently arisen over the journey of the German Embassy
from Paris; and the French Mission in front of us was consequently not being allowed to cross the German frontier until

Failure of a Mission

the train with the German Embassy from Paris should also be safe in neutral territory. That was, I believe, the origin of the trouble; and, thanks to German suspicions and their mania for reciprocity, we were similarly detained until the steamship with the Germany Embassy from London on board arrived in Dutch territorial waters. We remained, therefore, at Rheine from the Monday evening till about 1:30 on the Tuesday afternoon. There was no discomfort or discourtesy about it, as there was fortunately a restaurant car attached to our train. We remained in a siding apart from even the curious; and, as I had brought some bridge cards with me, we were able to while the time away.

But the incident had one very unfortunate sequel. It gave the German Government an excuse for retaining a number of our consular officials as hostages in Germany until all the German consular officers from British territory all over the world had safely returned to their own country. It was not till Christmas that these British officials were finally allowed to depart. For us it was merely tiresome, and it was at Rheine that we learned from the German papers that the British Air Force had raided Wilhelmshaven and that the first leaflets had been dropped in Germany, some of them not far from where we were sitting in our siding.

Ultimately we crossed the German frontier at about 2 P.M. on Tuesday and arrived at Rotterdam at 7 P.M. There we were received with much hospitality by His Majesty's Minister at The Hague, Sir Nevile Bland. Forbes and I spent that night at the Legation, while the rest of the staff were found accommodation at Scheveningen, one of Holland's best-known seaside resorts a few miles away.

Departure from Berlin

All that remained to be done was to find a neutral steamer to take us to England. It was not so easy as it sounds, but eventually arrangements were made for us to travel by the Dutch S.S. *Batavier V*, which was leaving Rotterdam for London at dawn on the Thursday morning. We embarked the night before, a diminished party, as Holman and one other member of the staff remained behind to strengthen the personnel of the Legation at The Hague.

When we went on deck the next morning, we were provided with the exhilarating spectacle of three British destroyers, one on each side and one in front of us, which had been detailed to escort us back home and had met our ship as soon as it was outside Dutch waters. Every member of our party was affected, as I was, by the sight of these silent but blessed British warships. Throughout that beautifully sunny autumn day they remained in that formation, though one or other would at intervals abruptly put on full steam ahead and disappear into the blue to investigate, maybe into some other vessel or maybe some suspicious sound recorded on its submarine detector. But the only real excitement came when we were unfortunately all below at lunch time. Then all of a sudden the *Batavier V* was shaken from stem to stern by the explosion of three depth charges one after the other. They had been dropped by the leading destroyer, and quite three miles from our ship. We hopefully imagined a few moments later, that we heard a short burst of small-arm gunfire. But what had really happened, we were never to know. The destroyer returned to its station, and we at once wirelessed asking, "What luck?"

Failure of a Mission

The only answer we got was "Your message received." The Admiralty instructions were to give nothing away. I nevertheless told my staff that, if the customs authorities on arrival asked us if we had anything to declare, the only reply to give was, "One German U-boat."

As soon as we were in sight of Gravesend our escort left us and returned to its base, presumably at Chatham. Our journey was over. Spatts' agents were the first to board the ship on our arrival at Gravesend and carried off to quarantine the two dogs which we had brought with us. We ourselves landed about 7 P.M. There were practically no porters available; and the staff, headed by Forbes with his coat off, carried most of our luggage from the ship to the train themselves. Shortly after 8 P.M. on Thursday September 7th, we reached Victoria Station. It had taken us three days and eight hours to get from Berlin to London. My mission to Berlin had terminated, and the failure was complete.

APPENDIXES

APPENDIX I

Letter from the Reichschancellor to the Prime Minister.

(Translation.)

Dear Mr. Chamberlain,   Berlin, September 27, 1938.

I HAVE in the course of the conversations once more informed Sir Horace Wilson, who brought me your letter of the 26th September, of my final attitude. I should like, however, to make the following written reply to certain details in your letter:—

The Government in Prague feels justified in maintaining that the proposals in my memorandum of the 23rd September went far beyond the concession which it made to the British and French Governments and that the acceptance of the memorandum would rob Czechoslovakia of every guarantee for its national existence. This statement is based on the argument that Czechoslovakia is to give up a great part of her prepared defensive system before she can take steps elsewhere for her military protection. Thereby the political and economic independence of the country is automatically abolished. Moreover, the exchange of population proposed by me would turn out in practice to be a panic-stricken flight.

I must openly declare that I cannot bring myself to understand these arguments or even admit that they can be regarded as seriously put forward. The Government in Prague simply passes over the fact that the actual arrangement for the final settlement of the Sudeten German problem, in accordance with my proposals, will be made dependent not on a unilateral German petition (⁵) or on German measures of force, but rather, on the one hand, on a free vote under no outside influence, and, on the other hand, to a very wide degree on German-Czech agreement on matters of detail to be reached subsequently. Not only the exact definition of the territories in which the plebiscite is to

(⁵) ? decision.

take place, but the execution of the plebiscite and the delimitation of the frontier to be made on the basis of its result, are in accordance with my proposals to be met independently of any unilateral decision by Germany. Moreover, all other details are to be reserved for agreement on the part of a German-Czech commission.

In the light of this interpretation of my proposals and in the light of the cession of the Sudeten population areas, in fact agreed to by Czechoslovakia, the immediate occupation by German contingents demanded by me represents no more than a security measure which is intended to guarantee a quick and smooth achievement of the final settlement. This security measure is indispensable. If the German Government renounced it and left the whole further treatment of the problem simply to normal negotiations with Czechoslovakia, the present unbearable circumstances in the Sudeten German territories which I described in my speech yesterday would continue to exist for a period, the length of which cannot be foreseen. The Czechoslovak Government would be completely in a position to drag out the negotiations on any point they liked, and thus to delay the final settlement. You will understand after everything that has passed that I cannot place such confidence in the assurances received from the Prague Government. The British Government also would surely not be in a position to dispose of this danger by any use of diplomatic pressure.

That Czechoslovakia should lose a part of her fortifications is naturally an unavoidable consequence of the cession of the Sudeten German territory agreed to by the Prague Government itself. If one were to wait for the entry into force of the final settlement in which Czechoslovakia had completed new fortifications in the territory which remained to her, it would doubtless last months and years. But this is the only object of all the Czech objections. Above all, it is completely incorrect to maintain that Czechoslovakia in this manner would be crippled in her national existence or in her political and economic independence. It is clear from my memorandum that the German occupation would only extend to the given line, and that the final delimitation of the

Appendixes

frontier would take place in accordance with the procedure which I have already described. The Prague Government has no right to doubt that the German military measures would stop within these limits. If, nevertheless, it desires such a doubt to be taken into account the British and, if necessary, also the French Government can guarantee the quick fulfillment of my proposal. I can, moreover, only refer to my speech yesterday in which I clearly declared that I regret the idea of any attack on Czechoslovak territory, and that under the condition which I laid down I am even ready to give a formal guarantee for the remainder of Czechoslovakia. There can, therefore, be not the slightest question whatsoever of a check to the independence of Czechoslovakia. It is equally erroneous to talk of an economic rift. It is, on the contrary, a well-known fact that Czechoslovakia after the cession of the Sudeten German territory would constitute a healthier and more unified economic organism than before.

If the Government in Prague finally evinces anxiety also in regard to the state of the Czech population in the territories to be occupied, I can only regard this with surprise. It can be sure that, on the German side, nothing whatever will occur which will preserve for those Czechs a similar fate to that which has befallen the Sudeten Germans consequent on the Czech measures.

In these circumstances, I must assume that the Government in Prague is only using a proposal for the occupation by German troops in order, by distorting the meaning and object of my proposal, to mobilize those forces in other countries, in particular in England and France, from which they hope to receive unreserved support for their aim and thus to achieve the possibility of a general warlike conflagration. I must leave it to your judgment whether, in view of these facts, you consider that you should continue your effort, for which I should like to take this opportunity of once more sincerely thanking you, to spoil such maneuvers and bring the Government in Prague to reason at the very last hour.

ADOLF HITLER.

[17961 9/38] Wt. 1810/2223 3M 11/38 F.O.P. 18124 Gp. 340

APPENDIX II

Letter of August 22, 1939, from the Prime Minister to the German Chancellor.

10 *Downing Street, August* 22, 1939.

Your Excellency,

YOUR Excellency will have already heard of certain measures taken by His Majesty's Government, and announced in the press and on the wireless this evening.

These steps have, in the opinion of His Majesty's Government, been rendered necessary by the military movements which have been reported from Germany, and by the fact that apparently the announcement of a German-Soviet Agreement is taken in some quarters in Berlin to indicate that intervention by Great Britain on behalf of Poland is no longer a contingency that need be reckoned with. No greater mistake could be made. Whatever may prove to be the nature of the German-Soviet Agreement, it cannot alter Great Britain's obligation to Poland which His Majesty's Government have stated in public repeatedly and plainly, and which they are determined to fulfill.

It has been alleged that, if His Majesty's Government had made their position more clear in 1914, the great catastrophe would have been avoided. Whether or not there is any force in that allegation, His Majesty's Government are resolved that on this occasion there shall be no such tragic misunderstanding.

If the case should arise, they are resolved, and prepared, to employ without delay all the forces at their command, and it is impossible to foresee the end of hostilities once engaged. It would be a dangerous illusion to think that, if war once starts, it will come to an early end even if a success on any one of the several fronts on which it will be engaged should have been secured.

Having thus made our position perfectly clear, I wish to repeat to you my conviction that war between our two peoples would be the greatest calamity that could occur. I am certain that it is desired neither by our people, nor by yours, and I cannot see that there is anything in the questions arising between Germany and Poland which could not and should not be resolved without the use of force, if only a situation of confidence could be restored to enable discussions to be carried on in an atmosphere different from that which prevails today.

We have been, and at all times will be, ready to assist in creating conditions in which such negotiations could take place, and in which it might be possible concurrently to discuss the wider problems affecting the future of international relations, including matters of interest to us and to you.

The difficulties in the way of any peaceful discussion in the present state of tension are, however, obvious, and the longer that tension is maintained, the harder will it be for reason to prevail.

These difficulties, however, might be mitigated, if not removed, provided that there could for an initial period be a truce on both sides—and indeed on all sides—to press polemics and to all incitement.

If such a truce could be arranged, then, at the end of that period, during which steps could be taken to examine and deal with complaints made by either side as to the treatment of minorities, it is reasonable to hope that suitable conditions might have been established for direct negotiations between Germany and Poland upon the issues between them (with the aid of a neutral intermediary, if both sides should think that that would be helpful).

But I am bound to say that there would be slender hope of bringing such negotiations to successful issue unless it were understood beforehand that any settlement reached would, when concluded, be guaranteed by other Powers. His Majesty's Government would be ready, if desired, to make such contribution as they could to the effective operation of such guarantees.

At this moment I confess I can see no other way to avoid a catastrophe that will involve Europe in war.

In view of the grave consequences to humanity, which may follow from the action of their rulers, I trust that Your Excellency will weigh with the utmost deliberation the considerations which I have put before you.

Yours sincerely,
NEVILLE CHAMBERLAIN.

APPENDIX III

Communication from the German Chancellor to the Prime Minister, handed to His Majesty's Ambassador on August 23, 1939.

(Translation.)

Your Excellency,

THE British Ambassador has just handed to me a communication in which your Excellency draws attention in the name of the British Government to a number of points which in your estimation are of the greatest importance.

I may be permitted to answer your letter as follows:—

1. Germany has never sought conflict with England and has never interfered in English interests. On the contrary, she has for years endeavored—although unfortunately in vain—to win England's friendship. On this account she voluntarily assumed in a wide area of Europe the limitations on her own interests which from a national-political point of view it would have otherwise been very difficult to tolerate.

2. The German Reich, however, like every other State possesses certain definite interests which it is impossible to renounce. These do not extend beyond the limits of the necessities laid down by former German history and deriving from vital economic pre-requisites. Some of these questions held and still hold a significance both of a national-political and a psychological character which no German Government is able to ignore.

To these questions belong the German City of Danzig, and the connected problem of the Corridor. Numerous statesmen, historians and men of letters even in England have been conscious of this at any rate up to a few years ago. I would add that all these territories lying in the aforesaid German sphere of interest and in particular those lands which returned to the Reich eighteen months ago received their cultural development at the hands not of the English but exclusively of the Germans and this, moreover, already from a time dating back over a thousand years.

3. Germany was prepared to settle the questions of Danzig

and of the Corridor by the method of negotiation on the basis of a proposal of truly unparalleled magnanimity. The allegations disseminated by England regarding a German mobilization against Poland, the assertion of aggressive designs towards Roumania, Hungary, etc., as well as the so-called guarantee declarations which were subsequently given had, however, dispelled Polish inclination to negotiate on a basis of this kind which would have been tolerable for Germany also.

4. The unconditional assurance given by England to Poland that she would render assistance to that country in all circumstances regardless of the causes from which a conflict might spring, could only be interpreted in that country as an encouragement thenceforward to unloosen, under cover of such a charter, a wave of appalling terrorism against the one and a half million German inhabitants living in Poland. The atrocities which since then have been taking place in that country are terrible for the victims, but intolerable for a Great Power such as the German Reich which is expected to remain a passive onlooker during these happenings. Poland has been guilty of numerous breaches of her legal obligations towards the Free City of Danzig, has made demands in the character of ultimata, and has initiated a process of economic strangulation.

5. The Government of the German Reich therefore recently caused the Polish Government to be informed that it was not prepared passively to accept this development of affairs, that it will not tolerate further addressing of notes in the character of ultimata to Danzig, that it will not tolerate a continuance of the persecutions of the German minority, that it will equally not tolerate the extermination of the Free City of Danzig by economic measures, in other words, the destruction of the vital bases of the population of Danzig by a kind of Customs blockade, and that it will not tolerate the occurrence of further acts of provocation directed against the Reich. Apart from this, the questions of the Corridor and of Danzig must and shall be solved.

6. Your Excellency informs me in the name of the British Government that you will be obliged to render assistance to

Poland in any such case of intervention on the part of Germany. I take note of this statement of yours and assure you that it can make no change in the determination of the Reich Government to safeguard the interests of the Reich as stated in paragraph 5 above. Your assurance to the effect that in such an event you anticipate a long war is shared by myself. Germany, if attacked by England, will be found prepared and determined. I have already more than once declared before the German people and the world that there can be no doubt concerning the determination of the new German Reich rather to accept, for however long it might be, every sort of misery and tribulation than to sacrifice its national interests, let alone its honor.

7. The German Reich Government has received information to the effect that the British Government has the intention to carry out measures of mobilization which, according to the statements contained in your own letter, are clearly directed against Germany alone. This is said to be true of France as well. Since Germany has never had the intention of taking military measures other than those of a defensive character against England or France, and, as has already been emphasized, has never intended, and does not in the future intend, to attack England or France, it follows that this announcement as confirmed by you, Mr. Prime Minister, in your own letter, can only refer to a contemplated act of menace directed against the Reich. *I therefore inform your Excellency that, in the event of these military announcements being carried into effect, I shall order immediate mobilization of the German forces.*

8. The question of the treatment of European problems on a peaceful basis is not a decision which rests on Germany but primarily on those who since the crime committed by the Versailles dictate have stubbornly and consistently opposed any peaceful revision. Only after a change of spirit on the part of the responsible Powers can there be any real change in the relationship between England and Germany. I have all my life fought for Anglo-German friendship; the attitude adopted by British diplomacy—at any rate up to the present—has, however, con-

vinced me of the futility of such an attempt. Should there be any change in this respect in the future nobody could be happier than I.

ADOLF HITLER.

APPENDIX IV

Supplementary Communication from the German Chancellor handed to His Majesty's Ambassador on August 25, 1939.

THE following is a translation of the text of a verbal communication made to Sir Nevile Henderson by Herr Hitler at his interview on the 25th August:—

"By way of introduction the Führer declared that the British Ambassador had given expression at the close of the last conversation to the hope that, after all, an understanding between Germany and England might yet be possible. He (the Führer) had therefore turned things over in his mind once more and desired to make a move as regards England which should be as decisive as the move as regards Russia which had led to the recent agreement. Yesterday's sitting in the House of Commons and the speeches of Mr. Chamberlain and Lord Halifax had also moved the Führer to talk once more to the British Ambassador. The assertion that Germany affected to conquer the world was ridiculous. The British Empire embraced 40 million square kilometers, Russia 19 million square kilometers, America 9½ million square kilometers, whereas Germany embraced less than 600,000 square kilometers. It is quite clear who it is who desires to conquer the world.

"The Führer makes the following communication to the British Ambassador:—

"1. Poland's actual provocations have become intolerable. It makes no difference who is responsible. If the Polish Government denies responsibility, that only goes to show that it no longer itself possesses any influence over its subordinate military authorities. In the preceding night there had been a fur-

ther twenty-one new frontier incidents; on the German side
the greatest discipline had been maintained. All incidents had
been provoked from the Polish side. Furthermore, commercial
aircraft had been shot at. If the Polish Government stated that
it was not responsible, it showed that it was no longer capable
of controlling its own people.

"2. Germany was in all the circumstances determined to
abolish these Macedonian conditions on her eastern frontier
and, what is more, to do so in the interests of quiet and order,
but also in the interests of European peace.

"3. The problem of Danzig and the Corridor must be
solved.—The British Prime Minister had made a speech which
was not in the least calculated to induce any change in the
German attitude. At the most, the result of this speech could
be a bloody and incalculable war between Germany and England. Such a war would be bloodier than that of 1914 to 1918.
In contrast to the last war, Germany would no longer have to
fight on two fronts. Agreement with Russia was unconditional
and signified a change in foreign policy of the Reich which
would last a very long time. Russia and Germany would never
again take up arms against each other. Apart from this, the
agreements reached with Russia would also render Germany
secure economically for the longest possible period of war.

"The Führer had always wanted an Anglo-German understanding. War between England and Germany could at the
best bring some profit to Germany but none at all to England.

"The Führer declared that the German-Polish problem must
be solved and will be solved. He is, however, prepared and
determined after the solution of this problem to approach
England once more with a large comprehensive offer. He is a
man of great decisions, and in this case also he will be capable
of being great in his action. He accepts the British Empire and
is ready to pledge himself personally for its continued existence
and to place the power of the German Reich at its disposal if—

"(1) His colonial demands which are limited and can be
negotiated by peaceful methods are fulfilled and in
this case he is prepared to fix the longest time limit.

Appendixes

"(2) His obligations towards Italy are not touched; in other words, he does not demand that England gives up her obligations towards France and similarly for his own part he cannot withdraw from his obligations towards Italy.

"(3) He also desires to stress the irrevocable determination of Germany never again to enter into conflict with Russia. The Führer is ready to conclude agreements with England which, as has already been emphasized, would not only guarantee the existence of the British Empire in all circumstances as far as Germany is concerned, but also if necessary an assurance to the British Empire of German assistance regardless of where such assistance should be necessary. The Führer would then also be ready to accept a reasonable limitation of armaments which corresponds to the new political situation, and which is economically tolerable. Finally, the Führer renewed his assurances that he is not interested in Western problems and that a frontier modification in the West does not enter into consideration. Western fortifications which have been constructed at a cost of milliards were final Reich frontier on the West.

"If the British Government would consider these ideas a blessing for Germany and also for the British Empire might result. If it rejects these ideas there will be war. In no case would Great Britain emerge stronger; the last war proved this.

"The Führer repeats that he is a man of *ad infinitum* decisions by which he himself is bound and that this is his last offer. Immediately after solution of the German-Polish question he would approach the British Government with an offer."

APPENDIX V

*Reply of His Majesty's Government dated August 28, 1939, to the German Chancellor's Communications of August 23 and 25, 1939.**

His Majesty's Government have received the message conveyed to them from the German Chancellor by His Majesty's Ambassador in Berlin, and have considered it with the care which it demands.

They note the Chancellor's expression of his desire to make friendship the basis of the relations between Germany and the British Empire and they fully share this desire. They believe with him that if a complete and lasting understanding between the two countries could be established it would bring untold blessings to both peoples.

2. The Chancellor's message deals with two groups of questions: those which are the matters now in dispute between Germany and Poland and those affecting the ultimate relations of Germany and Great Britain. In connexion with these last, His Majesty's Government observe that the German Chancellor has indicated certain proposals which, subject to one condition, he would be prepared to make to the British Government for a general understanding. These proposals are, of course, stated in very general form and would require closer definition, but His Majesty's Government are fully prepared to take them, with some additions, as subjects for discussion and they would be ready, if the differences between Germany and Poland are peacefully composed, to proceed so soon as practicable to such discussion with a sincere desire to reach agreement.

3. The condition which the German Chancellor lays down is that there must first be a settlement of the differences between Germany and Poland. As to that, His Majesty's Government entirely agree. Everything, however, turns upon the nature of the settlement and the method by which it is to be reached. On

* Nos. 60 and 68.

these points, the importance of which cannot be absent from the Chancellor's mind, his message is silent, and His Majesty's Government feel compelled to point out than an understanding upon both of these is essential to achieving further progress. The German Government will be aware that His Majesty's Government have obligations to Poland by which they are bound and which they intend to honor. They could not, for any advantage offered to Great Britain, acquiesce in a settlement which put in jeopardy the independence of a State to whom they have given their guarantee.

4. In the opinion of His Majesty's Government a reasonable solution of the differences between Germany and Poland could and should be effected by agreement between the two countries on lines which would include the safeguarding of Poland's essential interests, and they recall that in his speech of the 28th April last the German Chancellor recognized the importance of these interests to Poland.

But, as was stated by the Prime Minister in his letter to the German Chancellor of the 22nd August, His Majesty's Government consider it essential for the success of the discussions which would precede the agreement that it should be understood beforehand that any settlement arrived at would be guaranteed by other Powers. His Majesty's Government would be ready if desired to make their contribution to the effective operation of such a guarantee.

In the view of His Majesty's Government it follows that the next step should be the initiation of direct discussions between the German and Polish Governments on a basis which would include the principles stated above, namely, the safeguarding of Poland's essential interests and the securing of the settlement by an international guarantee.

They have already received a definite assurance from the Polish Government that they are prepared to enter into discussions on this basis, and His Majesty's Government hope the German Government would for their part also be willing to agree to this course.

If, as His Majesty's Government hope, such discussion led to agreement the way would be open to the negotiation of that wider and more complete understanding between Great Britain and Germany which both countries desire.

5. His Majesty's Government agree with the German Chancellor that one of the principal dangers in the German-Polish situation arises from the reports concerning the treatment of minorities. The present state of tension, with its concomitant frontier incidents, reports of maltreatment and inflammatory propaganda, is a constant danger to peace. It is manifestly a matter of the utmost urgency that all incidents of the kind should be promptly and rigidly suppressed and that unverified reports should not be allowed to circulate, in order that time may be afforded, without provocation on either side, for a full examination of the possibilities of settlement. His Majesty's Government are confident that both the Governments concerned are fully alive to these considerations.

6. His Majesty's Government have said enough to make their own attitude plain in the particular matters at issue between Germany and Poland. They trust that the German Chancellor will not think that, because His Majesty's Government are scrupulous concerning their obligations to Poland, they are not anxious to use all their influence to assist the achievement of a solution which may commend itself both to Germany and to Poland.

That such a settlement should be achieved seems to His Majesty's Government essential, not only for reasons directly arising in regard to the settlement itself, but also because of the wider considerations of which the German Chancellor has spoken with such conviction.

7. It is unnecessary in the present reply to stress the advantage of a peaceful settlement over a decision to settle the questions at issue by force of arms. The results of a decision to use force have been clearly set out in the Prime Minister's letter to the Chancellor of the 22nd August, and His Majesty's Government do not doubt that they are as fully recognized by the Chancellor as by themselves.

On the other hand, His Majesty's Government, noting with interest the German Chancellor's reference in the message now

Appendixes

under consideration to a limitation of armaments, believe that, if a peaceful settlement can be obtained, the assistance of the world could confidently be anticipated for practical measures to enable the transition from preparation for war to the normal activities of peaceful trade to be safely and smoothly effected.

8. A just settlement of these questions between Germany and Poland may open the way to world peace. Failure to reach it would ruin the hopes of better understanding between Germany and Great Britain, would bring the two countries into conflict, and might well plunge the whole world into war. Such an outcome would be a calamity without parallel in history.

APPENDIX VI

Reply of the German Chancellor to the Communication of August 28, 1939, from His Majesty's Government.* This reply was handed to Sir N. Henderson by Herr Hitler during the evening of August 29, 1939.

(Translation.)

THE British Ambassador in Berlin has submitted to the British Government suggestions which I felt bound to make in order—

(1) to give expression once more to the will of the Reich Government for sincere Anglo-German understanding, cooperation and friendship;
(2) to leave no room for doubt as to the fact that such an understanding could not be bought at the price of a renunciation of vital German interests, let alone the abandonment of demands which are based as much upon common human justice as upon the national dignity and honor of our people.

The German Government have noted with satisfaction from the reply of the British Government and from the oral explana-

* No. 74.

tions given by the British Ambassador that the British Government for their part are also prepared to improve the relationship between Germany and England and to develop and extend it in the sense of the German suggestion.

In this connexion, the British Government are similarly convinced that the removal of the German-Polish tension, which has become unbearable, is the pre-requisite for the realization of this hope.

Since the autumn of the past year, and on the last occasion in March, 1939, there were submitted to the Polish Government proposals, both oral and written, which, having regard to the friendship then existing between Germany and Poland, offered the possibility of a solution of the questions in dispute acceptable to both parties. The British Government are aware that the Polish Government saw fit, in March last, finally to reject these proposals. At the same time, they used this rejection as a pretext or an occasion for taking military measures which have since been continuously intensified. Already in the middle of last month Poland was in effect in a state of mobilization. This was accompanied by numerous encroachments in the Free City of Danzig due to the instigation of the Polish authorities; threatening demands in the nature of ultimata, varying only in degree, were addressed to that City. A closing of the frontiers, at first in the form of a measure of customs policy but extended later in a military sense affecting also traffic and communications, was imposed with the object of bringing about the political exhaustion and economic destruction of this German community.

To this were added barbaric actions of maltreatment which cry to Heaven, and other kinds of persecution of the large German national group in Poland which extended even to the killing of many resident Germans or to their forcible removal under the most cruel conditions. This state of affairs is unbearable for a Great Power. It has now forced Germany, after remaining a passive onlooker for many months, in her turn to take the necessary steps for the safeguarding of justified German interests. And indeed the German Government can but assure the British Government in the most solemn manner that a condition of affairs has now been reached which can no longer be accepted or observed with indifference.

The demands of the German Government are in conformity with the revision of the Versailles Treaty in regard to this territory which has always been recognized as being necessary: viz., return of Danzig and the Corridor to Germany, the safeguarding of the existence of the German national group in the territories remaining to Poland.

The German Government note with satisfaction that the British Government also are in principle convinced that some solution must be found for the new situation which has arisen.

They further feel justified in assuming that the British Government too can have no doubt that it is a question now of conditions, for the elimination of which there no longer remain days, still less weeks, but perhaps only hours. For in the disorganized state of affairs obtaining in Poland, the possibility of incidents intervening which it might be impossible for Germany to tolerate, must at any moment be reckoned with.

While the British Government may still believe that these grave differences can be resolved by way of direct negotiations, the German Government unfortunately can no longer share this view as a matter of course. For they have made the attempt to embark on such peaceful negotiations, but, instead of receiving any support from the Polish Government, they were rebuffed by the sudden introduction of measures of a military character in favor of the development alluded to above.

The British Government attach importance to two considerations: (1) that the existing danger of an imminent explosion should be eliminated as quickly as possible by direct negotiation, and (2) that the existence of the Polish State, in the form in which it would then continue to exist, should be adequately safeguarded in the economic and political sphere by means of international guarantees.

On this subject the German Government makes the following declaration:—

Failure of a Mission

Though sceptical as to the prospects of a successful outcome, they are nevertheless prepared to accept the English proposal and to enter into direct discussions. They do so, as has already been emphasized, solely as the result of the impression made upon them by the written statement received from the British Government that they too desire a pact of friendship in accordance with the general lines indicated to the British Ambassador.

The German Government desire in this way to give the British Government and the British nation a proof of the sincerity of Germany's intentions to enter into a lasting friendship with Great Britain.

The Government of the Reich felt, however, bound to point out to the British Government that in the event of a territorial rearrangement in Poland they would no longer be able to bind themselves to give guarantees or to participate in guarantees without the U.S.S.R. being associated therewith.

For the rest, in making these proposals the German Government have never had any intention of touching Poland's vital interests or questioning the existence of an independent Polish State. The German Government, accordingly, in these circumstances agree to accept the British Government's offer of their good offices in securing the despatch to Berlin of a Polish Emissary with full powers. They count on the arrival of this Emissary on Wednesday, the 30th August, 1939.

The German Government will immediately draw up proposals for a solution acceptable to themselves and will, if possible, place these at the disposal of the British Government before the arrival of the Polish negotiator.

Appendixes

APPENDIX VII

Text of German proposals to the Polish Government which were never communicated to them officially, together with explanatory statement.

Message which was communicated to H.M. Ambassador in Berlin by the State Secretary on August 31, 1939, at 9:15 P.M.

(Translation.)

His Majesty's Government informed the German Government, in a note dated the 28th August, 1939,* of their readiness to offer their mediation towards direct negotiations between Germany and Poland over the problems in dispute. In so doing they made it abundantly clear that they, too, were aware of the urgent need for progress in view of the continuous incidents and the general European tension. In a reply dated the 29th August,† the German Government, in spite of being sceptical as to the desire of the Polish Government to come to an understanding, declared themselves ready in the interests of peace to accept the British mediation or suggestion. After considering all the circumstances prevailing at the time, they considered it necessary in their note to point out that, if the danger of a catastrophe was to be avoided, then action must be taken readily and without delay. In this sense they declared themselves ready to receive a personage appointed by the Polish Government up to the evening of the 30th August, with the proviso that the latter was, in fact, empowered not only to discuss but to conduct and conclude negotiations.

Further, the German Government pointed out that they felt able to make the basic points regarding the offer of an understanding available to the British Government by the time the Polish negotiator arrived in Berlin.

Instead of a statement regarding the arrival of an authorized Polish personage, the first answer the Government of the Reich received to their readiness for an understanding was the news of

* No. 74.   † No. 78.

329

the Polish mobilization, and only towards 12 o'clock on the night of the 30th August, 1939, did they receive a somewhat general assurance of British readiness to help towards the commencement of negotiations.

Although the fact that the Polish negotiator expected by the Government of the Reich did not arrive removed the necessary condition for informing His Majesty's Government of the views of the German Government as regards possible bases of negotiation, since His Majesty's Government themselves had pleaded for *direct* negotiations between Germany and Poland, the German Minister for Foreign Affairs, Herr von Ribbentrop, gave the British Ambassador on the occasion of the presentation of the last British note precise information as to the text of the German proposals which would be regarded as a basis of negotiation in the event of the arrival of the Polish plenipotentiary.

The Government of the German Reich considered themselves entitled to claim that in these circumstances a Polish personage would immediately be nominated, at any rate retroactively.

For the Reich Government cannot be expected for their part continually not only to emphasize their willingness to start negotiations, but actually to be ready to do so, while being from the Polish side merely put off with empty subterfuges and meaningless declarations.

It has once more been made clear as a result of a *démarche* which has meanwhile been made by the Polish Ambassador that the latter himself has no plenary powers either to enter into any discussion, or even to negotiate.

The Führer and the German Government have thus waited two days in vain for the arrival of a Polish negotiator with plenary powers.

In these circumstances the German Government regard their proposals as having this time too been to all intents and purposes rejected, although they considered that these proposals, in the form in which they were made known to the British Government also, were more than loyal, fair and practicable.

The Reich Government consider it timely to inform the public of the bases for negotiation which were communicated to the

Appendixes

British Ambassador by the Minister for Foreign Affairs, Herr von Ribbentrop.

The situation existing between the German Reich and Poland is at the moment of such a kind that any further incident can lead to an explosion on the part of the military forces which have taken up their position on both sides. Any peaceful solution must be framed in such a way as to ensure that the events which lie at the root of this situation cannot be repeated on the next occasion offered, and that thus not only the East of Europe, but also other territories shall not be brought into such a state of tension. The causes of this development lie in: (1) the impossible delineation of frontiers, as fixed by the Versailles dictate; (2) the impossible treatment of the minority in the ceded territories.

In making these proposals, the Reich Government are, therefore, actuated by the idea of finding a lasting solution which will remove the impossible situation created by frontier delineation, which may assure to both parties their vitally important line of communication, which may—as far as it is at all possible—remove the minority problem and, in so far as this is not possible, may give the minorities the assurance of a tolerable future by means of a reliable guarantee of their rights.

The Reich Government are content that in so doing it is essential that economic and physical damage done since 1918 should be exposed and repaired in its entirety. They, of course, regard this obligation as being binding for both parties.

These considerations lead to the following practical proposals:—

(1) The Free City of Danzig shall return to the German Reich in view of its purely German character, as well as of the unanimous will of its population;

(2) The territory of the so-called Corridor which extends from the Baltic Sea to the line Marienwerder-Graudenz-Kulm-Bromberg (inclusive) and thence may run in a westerly direction to Schönlanke, shall itself decide as to whether it shall belong to Germany or Poland;

(3) For this purpose a plebiscite shall take place in this territory. The following shall be entitled to vote: all Germans who were either domiciled in this territory on the 1st January, 1918,

or who by that date have been born there, and similarly of Poles, Kashubes, etc., domiciled in this territory on the above day (the 1st January, 1918) or born there up to that date. The Germans who have been driven from this territory shall return to it in order to exercise their vote with a view to ensuring an objective plebiscite, and also with a view to ensuring the extensive preparation necessary therefor. The above territory shall, as in the case of the Saar territory, be placed under the supervision of an international commission to be formed immediately, on which shall be represented the four Great Powers—Italy, the Soviet Union, France and England. This commission shall exercise all the rights of sovereignty in this territory. With this end in view, the territory shall be evacuated within a period of the utmost brevity, still to be agreed upon, by the Polish armed forces, the Polish police, and the Polish authorities;

(4) The Polish port of Gdynia, which fundamentally constitutes Polish sovereign territory so far as it is confined territorially to the Polish settlement, shall be excluded from the above territory. The exact frontiers of this Polish port should be determined between Germany and Poland, and, if necessary, delimited by an international committee of arbitration;

(5) With a view to assuring the necessary time for the execution of the extensive work involved in the carrying out of a just plebiscite, this plebiscite shall not take place before the expiry of twelve months;

(6) In order to guarantee unrestricted communication between Germany and East Prussia and between Poland and the sea during this period, roads and railways shall be established to render free transit traffic possible. In this connection only such taxes as are necessary for the maintenance of the means of communication and for the provision of transport may be levied;

(7) The question as to the party to which the area belongs is to be decided by simple majority of the votes recorded;

(8) In order to guarantee to Germany free communication with her province of Danzig-East Prussia, and to Poland her connection with the sea after the execution of the plebiscite—regardless of the results thereof—Germany shall, in the event of

the plebiscite area going to Poland, receive an extra-territorial traffic zone, approximately in a line from Bütow to Danzig or Dirschau, in which to lay down an autobahn and a 4-track railway line. The road and the railway shall be so constructed that the Polish lines of communication are not affected, *i.e.*, they shall pass either over or under the latter. The breadth of this zone shall be fixed at 1 kilometer, and it is to be German sovereign territory. Should the plebiscite be favorable to Germany, Poland is to obtain rights, analogous to those accorded to Germany, to a similar extra-territorial communication by road and railway for the purpose of free and unrestricted communication with her port of Gdynia;

(9) In the event of the Corridor returning to the German Reich, the latter declares its right to proceed to an exchange of population with Poland to the extent to which the nature of the Corridor lends itself thereto;

(10) Any special right desired by Poland in the port of Danzig would be negotiated on a basis of territory against similar rights to be granted to Germany in the port of Gdynia;

(11) In order to remove any feeling in this area that either side was being threatened, Danzig and Gdynia would have the character of exclusively mercantile towns, that is to say, without military installations and military fortifications;

(12) The peninsula of Hela, which as a result of the plebiscite might go either to Poland or to Germany, would in either case have similarly to be demilitarized;

(13) Since the Government of the German Reich has the most vehement complaints to make against the Polish treatment of minorities, and since the Polish Government for their part feel obliged to make complaints against Germany, both parties declare their agreement to have these complaints laid before an international committee of enquiry, whose task would be to examine all complaints as regards economic or physical damage, and any other acts of terrorism. Germany and Poland undertake to make good economic or other damage done to minorities on either side since the year 1918, or to cancel expropriation as the case may

be, or to provide complete compensation to the persons affected for this and any other encroachments on their economic life;

(14) In order to free the Germans who may be left in Poland and the Poles who may be left in Germany from the feeling of being outlawed by all nations, and in order to render them secure against being called upon to perform action or to render services incompatible with their national sentiments, Germany and Poland agree to guarantee the rights of both minorities by means of the most comprehensive and binding agreement, in order to guarantee to these minorities the preservation, the free development and practical application of their nationality (Volkstum), and in particular to permit for this purpose such organization as they may consider necessary. Both parties undertake not to call upon members of the minority for military service;

(15) In the event of agreement on the basis of these proposals, Germany and Poland declare themselves ready to decree and to carry out the immediate demobilization of their armed forces;

(16) The further measures necessary for the more rapid execution of the above arrangement shall be agreed upon by both Germany and Poland conjointly.